IF AT FIRST YOU DON'T SUCCEED? WRITING, RHETORIC, AND THE QUESTION OF FAILURE

PERSPECTIVES ON WRITING
Series Editors: Rich Rice and J. Michael Rifenburg
Consulting Editor: Susan H. McLeod
Associate Editors: Johanna Phelps, Jonathan M. Marine, and Qingyang Sun

The Perspectives on Writing series addresses writing studies in a broad sense. Consistent with the wide ranging approaches characteristic of teaching and scholarship in writing across the curriculum, the series presents works that take divergent perspectives on working as a writer, teaching writing, administering writing programs, and studying writing in its various forms.

The WAC Clearinghouse and University Press of Colorado are collaborating so that these books will be widely available through free digital distribution and low-cost print editions. The publishers and the series editors are committed to the principle that knowledge should freely circulate and have embraced the use of technology to support open access to scholarly work.

Recent Books in the Series

Ryan J. Dippre and Talinn Phillips (Eds.), *Improvisations: Methodologies in Lifespan Writing Research* (2024)

Ashley J. Holmes and Elise Verzosa Hurley (Eds.), *Learning from the Mess: Method/ological Praxis in Rhetoric and Writing Studies* (2024)

Diane Kelly-Riley, Ti Macklin, and Carl Whithaus (Eds.), *Considering Students, Teachers, and Writing Assessment: Volumes 1 and 2* (2024)

Amy Cicchino and Troy Hicks (Eds.), *Better Practices: Exploring the Teaching of Writing in Online and Hybrid Spaces* (2024)

Genesea M. Carter and Aurora Matzke (Eds.), *Systems Shift: Creating and Navigating Change in Rhetoric and Composition Administration* (2023)

Michael J. Michaud, *A Writer Reforms (the Teaching of) Writing: Donald Murray and the Writing Process Movement, 1963–1987* (2023)

Michelle LaFrance and Melissa Nicolas (Eds.), *Institutional Ethnography as Writing Studies Practice* (2023)

Phoebe Jackson and Christopher Weaver (Eds.), *Rethinking Peer Review: Critical Reflections on a Pedagogical Practice* (2023)

Megan J. Kelly, Heather M. Falconer, Caleb L. González, and Jill Dahlman (Eds.), *Adapting the Past to Reimagine Possible Futures: Celebrating and Critiquing WAC at 50* (2023)

William J. Macauley, Jr. et al. (Eds.), *Threshold Conscripts: Rhetoric and Composition Teaching Assistantships* (2023)

IF AT FIRST YOU DON'T SUCCEED? WRITING, RHETORIC, AND THE QUESTION OF FAILURE

Edited by Steven J. Corbett

The WAC Clearinghouse
wac.colostate.edu
Fort Collins, Colorado

University Press of Colorado
upcolorado.com
Denver, Colorado

The WAC Clearinghouse, Fort Collins, Colorado 80523

University Press of Colorado, Denver, Colorado 80203

© 2024 by Steven J. Corbett. This work is licensed under a Creative Commons Attribution-NonCommercial-NoDerivatives 4.0 International license.

ISBN 978-1-64215-249-4 (PDF) 978-1-64215-250-0 (ePub) 978-1-64642-735-2 (pbk.)

DOI 10.37514/PER-B.2024.2494

Produced in the United States of America

Library of Congress Cataloging-in-Publication Data

Names: Corbett, Steven J., 1970– editor
Title: If at first you don't succeed? : writing, rhetoric, and the question of failure / edited by Steven J. Corbett.
Other titles: If at first you do not succeed?
Description: Fort Collins, Colorado : The WAC Clearinghouse, 2025. | Series: Perspectives on writing | Includes bibliographical references.
Identifiers: LCCN 2025000007 (print) | LCCN 2025000008 (ebook) | ISBN 9781646427352 paperback | ISBN 9781642152494 adobe pdf | ISBN 9781642152500 epub
Subjects: LCSH: English language—Rhetoric—Psychological aspects | English language—Rhetoric—Study and teaching—Psychological aspects | Failure (Psychology) | LCGFT: Essays
Classification: LCC PE1403 .I3 2025 (print) | LCC PE1403 (ebook) | DDC 808—dc23/eng/20250408
LC record available at https://lccn.loc.gov/2025000007
LC ebook record available at https://lccn.loc.gov/2025000008

Copyeditor: Samantha Maloney
Designer: Mike Palmquist
Cover Photo: Rawpixel image 12084619. Licensed.
Series Editors: Rich Rice and J. Michael Rifenburg
Consulting Editor: Susan H. McLeod
Associate Editors: Johanna Phelps, Jonathan M. Marine, and Qingyang Sun

The WAC Clearinghouse supports teachers of writing across the disciplines. Hosted by Colorado State University, it brings together scholarly journals and book series as well as resources for teachers who use writing in their courses. This book is available in digital formats for free download at wac.colostate.edu.

Founded in 1965, the University Press of Colorado is a nonprofit cooperative publishing enterprise supported, in part, by Adams State University, Colorado State University, Fort Lewis College, Metropolitan State University of Denver, University of Alaska Fairbanks, University of Colorado, University of Denver, University of Northern Colorado, University of Wyoming, Utah State University, and Western Colorado University. For more information, visit upcolorado.com.

Citation Information: Corbett, Steven J. (Ed.). (2024). *If at First You Don't Succeed? Writing, Rhetoric, and the Question of Failure.* The WAC Clearinghouse; University Press of Colorado. https://doi.org/1010.37514/PER-B.2024.2494

Land Acknowledgment. The Colorado State University Land Acknowledgment can be found at landacknowledgment.colostate.edu.

CONTENTS

Acknowledgments vii

Introduction. Choice, Control, and Performance: Writing Studies and the Rhetoric of Failure 3
    Steven J. Corbett

PART 1. HISTORICIZING AND THEORIZING FAILURE 19

Chapter 1. A Genealogy of Failure 21
    Paul Cook

Chapter 2. Counterpoint: Why Not Intellectual Risk? 47
    Alexis Teagarden, Justin Mando, and Carolyn Commer

Chapter 3. Theorizing Failure Through Teacher Response 65
    Shane A. Wood

PART 2. CASE STUDIES AND PROFESSIONAL PROFILES OF FAILURE IN ACTION 89

Chapter 4. Fail Memes and Writing as Performance: Popular Portrayals of Writing in Internet Culture 91
    Ruth Mirtz

Chapter 5. "I'm a Bad Writer": How Students' Mindsets Influence Their Writing Processes and Performances 105
    Laura K. Miller

Chapter 6. Recognizing Feminist Resilience Rather Than Seeking Success in Response to Failure 125
    Karen R. Tellez-Trujillo

Chapter 7. Teaching to Fail? Three Female Faculty Narratives about the Racial and Gender Inequalities of SETs 137
    Mary Lourdes Silva, Josephine Walwema, and Suzie Null

PART 3. SHORT (BUT BITTER/SWEET) NARRATIVE SNIPPETS OF FAILURE 159

Chapter 8. Imposter, Performer, Professional 161
    Teagan Decker

Contents

Chapter 9. Self-Sponsored Writing & Academicized Space in FYW (Or, A Failure in Three Moves) 167
    Tyler Gillespie

Chapter 10. The Afterlife of Unfinished Writing 171
    William Duffy

Chapter 11. In Pursuit of Industry Knowledge: Always Learning by Often Failing 175
    Michal Horton

Chapter 12. Opening Doors to the Ivory Tower: Helping Students Feel Welcome to Engage in Academic Discourse 181
    Sean Fenty

Chapter 13. Standardized Test Writing and the Fear of Failing 187
    Elizabeth Blomstedt

Chapter 14. Failure to Launch? Theorizing Rhetorics of Rejection from Graduate Student Perspectives 191
    Jerrice Renita Donelson and Anicca Cox

Chapter 15. The CV of Failure: Making Rejection Visible and Cultivating Growth Mindsets in Doctoral Writers 197
    Dana Lynn Driscoll

Chapter 16. Reaping What You Sow: Reframing Academic Rejection as a Community Garden for Writing Studies 203
    Laura Decker

Chapter 17. Using X as Applied Learning in a First-Year Writing Classroom 209
    Jeffrey L. Jackson

Chapter 18. "Trust the Process": Dissertation Gatekeeping, Failure, and Graduate Student Writing 215
    Mario A. D'Agostino

Afterword. Failure: A Dwelling 223
    Allison D. Carr

Contributors 231

ACKNOWLEDGMENTS

I'd like to begin by thanking our series editors, J. Michael Rifenburg, Rich Rice, and Heather Falconer, for initially entertaining—and then fully supporting—this project every step of the way. Big thank you to our anonymous reviewers, who contributed crucial feedback from the early stages of the proposal all the way to the feedback on the full manuscript. And huge appreciation (once more) to Mike Palmquist for everything he unfailingly does and has done on a day-to-day basis for the betterment of our field and everyone in it. Wishing you all the happiness and free time you truly deserve, Mike.

Thank you to all the contributors to this collection. Your honesty, courage, perseverance, patience, and (sometimes) even surrender beautifully illustrate the concepts of choice, control, and performance that dwell within the heart of this collection.

Thank you to my colleagues at Methodist University, Suzanne Blum Malley and J. R. Hustwit (as well as the amazing Anicca Cox), for bringing me aboard and enabling me to realize personal happiness and fulfillment.

Finally, thank you to the friends, family, and loved ones who inspire and enrich my life every day: Teagan, Emma, Blake, Jordan, Will, Addison, Floyd, Garfunkel, Tory, Stephen, Niko, Sophia, Evan, Lynn, Barry, Zach, Betsy, Mom, John, Dave, Marci, Shena, PJ, Kat, Marshall, Annette, Jody, Michele, Dan, Diana, Abby, Tony, and Martin.

IF AT FIRST YOU DON'T SUCCEED? WRITING, RHETORIC, AND THE QUESTION OF FAILURE

INTRODUCTION.
CHOICE, CONTROL, AND PERFORMANCE: WRITING STUDIES AND THE RHETORIC OF FAILURE

Steven J. Corbett
Methodist University

> Failure is a feeling long before it becomes an actual result. It's vulnerability that breeds with self-doubt and then is escalated, often deliberately, by fear.
> – Michelle Obama

> Failure is a bruise, not a tattoo.
> – Jon Sinclair

As a nontraditional community college student in late-1990s Seattle, I failed my math requirement twice before finally (and barely) passing it the third time.[1] In 1997, I started my first academic job as a writing center tutor at the same community college. Seeing so many fellow students struggle and worry, I started to obsess over the idea of what it means to fail a writing course or assignment as a *student* versus what it means to fail a student in a writing course or assignment as a *teacher*. In 2005, my first attempt at passing the PhD exams failed, though . . . I promise you . . . I earnestly tried. What *does* it mean to fail at an important performance, to be a failure, or to fail someone at something?

Rachel Hodin (2013) reports on 35 people who (famously) failed or were painfully rejected before becoming legendary in their fields and professions. Some of these notable "failures"?

- Abraham Lincoln entered the army as a captain and left as a private. He also tried to start several businesses before becoming president, all of which failed.
- Lady Gaga, after finally being signed by a major record label, was dropped after only three months.

---

[1] Portions of this introduction originally appeared in Corbett and Kunkel (2017) and LaFrance and Corbett (2020).

DOI: https://doi.org/10.37514/PER-B.2024.2494.1.3

- Vincent van Gogh only sold one painting during his lifetime, and that was to a friend for very little money.
- Steven Spielberg applied to, and was rejected three times from, the University of Southern California School of Theater, Film and Television.
- J. K. Rowling was fired from her London-based Amnesty International job for writing stories all day on her work computer.
- Stephen King's first book, *Carrie*, was rejected 30 times.

In 1968, writing process pioneer Donald Murray argued that the most important experience of all for a writer is the experience of failure. For Murray, the process of writing is laden with failure: "The writer tries to say something, and fails, and through failure tries to say it better, and fails, but perhaps, eventually, he says it well enough" (p. 119). Forty-five years later, Allison Carr (2013) urged compositionists to fully explore the pedagogical potential of the concept of failure. About ten years later, she revisited and reflected upon that notion (Carr, 2024; Carr, this volume). Writing studies scholars have paid increasing attention to failure in multiple contexts, including in relation to threshold concepts (Downs & Robertson, 2015; Anson, 2015; Brooke & Carr, 2015); retention (Powell, 2014); grading and assessment practices (Caswell, 2014; Inoue, 2014, 2022; Babb & Corbett, 2016; Inoue & Bailey, 2024); graduate writing (LaFrance & Corbett, 2020); imposter syndrome (Thoune, 2020); race, gender, and class intersections (Inoue, 2020; West-Pucket et al., 2023; Inoue & Bailey, 2024); and learning transfer (e.g., Donahue, 2012; Beaufort, 2012; Wardle, 2012; Driscoll & Wells, 2012; Yancey et al., 2014; Anson, 2016; Corbett & Kunkel, 2017; Corbett, 2018). Failure is a universal concept widely applicable to every aspect of writing studies. Perhaps it is *the* most universal concept applicable to writing studies (or life, for that matter).

One way to frame failure, as exhibited, for example, in the narratives of Part Three of this volume, is to think about failure in terms of individual human agency as well as sociocultural factors. In the Obama (2021) quote above, when she says that fear "is escalated, often deliberately, by fear," she is pointing to the aspect of social control, how outside forces can "often deliberately" cause us to experience deep feelings of fear, which frequently cause us to fail. When combined with the Sinclair quote, Obama's individual "vulnerability" and "self-doubt" meet Sinclair's personal "bruise" that does not have to become a more permanent "tattoo" of stigmatized failure. In this sense, questions of *control* (see Figure 1) become important in conceptualizing failure, with failure occupying one end of a broad and deep continuum of success/failure: How much control do you have over a situation? How much control does someone or something else have in a situation? When is it harder to identify the locus of control or how much *choice* you have in a given situation?

Introduction. Choice, Control, and Performance

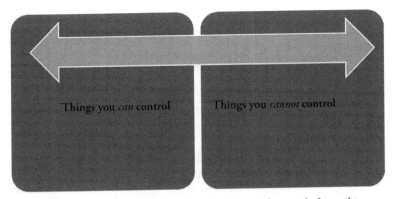

Figure 1. Continuum of success/failure and the locus of control, from things you can control to things you cannot control.

But what it means to fail can also mean vastly different things to vastly different people at vastly different times. Classical rhetoricians described the role of failed performances in rhetorical training. For example, Quintilian (ca. 95/1921) called for a socially-interactive rhetoric classroom where (white, male, citizen) students were explicitly called upon to showcase their communicative strengths while coming to terms with their own weaknesses—and performance failures—and those of their peers. Quintilian strongly believed that in order to do justice in preparing his students for the ups and downs of an often brutally competitive world, he needed to socialize them accordingly. Quintilian describes how both stronger and weaker students received rigorous rhetorical training in dealing with defeat and failure (and witnessing how their peers also dealt with defeat and failure) during oratorical performances:

> Having distributed the boys in classes, they made the order in which they were to speak depend on their ability, so that the boy who had made most progress in his studies had the privilege of declaiming first. The performances on these occasions were criticised. To win commendation was a tremendous honour, but the prize most eagerly coveted was to be the leader of the class. Such a position was not permanent. Once a month the defeated competitors were given a fresh opportunity of competing for the prize. Consequently success did not lead the victor to relax his efforts, while the vexation caused by defeat served as an incentive to wipe out the disgrace. (I.1.23–25)

For Quintilian and his contemporaries, there was great benefit in putting students on the spot, in providing them with rigorous rhetorical practice, giving and taking criticism in their speaking and writing performances—and, in the process, also learning how to cope with and manage fear of failure. The role of the instructor becomes that of the coach, encouraging rhetorical acumen, win or lose, as described by Quintilian: "If he speaks well, he has lived up to the ideals of his art, even if he is defeated" (II.17.23). And if "he" is defeated but has learned enough from that failure, then he might have the opportunity to someday prove victorious.

Given, then, crucial aspects of *kairos* and *chronos* when conceptualizing such a slippery notion as failure, a particularly useful way of thinking about the concept of failure for writing studies might be to apply a classical rhetorical frame. The authors of Chapter 2 (this volume), Alexis Teagarden, Justin Mando, and Carolyn Commer, offer a useful three-part frame with their theorizing of failure vs. risk-taking based on the "classical genres of oratory and their orientation toward time: the forensic (focused on the past), the epideictic (focused on the present), and the deliberative (focused on the future)" (see Figure 2).

With this orientation toward failure, questions of *time* become mandatory: When, in the past, have I experienced moments of failure? How did that failure affect my present, or (if I so choose) what can I do now to try to remedy that past failure? How can I look to the (possible) future to anticipate elements of (possible) failure, even as I look to the past and attempt to control my present? These can be tough questions to try to answer at any time in a person's life experience. But with time might come wisdom. For example, many contributors to this collection seem to dance an attitude of looking back to relatively recent past failures—in a relatively early or precarious career in the field (pre-tenure or contingent status and relatively few academic professional successes)—hoping to find lessons on how to not repeat those failures. Other contributors seem to reflect on temporally more distant past failures with an attitude—from relatively successful mid-to-late professional academic careers in the field (tenure and a critical mass of professional successes)—that they can continue to successfully manage any remaining critical incidents that come their way.

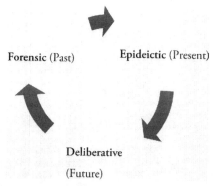

Figure 2. *"Classical Genres of Oratory and Their Orientation Toward Time."*

STUDYING OTHER'S CRITICAL MOMENTS OF FAILURE . . . AND LOOKING IN THE MIRROR

The frequently used concept of "discourse communities" is just one variable to consider in relation to the locus of control, orientations toward time, and failure. In *Writing across Contexts*, Kathleen Blake Yancey, Liane Robertson, and Kara Taczak (2014)—with their notion of "critical incidents"—offer an unpacking of negative transfer in the negotiation of discourse communities. The authors define a critical incident as "a situation where efforts either do not succeed at all or succeed only minimally" (Yancey et al., 2014, p. 120). They illustrate this concept through the extended study of Rick, a first-year physics and astrophysics major, who struggled to write about science for a general audience in his writing course then failed to write an acceptable lab report for his chemistry professor based on what he learned from writing about science for a more general audience. Ultimately, Rick learned—through persistence and accepting responsibility for his own learning—to make moments of failure opportunities for growth and improvement.

Prominent scholars in writing studies have also reported on coming to terms with their own professional "failures." Anne Beaufort (2012) reflects back on some of the issues she failed to fully account for, in terms of positive knowledge transfer, in the sample curriculum and pedagogy suggestions of her longitudinal study *College Writing and Beyond* (2007). Like Yancey, Robertson, and Taczak, Beaufort reported on a student, Tim, who, much like Rick, left his freshman writing course believing he had learned strategies for writing applicable to the other discourse communities he would subsequently encounter. Yet, as Beaufort describes, Tim failed to come to terms with the multifarious communicative situations he faced and apparently took much longer in his realization of the complex nature of discourse communities. But Beaufort lingers on her own researcherly shortcomings as well, relaying what (she realized) finally had to occur for Tim to begin to realize some sense of how all the communicative pieces might come together for him to experience success, his first professional job with an engineering firm.

While the concept of discourse communities can account for a lot of the socio-rhetorical reasons why we might experience a critical incident, we also need to consider more personalistic and individualistic variables. Asao Inoue (2020), in the "Afterword: Failure and Letting Go" for the collection *Failure Pedagogies: Learning and Unlearning What It Means to Fail*, intimates how—as successful, widely published, and respected as he is in the field—he has not succeeded in publishing anything in our flagship journal *College Composition and Communication*. He describes how an experience with a highly unsympathetic review of a manuscript he submitted to a journal early in his career caused him to (harking back to the Michelle Obama quote above) *fear* submitting anything for consideration since causing him to "fail at giving up that past failure" (Inoue, 2020, p. 261). But Inoue's fear of failure does not stop with his scholarship.

Like others in the collection *Narratives of Joy and Failure in Antiracist Assessment: Exploring Collaborative Writing Assessments,* Inoue (2024) has also questioned whether he has *failed* some of his students from time to time. Inoue describes how he may have failed while working with a young Black female student, Brea, from a working-class family in the Seattle-Tacoma area in a first-year composition course. Inoue had to come to terms with the ambiguity of Brea's performance in relation to his antiracist assessment ecology when she seemed not to directly engage with what he intended to be antiracist collaborative and linguistic aspects of certain assignments. Inoue was uncertain if Brea was performing a certain amount of resistance to Habits of White Language (HOWL) aspects of assignments by choice and if there was anything he was doing that might have been too pedagogically or conceptually controlling. While Inoue expresses unsureness about whether their pedagogical interactions were a complete failure, he also expresses unsureness about whether their interactions were a complete success. In the same volume, Sarah Prielipp (2024) also questions her own antiracist pedagogies in relation to HOWL student learning outcomes (SLOs) and whether or not students failed certain aspects of assignments or whether her system of assessment somehow failed these students. Ultimately, feeling that she needed to do a better job of helping students learn from failure, she needed to listen to their impressions of their own performances better:

> Rather than focusing on SLOs, I now ask students to measure their success by their own learning goals: What did you want to learn? How did you do it? What worked and didn't work? What do you still want to learn? Their language determines how they will be assessed, and this focus on the students' goals for their assessment holds me more accountable to their learning needs as we adjust what we should do in class based on their goals . . . Like my students, I, too, must learn from my failure and continually seek to improve my practice. (Prielipp, 2024, p. 188; cf. Babb & Corbett, 2016; Corbett & Kunkel, 2017; Corbett & Villarreal, 2022; Wood, this volume; Fenty, this volume)

In short, both Inoue and Prielipp are rightfully worrying about—and actively striving toward—building reciprocal trust and empowerment in their teaching and the reporting of their teaching.

Dana Driscoll and Jennifer Wells (2012), in relation to failed moments of knowledge transfer, argue that individual dispositions—like motivation, values, self-efficacy, and self-regulation—need to be accounted for much more when trying to account for any failed performance. For example, in considering the value of a more individually-focused lens for Beaufort's student Tim, discussed above, the authors observe:

> While Beaufort's study focuses on Tim's perceptions of his discourse communities, she does not focus on the dispositional aspects Tim has that may be causing those perceptions (such as locus of control, motivation, etc.). Beaufort also does not discuss anything about Tim as a person outside of the educational setting.

Turning our lens toward the personal and individual might nudge us to ask different types of questions regarding Tim's specific critical incidents and the idea of failed performance in general. Could there have been personal reasons that caused some of the trouble Tim had in negotiating in and between the discourse communities of first-year composition, history, and engineering? Too many commitments like a job, family, or illness might have played a part. A simple lack of motivation and effort may have been a culprit. Perhaps by the time Tim finally saw the "end" of his education, when he finally succeeded in landing a professional engineering job, all the dispositional pieces came together (or started to come together) more synergistically with that particular discourse community. A concept Driscoll and Wells build into their disposition theorizing is the theory of attribution, which can help us begin to make connections between individual agency and motivation and the outside force of discourse communities. Simply put, attribution theory deals with how much control a person believes they have over a situation and how much the cause of success or failure is a result of their own actions or circumstances beyond their control (Turner, 2007). Drawing on Pierre Bourdieu's concept of *habitus*, Elizabeth Wardle (2012) speculates that perhaps fields themselves warrant attribution consideration for frequently inculcating students with problem-solving attitudes and dispositions at the expense of problem-exploring dispositions. The author believes that this dichotomy forces students into a "psychological double-bind" that can result in confusion and failure. In many ways, then, the students we discussed above with Yancey et al. (2014), Beaufort (2012), and Driscoll and Wells (2012)—as well as teacher-scholars like Corbett and Villarreal (2022), Inoue (2024), and Prielipp (2024)—are understandably facing both immense socio-rhetorical as well as psycho-rhetorical forces they are doing their best to negotiate in the quest to survive and make sense of the critical incidents, and the accompanying chance of a failed teaching-or-learning performance, we all must inevitably face.[2]

Finally, and to further complicate this analytical frame, we would do well to remember Erving Goffman's thoughts on failed performance. In *The Presentation of Self in Everyday Life*, Goffman (1959) writes, "We must be prepared to see that the impression of reality fostered by a performance is a delicate, fragile thing that can be shattered by a very minor mishap" (p. 56). Goffman suggests the ways in which socio-rhetorical actors, rather than simply "attempting to achieve certain ends by acceptable means," also "can attempt to achieve the impression that they are achieving certain ends by acceptable means" (Goffman, 1959, p. 250). Hence, in relation to failure, the old admonishment: "Fake it, till you make it." Elsewhere, in his later work *Forms of Talk*, Goffman (1981) analyzes the consequences of failure to execute a successful performance. He explains how the very awareness and prospect of social control is a powerful means of social control, causing social actors to make preemptive moves (right or wrong) to avoid the stigma of failure at all costs. The plurality, often ambiguity, of the locus of control lends itself to the drama of human communication—including failed performances—and adds yet another layer to the many variables (see Figure 3) that can help us make sense of the vagaries of successful and failed performances.

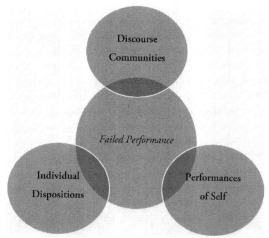

Figure 3. Overlapping Socio-Cognitive Elements of Failed Performance.

---

2   Here, we might think about individual dispositions and negotiation of discourse communities in terms of the *Framework for Success in Postsecondary Writing* habits of mind: curiosity, openness, engagement, creativity, persistence, flexibility, responsibility, and metacognition (Council of Writing Program Administrators, National Council of Teachers of English, and National Writing Project, 2011). While these dispositional traits might have been intended to apply to first-year writers, they also seem applicable to all professionals at any level.

Introduction. Choice, Control, and Performance

WHY THE POSSIBILITY OF FAILURE IS SO VERY PERSONAL . . . AND SO VERY SOCIAL

Whatever theories and frames we decide to use to try to make sense of failed performances, one thing for certain is that they involve people's stories of dealing with the *affect* of failure. Given the fact that contributors to this collection are going to be doing a lot of similar intersectional intimations, I'd like to offer readers a sense of my own coming to terms with the intertwining social and personal realities of failure, with a couple of brief snapshots from my own personal and professional experience.

I was a nontraditional, low-income, high-school dropout with an abusive and dysfunctional upbringing who returned to school at the age of 27 to earn my high school diploma and begin taking courses at Edmonds Community College near Seattle. Up to that point, it's not hard to argue that I was more-or-less a failure in life.[3] I worked hard as both an undergraduate (where I often worked multiple jobs, including at our campus writing center) and a graduate student to professionalize. As an undergraduate, I started presenting papers at conferences, landed my first academic publication in the *Writing Lab Newsletter* (Corbett, 2002), and continued this creative academic momentum as a grad student. I served as graduate assistant director of both the Expository Writing Program and the English Department Writing Center at the University of Washington, Seattle. Perhaps somewhere inside, I was attempting to allay any doubt that I was a legitimate academic performer.

Oftentimes, what seem to be crushing defeats can—in time—prove really only *major* setbacks . . . But they sure don't feel that way at first . . . When I initially failed my PhD qualifying exams in 2005, I wondered and worried if that was the end of my academic ambitions. Faced with my three—suddenly stern—mentors/committee members to orally defend my written exams, I found myself truly afraid and on the defense (c.f. Blomstedt, this volume; Donelson & Cox, this volume; D'Agostino, this volume). I floundered my way through three hours

---

3 As I reported on our writing center workshop (Corbett, Decker & Halpin, 2005), in a *Writing Lab Newsletter* article (Corbett, 2005): In a surprising, provocative testimonial, unbeknownst to both my colleagues (though they knew full-well the subject matter), I punctuated the alternative tone of our presentation when I began, "I am a PhD student, the principal investigator in an ongoing Human Subjects Division approved research study on peer tutor training, a classroom composition instructor, and the founding director of a writing center. But nine years ago, I was a high school drop-out sitting in jail for distribution of marijuana." With this last line I watched the eyes in the room, including my fellow presenters, grow large and intently focused as I continued to relate my personal transition from the subterranean world I knew to the academic one I now inhabit. I talked about anxieties, but also teachers who were patient enough to dispel them at least enough for me to continue through, teachers who gave me the skills and knowledge I needed to continue on. (p. 6)

11

of brutal Q&A that left me feeling helplessly worried and deeply wounded. At the time, it felt like the biggest failure of my life, like there was something really wrong with me—that I had been unmasked and finally found out . . .

But what I really needed to understand was the loose, baggy monster that is the genre of the exam essay. I needed to realize that it wasn't just ME (the actor); it was also YOU (the scene). It is well-understood in writing studies that students unfamiliar with a new writing situation or genre will fall back (regress) often on summary rather than argumentation and analysis. What my committee wanted were smart, sophisticated, argumentative essays. Sure, they wanted a reasonable amount of evidentiary support, but when I started to really study other people's exams, what I noticed was that they might only have ten or fifteen—strategically well-chosen—sources for each essay, rather than, say, the thirty or forty I had ridiculously tried to stuff in.

The lesson here? When faced with an unfamiliar writing situation, I study models of the genre I am about to write in. I don't just peruse—I study. After meeting with my dissertation chair, I realized I should have also talked more with all my committee members about precisely what they would be looking for. How much summary did they want? How much argumentation did they want? Etc.

Then came the new rhetorical situations of the job search. I learned a hard lesson during my exams; one that I'll never forget. In preparation for the job search, I did all the things right, textually, that I did wrong during the exams. I took all the sample materials I could get and studied them, especially the cover letter. The first draft of my cover letter was very vague about my experiences, publications, accomplishments. Too much "aw shucks" and not enough "look at this!" perhaps. But after studying, especially my chair's cover letter from his uber-successful job search eight or so years before, I knew exactly what I needed to do. (The ancient rhetorical art of imitation in the service of invention must never be taken for granted.) I noticed that he didn't hold back in describing the details of his publications, presentations, administrative positions, research activities in his cover letter—the significance of them, what they mean to our field, what they did for his teaching and learning, what they could mean for the institution he was trying so skillfully to persuade that they needed him. Once I felt I had a stronger draft of the letter, I asked all my committee members to read it and give me feedback. I took it through several successive drafts; I babied it and compulsively worked every paragraph, every sentence, every word until I felt satisfied. And as the job search progressed, I tweaked it as I tried to better fit the needs of the particular audience I felt I was writing for.

In both the PhD exams and the job search I made deliberate choices to toe the line, to conform. I made conscientious choices in my attempts to *avoid failure* by studying and performing more "expert," "smart" communicative moves that would not shock the minds and memories of my various audiences. Goffman (1959) analyzes the many complicated ways social actors judge and prepare to be judged or legitimized. He writes, "Paradoxically, the more closely the impostor's performance approximates to the real thing, the more intensely we may be threatened, for a competent performance by someone who proves to be an impostor may weaken in our minds the moral connection between legitimate authorship to play a part and the capacity to play it" (Goffman, 1959, p. 59). The further I moved through my processes of becoming an academic professional, the more proficient I became at writing my way through the academic hoops I was learning to jump through. The more competent my authorial performances became, the more I felt I was opening myself up to unmasking, to judging, to de-legitimization. I tried my best to *control* my actions in ways becoming of a budding teacher-scholar. Then, I made the *choice* to prepare myself to fail at making everyone who read my materials love me and want to hire me.

PERFORMANCES (AND REALIZATIONS) OF SELF: RISKING IT ALL ON FAILURE

Harking back a few decades, many centuries, (and to the start of this introduction), Donald Murray (1968/1982) urged that the writing course should be an experimental one:

> A course in practicing, a course in trying, a course in *choice* [emphasis added], a course in craft. Failure should not be accepted passively, but failure should never be defeat. The student should learn to exploit his failures as he rediscovers his subject, re-searches his information, redesigns his form, rewrites and edits every sentence. (p. 119–120)

We might just as easily argue that the curriculum and pedagogy in writing studies must, therefore, also be a curriculum and pedagogy with the notion of failure at its core. But one wherein students and teachers learn to metacognitively come to terms with the concept of failure, to manage their own experiences with failure, and to exploit the notion for its full worth. And this applies just as relevantly to the career path of the student or the teacher.

What might it mean, then, to negotiate the often-fuzzy interstices of choice and control in failure, adversity, and success in relation to conformity, resistance, risk or boundary-pushing, and performances (and realizations) of self? What if you might be too poor, or too Black, or too Latinx, or just too queer? The work of queer theorists can aid us further in these complex calls to personal growth and becoming, offering foundational insights into our attempts to negotiate time, space, control, and choice. To queer something can mean to take an alternate path, to disturb the order of things, to "fail" in or "dis" traditional orientations and ways of knowing and ways of acting and performing (Ahmed, 2006; see also Johnson & Sheehan, 2020; West-Pucket et al., 2023). Judith (Jack) Halberstam (2011), in *The Queer Art of Failure*, offers what might be called a theoretical blueprint for how academics often learn to balance exactly the tensions they experience between needing to conform to conventions and expectations in order to succeed and the desire to resist and take risks. Making the choice to take intellectual risks is an important piece of the growth of a writer or teacher of writing (see Teagarden, Mando & Commer, this volume). Planning for more purposeful failures can then be a part of our intentional and strategic growth as learners and writers. For Halberstam (2011), failure and risk-taking offer their own rewards: "Under certain circumstances failing, losing, forgetting, unmasking, undoing, unbecoming, not knowing may in fact offer more creative, more cooperative, more surprising ways of being in the world" (pp. 2–3). Halberstam believes that one can realize a state of being "in but not of" (p. 11) the university, that even though we are—indeed more-or-less by choice—part of the socially engineered world of the modern university, we might still *realize* our own local, esoteric knowledges, and that these unbridled knowings might just do their part to push the boundaries of the serious, stuffy academy where any sort of resistance by force may seem futile. In short, Halberstam urges academics to make choices in how they "fail" to be "normal(ized)."

If fortune does indeed favor the brave (and, sometimes, the queer), then scholars in writing studies can learn a lot—and sometimes risk a lot—by using failure as a conceptual lens to study and reflect upon all aspects of the complex intersectional work we do. In this collection, writing researchers from all subfields of writing studies share their thoughts, experiences, and studies on the concept of failure. This collection is intended for teachers and researchers of writing across the disciplines. The 18 original chapters, as well as the Afterword by (none other than the most-cited scholar on the topic of writing studies and failure in this collection) Allison Carr, will expand and complicate concepts and ideas related to the topic of writing and failure, like the ones explored in Carr and Laura Micciche's (2020) *Failure Pedagogies*; Stephanie West-Pucket, Nicole Caswell, and William Bank's (2023) *Failing Sideways: Queer Possibilities for Writing Assessment*; and Inoue and Kristin DeMint Bailey's (2024) *Narratives of Joy and Failure in Antiracist Assessment,* especially in terms of pedagogy and identity. It is divided into three interanimating parts: Part One: Historicizing and Theorizing Failure; Part Two: Case Studies and Professional Profiles of Failure in Action; and Part Three: Short (but Bitter/Sweet) Narrative Snippets of Failure.

REFERENCES

Ahmed, S. (2006). *Queer phenomenology: Orientations, objects, others*. Duke University Press.

Anson, C. M. (2015). Crossing thresholds: What's to know about writing across the curriculum? In L. Adler-Kassner & E. Wardle (Eds.), *Naming what we know: Threshold concepts of writing studies* (pp. 203–219). Utah State University Press.

Anson, C. M. (2016). The Pop Warner chronicles: A case study in contextual adaptation and the transfer of writing ability. *College Composition and Communication, 67*(4), 518–549. https://doi.org/10.58680/ccc201629612.

Babb, J. & Corbett, S. J. (2016). From zero to sixty: A survey of college writing teachers' grading practices and the affect of failed performance. *Composition Forum, 34*. https://compositionforum.com/issue/34/zero-sixty.php.

Beaufort, A. (2007). *College writing and beyond: A new framework for university writing instruction*. Utah State University Press.

Beaufort, A. (2012). *College writing and beyond*: Five years later. *Composition Forum, 26*. http://compositionforum.com/issue/26/college-writing-beyond.php.

Brooke, C. & Carr A. D. (2015). Failure can be an important part of writing development. In L. Adler-Kassner & E. Wardle (Eds.), *Naming what we know: Threshold concepts of writing studies* (pp. 62–64). Utah State University Press.

Carr, A. D. (2013). In support of failure. *Composition Forum, 27*. https://compositionforum.com/issue/27/failure.php.

Carr, A. D. (2024). Following failure. *Composition Forum, 53*. https://compositionforum.com/issue/53/following-failure.php.

Carr, A. D. & Micciche, L. R. (Eds.). (2020). *Failure pedagogies: Learning and unlearning what it means to fail*. Peter Lang.

Caswell, N. I. (2014). Dynamic patterns: Emotional episodes within teachers' response practices. *Journal of Writing Assessment 7*(1). https://escholarship.org/uc/item/7gz1c60w.

Corbett, S. J. (2002). The role of the emissary: Helping to bridge the communication canyon between instructors and students. *The Writing Lab Newsletter, 27*(2), 10–11. https://wac.colostate.edu/docs/wln/v27/27.2.pdf.

Corbett, S. J. (2005). Report from the 4Cs: Familiar faces and a few surprises. *The Writing Lab Newsletter, 29*(9), 6–9. https://wac.colostate.edu/docs/wln/v29/29.9.pdf.

Corbett, S. J., Decker, T. E. & Halpin, J. (2005, March). Never too old to do it: Returning student success and writing centers [Pre-C's Workshop]. 56th Annual Conference on College Composition and Communication, San Francisco, CA.

Corbett, S. J. (2018). Processes of administrative (un)becoming: Learning to fail while trying to fly. In C. A. Wooten, J. Babb, and B. Ray (Eds.), *WPAs in transition: Navigating educational leadership positions* (pp. 139–152). Utah State University Press.

Corbett, S. J. & Kunkel J. (2017). "Did you ever take that test yourself?" Failed knowledge transfer and the *framework* habits of mind as two-way street. In P. Portanova, J. M. Rifenburg & D. Roen (Eds.), *Contemporary perspectives on cognition and writing* (pp. 247–267). The WAC Clearinghouse; University Press of Colorado. https://doi.org/10.37514/PER-B.2017.0032.2.13.

Corbett, S. J. & Villarreal, K. (2022). Listening about listening: Narratives of affect, diversity, and feminist listening in writing center research reporting. In J. Morris & K. A. Concannon (Eds.), *Emotions and affect in writing centers*, (pp. 219–236). Parlor Press.

Council of Writing Program Administrators, National Council of Teachers of English & National Writing Project. (2011). *Framework for success in postsecondary writing.* https://wpacouncil.org/aws/CWPA/asset_manager/get_file/350201?ver=7548.

Donahue, C. (2012). Transfer, portability, generalization: (How) does composition expertise "carry"? In K. Ritter & P. K. Matsuda (Eds.), *Exploring composition studies: Sites, issues, and perspectives* (pp. 145–166). Utah State University Press.

Downs, D. & Robertson, L. (2015). Threshold concepts in first-year composition. In L. Adler-Kassner & E. Wardle (Eds.), *Naming what we know: Threshold concepts of writing studies* (pp. 201–219). Utah State University Press.

Driscoll, D. L. & Wells, J. (2012). Beyond knowledge and skills: Writing transfer and the role of student dispositions. *Composition Forum, 26.* http://compositionforum.com/issue/26/beyond-knowledge-skills.php.

Goffman, E. (1959). *The presentation of self in everyday life.* Double Day.

Goffman, E. (1981). *Forms of talk.* University of Pennsylvania Press.

Halberstam, J. (2011). *The queer art of failure.* Duke University Press.

Hodin, R. (2013, October 14). *35 Famous people who were painfully rejected before making it big.* Thought Catalogue. https://thoughtcatalog.com/rachel-hodin/2013/10/35-famous-people-who-were-painfully-rejected-before-making-it-big/.

Inoue, A. B. (2014). Theorizing failure in US writing assessments. *Research in the Teaching of English, 48,* 330–352.

Inoue, A. B. (2022). *Labor-based grading contracts: Building equity and inclusion in the compassionate writing classroom* (2nd ed.). The WAC Clearinghouse; University Press of Colorado. https://doi.org/10.37514/PER-B.2022.1824.

Inoue, A. B. (2020). Afterword: Failure and letting go. In A. D. Carr & L. R. Micciche (Eds.), *Failure pedagogies: Learning and unlearning what it means to fail* (pp. 259–263). Peter Lang.

Inoue, A. B. (2024). More than a story of antiracist failure and hope. In A. B Inoue & K. D. Bailey (Eds.), *Narratives of joy and failure in antiracist assessment: Exploring collaborative writing assessments* (pp. 31–42). The WAC Clearinghouse; University Press of Colorado. https://doi.org/10.37514/PRA-B.2024.2227.2.01.

Inoue, A. B. & Bailey, K. D. (Eds.). (2024). *Narratives of joy and failure in antiracist assessment: Exploring collaborative writing assessments.* The WAC Clearinghouse; University Press of Colorado. https://doi.org/10.37514/PRA-B.2024.2227.

Johnson, G. P. & Sheehan, R. (2020). The uses of queer failure: Navigating the pedagogical mandate of happiness. In A. D. Carr & L. R. Micciche (Eds.), *Failure pedagogies: Learning and unlearning what it means to fail* (pp. 127–140). Peter Lang.

LaFrance, M. & Corbett, S. J. (2020). Discourse community fail! Negotiating choices in success/failure and graduate level writing development. In M. Brooks-Gillies, E. G. Garcia, S. H. K. K. Manthey & T. G. Smith (Eds.), *Graduate writing across the disciplines: Identifying, teaching, supporting.* (pp. 295–314). The WAC

Clearinghouse; University Press of Colorado. https://doi.org/10.37514/ATD-B.2020.0407.2.12.

Murray, D. M. (1982). The process of teaching. In D. M. Murray (Ed.), *Learning by teaching: Selected articles on writing and teaching* (pp. 115–120). Boynton/Cook. (Original work published 1968)

Obama, M. (2021). *Becoming*. New York: Crown.

Powell, P. R. (2014). *Retention and resistance: Writing instruction and students who leave.* Logan: Utah State University Press.

Prielipp, S. (2024). Tensions and failures: A story of assessment. In A. B. Inoue & K. D. Bailey (Eds.), *Narratives of joy and failure in antiracist assessment: Exploring collaborative writing assessments* (pp. 177–190). The WAC Clearinghouse; University Press of Colorado. https://doi.org/10.37514/PRA-B.2024.2227.2.10.

Quintilian, M. F. (1921) *The institutio oratoria.* (H. E. Butler, Trans). G. P. Putnam's Sons. (Original work published ca.95)

Thoune, D. L. (2020). Failure potential: Using failure as feedback. In A. D. Carr & L. R. Micciche (Eds.), *Failure pedagogies: Learning and unlearning what it means to fail* (pp. 53–62). Peter Lang.

Turner, J. H. (2007). *Human emotions: A sociological theory*. Routledge.

Wardle, E. (2012). Creative repurposing for expansive learning. *Composition Forum, 26*. http://compositionforum.com/issue/26/creative-repurposing.php.

West-Puckett, S., Caswell, N. I. & Banks, W. P. (2023). *Failing sideways: Queer possibilities for writing assessment.* Utah State University Press.

Yancey, K. B., Robertson, L. & Taczak, K. (2014). *Writing across contexts: Transfer, composition, and sites of writing.* Utah State University Press.

PART 1.

HISTORICIZING AND THEORIZING FAILURE

Part One offers chapters that help contextualize the rest of the collection with histories and theories of failure. Contributors provide breadth and depth to the question of failure, including continuing to take us back thousands of years in the rhetorical tradition with a genealogy of failure, detailing a rhetorical approach to the idea of intellectual risk-taking as a conceptual counterpoint to failure, and theorizing failure in relation to feedback to student writing.

In **Chapter 1**, "A Genealogy of Failure," Paul Cook takes a broad historical view of the concept of failure from the *arete* of the ancient Greeks to the earliest Medieval universities with their agonistic oral disputations to the present era of hyper-anxiety surrounding college admissions—complete with celebrity cheating scandals. This chapter, lauded by Allison Carr (this volume) as "the most comprehensive review of failure's systemic meaning that has been written," maps this history through the Nietzschean-Foucauldian method of genealogy in order to illuminate its workings alongside the development of capitalism and the gradual development of the university as a significant social institution. Cook provides a compelling historical account of how failure became an internalized, individualized concept enmeshed in the logic of neoliberal capital and argues how this understanding of failure has limited our collective capacity to imagine other forms of success, especially as it pertains to the relationship between education and material achievement. The author concludes by suggesting concrete ways that we, as academics and writing teachers, can reframe success and failure in the 21st century in an effort to improve our relations with each other and the world. For example, how might these terms, so slippery in their familiarity, be refocused to encompass one's commitment to social justice, equity, and advocacy?

Chapter 2, "Counterpoint: Why Not Intellectual Risk?" authors Alexis Teagarden, Justin Mando, and Carolyn Commer draw on their previous work in developing a rhetorical approach to intellectual risk-taking to explore the conceptual and practical trade-offs related to approaching writing as a "risk" that relates to—or precedes—failure. In their previous study, the authors examined the problems posed by vague and often undefined uses of the term "intellectual risk." But their current inquiry asks how might its capaciousness as a term be of value as a flexible pedagogical concept that accounts for a variety of writing practices? This chapter suggests how framing writing as a process of deliberating over the *choices* involved in intellectual risks may offset or complement students' and writers' attitudes about putting *something* "on the line" that can fail.

Shane A. Wood, in **Chapter 3**, "Theorizing Failure through Teacher Response," engages compelling questions involving failure in and through teacher response. Does all feedback on student writing produce better, more accomplished writing? When does feedback fail to do the job a teacher expects it to do, and how do we account for the failure of teacher feedback? To explore these questions, this chapter introduces *feedback failure theory* and offers an examination of how feedback can fail through its *production* and *perception*, two sites where failure occurs in and through response. Wood describes a pedagogical practice that allows both students and teachers to focus on how teacher feedback, like student writing, somehow misses the mark, or fails, at least some of the time. The author ultimately frames failure as an opportunity to create more purposeful pedagogies through response.

CHAPTER 1.
A GENEALOGY OF FAILURE

Paul Cook
Indiana University, Kokomo

Failure is a compelling paradox.

On the one hand, few of life's vicissitudes are more familiar to us than failure: the bitter sting of failed careers, the end of cherished relationships, ego-draining professional or academic failures, the dramatized downfalls that fill popular fiction, the quotidian (and always untimely) failures of digital devices, cars, and other appliances. And who can deny the ultimate and unavoidable failures of our own human, all-too-human bodies?

There are also the macro-failures we share in a democratic society like the United States: our mostly bungled response to the COVID-19 pandemic, our repeated failure to do much of anything about mass shootings, our general inability to meaningfully address the existential threat of climate change in policy proposals, and—some would say—the encroaching failure of liberal democracy itself (Luce, 2018). Failures, large and small, are everywhere, all the time, just over the horizon.

And yet, for all of failure's lived ubiquity and closeness, how well do we really understand it?

Taking a broad historical view of the concept of failure from the *arete* of the ancient Greeks (Hawhee, 2004) to the earliest Medieval universities with their agonistic oral disputations (Clark, 2006) to the present era of hyper-anxiety surrounding college admissions (Cornwall, 2022)—complete with celebrity cheating scandals! (Medina et al., 2019)—this chapter attempts to map the history, present, and future of failure as it intersects with both neoliberal rationality and formal education. My primary goal is to illuminate how failure "works" alongside both the development of capitalism and the rise of the university as a significant social institution.

In what follows, I provide an eclectic, genealogical account of failure's discontinuities and mutations over time, especially as they pertain to how we understand success and failure, winning and losing, and competition. For the ancient Greeks, failure and victory alike could be found in the contestive, identity-forming struggle of the *agon*, whether in wrestling or in oratorical competition or on the field of battle. In the Middle Ages, oral disputation in the early university retained much of this agonism but shifted its focus from identity construction to ritualized questioning and the maintenance of canonical knowledge (Connors, 1997). To fail academically in the context of a medieval university was to deviate from the accepted, sacred knowledge of the canon.

But these were understandings of failure that played mostly on the surface of things. In the modern era, failure has burrowed deep into our psyches, becoming an internal, individualized experience enmeshed in what Brown (2015) calls the "sophisticated common sense" logic of neoliberalism (p. 35). With its celebration of the individual-as-entrepreneur and the extension of market rationality to all facets of existence, neoliberal rationality has intensified into a kind of hardened, common-sense dogma for individuals in late capitalism, perhaps especially in the era of ubiquitous digital connectivity and social media, even as its viability as a set of economic policy assumptions and prescriptions has waned since the global financial crisis of 2007–2008 (Sitaraman, 2019).

I conclude by sketching a vision for an academy in which success and failure have been reframed not around *winning* but around mutual support, collective action, and community. Here, I follow most closely the work of researchers like Feigenbaum (2021) and Kapur (2015), whose work on generative failure holds great promise for informing how we as educators might rethink our approaches to teaching and learning, even as we advocate for the kinds of large-scale structural changes that would ultimately be necessary to cultivate classrooms and workplaces where failure is truly accepted as both productive and part of the growth process. How might these binary terms—failure and success, losing and winning—so slippery in their familiarity and so limiting in their shaping of both private and public life, be refocused or even unbundled to encompass a commitment to social justice, equity, collective action, and advocacy?

This chapter, ultimately, is about more than grappling with the simplistic binary of success/failure. It is about more than even just our impoverished vocabulary for understanding success and failure. It is about power. How might power be (re)distributed, (re)thought, and/or (re)used for the collective good of the greatest number of people? How might (re)thinking our obsessions with failure (and success), with winning (and losing), and with competition and scarcity help us get there? How might a different understanding of failure—one informed by a genealogical reading of failure that defamiliarizes failure and reads against the grain of "official" histories (i.e., the rise of the bourgeois subject)—inform our present moment?

Seriously, what other choice do we have?

FEAR OF FAILING WITHOUT A NET

Neither the ubiquity nor proximity of failure provides any guarantee that we actually understand it, much less talk about it. The rise of academic Failure

Studies over the course of the last decade or so is an acknowledgment of this fact, as well as an earnest attempt by scholars and researchers from a variety of disciplines to draw failure out of its secret places, as it were, and into the open, so that it can be better analyzed and understood.[1] Carr and Micciche (2020b), writing in the introduction to their important edited collection *Failure Pedagogies: Learning and Unlearning What It Means to Fail*, identify the "growing, collective obsession with failure" in both academic and public discourse as a "trend [that] makes concrete the relationship between failure and success that has long played a role in bootstraps ideologies pervasive within American progress narratives" (p. 1). Like the sweet smell of success, failure, too, is ever-present, humming along in the background, always lurking in the recesses of our thoughts, occasionally muscling its way into the foreground of the cerebral cortex. It's telling and instructive that Carr and Micciche (2020b), borrowing a metaphor from Ahmed (2017), refer to failure as a "sweaty concept" (p. 2). Sweaty concepts are those that emerge from lived experiences and bear the marks—the sweat and discomfort—of their toil, refusing to hide the fact that they are the products of laboring bodies, bodies that must be seen, bodies "that are unsettled by the labor of dealing with systemic failures" (Carr & Micciche, 2020b, p. 2). A sweaty concept "shows the labor involved in its making," resisting the "reassuring takeaways" and uplifting bromides that we've been conditioned to trot out in polite company, perhaps especially in academic discourse (Carr & Micciche, 2020b, p. 2).

It's probably true that many of us avoid candidly discussing our own failures, at least openly or publicly, and then only if they can be reframed in a way that somehow enhances our identity, diversifies our personal "stock portfolio" of rich and formative experiences, or provides curious onlookers with a comforting uplift. Failures are generally only safe for public consumption if they can be recast as hard-earned comebacks, used to showcase an entrepreneurial spirit, or offered up as fodder for an appropriately cheery Instagram story, perhaps extolling the virtues of "never giving up" or "believing in yourself." Failure, in other words, though everywhere and always imposing itself on lived

---

[1] Several articles and book-length studies in a variety of disciplines, from rhetoric and composition studies to history to film and media studies, have emerged in the last decade that attempt to understand failure, several of which are examined in greater detail in this chapter (Appadurai & Alexander, 2020; Burger, 2012; Carr, 2013; Carr, 2017; Carr & Micciche, 2020a; Feigenbaum, 2021; Rickly, 2017; Sandage, 2005; Smith, 2010). An interesting corollary to the rise of what some have dubbed "Failure Studies" is "Quit Lit," a genre characterized by academics writing about their experiences leaving academia. It is worth noting that both Failure Studies and Quit Lit have emerged as recognizable genres of academic and public discourse in the last two decades, with a noticeable uptick after the global financial crisis of 2007–2008.

experience, can be a difficult concept to get at precisely because it is so familiar. As the notion of failure as a sweaty concept suggests, it's rare that we can just sit with failure, just *let it be*, without making it into something else: a lesson, a warning, a tactic. There is a logic behind this; it is the logic of neoliberalism and human capital.

In global capitalism—or more vividly, in what Odell (2019) pointedly calls our "blasted landscape of neoliberal determinism"—failure, like everything else, takes on an inescapably economic character (p. xii). The modern subject, conditioned by economic scarcity and a kind of gnawing, tenuous (or "sweaty") precarity, is indelibly shaped by the always-on, dehumanizing entrepreneurialization of human activity under neoliberalism. We are always and everywhere prepared, poised, and presented as market actors—"*homo oeconomicus*," following Foucault (1979/2003) in his lectures on biopolitics from the late 1970s. This means that what "counts" as success (and failure), as winning (and losing) now figures primarily—if not exclusively—within a hyper-competitive market-driven economic matrix of calculations, one in which the individual striver is constrained not only by the stigma associated with failure but also with the tangibly real possibility of total economic and material loss.[2]

The fact is that, for many people, due in large part to the United States' notoriously lousy social safety net (Aaron, 2020), these days, second chances are about as rare as a low-interest loan for a bad credit borrower. In fact, much of the current precarity in our society can be directly traced to the hollowing out of the social safety net in the United States and other developed nations over the last fifty years, coupled with the inherent instability of global financial capitalism and ubiquitous bootstraps sermons about bettering oneself through

---

2 As Brown (2015) notes, this is not to say that all aspects of life have been monetized or marketized under neoliberal rationality but that the *model* of the market has colonized all domains of life, even in contexts where money or markets are not explicitly involved (pp. 33–35). People on dating apps often approach their activities there as investors or entrepreneurs, diversifying their "dating portfolios" to net as many connections (or matches) as possible; similarly, parents obsess over school rankings and placement rates at K-12 schools and elite colleges. Neither of these examples is explicitly monetary in that the immediate goal is to generate wealth. Rather, they suggest how people are construed as market actors in nearly all facets of life, which underpins the ever-present fear of fiscal and material failure that characterizes contemporary existence. As far back as the 1980s, Ehrenreich (1989) diagnosed this anxiety as the American middle class's "fear of falling." More recently, Brown (2015) writes: "*Homo oeconomicus* as human capital is concerned with enhancing its portfolio value in all domains of its life, an activity undertaken through practices of self-investment and attracting investors. Whether through social media 'followers,' 'likes,' and 'retweets,' through ranking and ratings for every activity and domain, or through more directly monetized practices, the pursuit of education, training, leisure, reproduction, consumption, and more are increasingly configured as strategic decisions and practices related to enhancing the self's future value" (pp. 33–34; original emphasis).

hard work and savvy self-presentation.[3] These and other forces have conspired to create a situation where economic ruin is an ever-present threat from which none of us—even the moderately well-off—are ever truly immune. Ehrenreich (1989) refers to this as the uniquely middle-class "fear of falling." The majority of working Americans are a single paycheck away from financial hardship or ruin according to a study by the nonpartisan research organization NORC at the University of Chicago (Passy, 2019). Not surprisingly, BIPOC are among the most economically vulnerable Americans: "Right now the net wealth of a typical Black family in America is around one-tenth that of a white family" (Mineo, 2021).

Moreover, under the contemporary regime of neoliberal rationality, where "heretofore noneconomic domains, activities, and subjects" are transformed into economic calculations, and everyone is obsessed with "enhancing [their] portfolio value in all domains of . . . life," to fail economically is, in some rather obvious respects, to fail ultimately and decisively (Brown, 2015, pp. 31–32).[4] As Nealon (2008) pointedly puts it, life under 21st-century neoliberalism features the constant and "mundane reminder that many *successful* people in wealthy countries are still only a couple of paychecks or a serious illness away from the street" (p. 54; emphasis added).

Like precarious workers at all levels of society and industry (Sagan, 2016), is it any wonder that today's college students are afraid to take risks with their learning, majors, and coursework? The problem is not that today's students are dull or uninspired, or even necessarily that they have been shell-shocked by the pandemic (McMurtrie, 2022), but that they are deathly afraid to fail, which in the current environment of precarity can lead to increased debt and extreme economic hardship, especially for low-income students. Reporting on a recently concluded, large-scale study of over 1,000 students on ten campuses, Fischman & Gardner (2022) describe students' relationship with learning and schooling as a transactional one:

---

3 Add to this volatile mix the fact that a college degree, which for decades has proven to be one of the most durable pathways to the middle class in the US, keeps going up in price. As we will see in a later section, elite academic institutions can pretty well charge what they want, with some parents infamously paying hundreds of thousands of dollars to get their children in "through the side door," which was Rick Singer's term for bribing coaches, admissions officers, and other university representatives to shepherd the children of elites into top universities like Stanford and the University of Southern California (Thomason et al., 2020).

4 My examination of contemporary failure in this chapter is obviously and unapologetically U.S.-centric, especially in its examples and in the broad contours of its main arguments. While I do make several attempts to show how neoliberalism shapes subjectivity and failure in a global context, the majority of my examination is focused firmly on the U.S. context for reasons that I hope will become clear over the course of this chapter.

> We found that nearly half of [students] miss the point of college. They don't see value in what they are learning, nor do they understand why they take classes in different fields or read books that do not seem directly related to their major. They approach college with a "transactional" view—their overarching goal is to build a resumé with stellar grades, which they believe will help them secure a job post-college. Many see nothing wrong with using any means necessary to achieve the desired resumé, and most acknowledge that cheating is prevalent on campus. In short, they are more concerned with the pursuit of earning than the process of learning.

Similarly, Davidson (2017/2022), in a description that will be familiar to anyone who has been in a college classroom in the last decade or so, describes how students are "burdened by debt" and therefore "narrow their choices":

> They do not explore and test options for a productive potential career that intersects with their passions and interests. Instead, the financial strain of tuition debt turns college from an aspiration for a better future, alive with possibility, into a cynical enterprise, a union card, as people used to say, on the way to the best-paying job they can wrangle, *whether they like it or not.* (p. 166; emphasis added)

As a way to remedy this situation, educators have sought to lower the stakes of failure by changing the narrative and showing students that failure is a part of the process of growth and learning. Many instructors experiment with labor-based grading contracts, course menus, low-stakes assignments, and other curricular mechanisms to change the structure of their classes in ways that encourage risk-taking and experimentation. But as Feigenbaum (2021) notes, "these efforts do not challenge the ideology of hypercompetitive individualism; in other words, lowering the stakes of failure is not the same as *de-stigmatizing* failure" (22; original emphasis). Hallmark (2018) argues that the "Failure is OK" narrative is damaging to low-income and first-generation college students, many of whom are economically vulnerable and, realistically, unable to fail. Scholarships can be lost, utilities can be disconnected, family members can suffer. For the most vulnerable among us, failure can have very real material consequences that are difficult or even impossible to undo. Telling these students that "Failure is essential to success," while perhaps true on some level and for some (privileged) students, conveniently ignores the reality of privilege and rampant inequality in American society while bracketing the material consequences of failure in a "precarious meritocracy" like the US (Feigenbaum, 2021, p. 18). "Precarious meritocracy" names the neoliberal ideology that "portrays academic and professional success as a matter of personal accountability rather than an outcome engendered by systemic forces" (Feigenbaum, 2021, pp. 18–19).

Our own historically specific (and quite recent) understanding of failure has limited our collective capacity to imagine other forms of success, or even happiness, particularly as it pertains to the relationship between education and material achievement. At the same time, as Duina (2011) convincingly argues in a book-length exploration of the American obsession with winning, "The power and prevalence in American society of the language of winning and losing means that we do not engage in . . . self-discovery and that we settle, in turn, with an approach to life that is tiring and fails to fulfill us fully" (p. 202). Much of this lack of imagination can, I suggest, be chalked up to the aforementioned precarity and the lack of a robust social safety net that would enable greater risk-taking and make it possible for people to rise above the claustrophobic confines of neoliberalism's all-encompassing market logic and view themselves as more than merely human capital.

Within the paradigm of neoliberalism, it has become laughable to suggest alternative, collective forms of resistance to the ever-intensifying demands placed on students, workers, professionals, and others. Much of this has to do with the frailty of the human ego and the collective failure of our political imaginations. Much of it has to do with our impoverished vocabulary for articulating alternative conceptions of success and fulfillment outside the narrow confines of what actor Charlie Sheen so memorably encapsulated over a decade ago (*"winning!"*). The beauty of the human animal and the experience of life itself—our originality, our uniqueness, our many-splendored talents and higher natures—are swallowed up and rendered insignificant and speck-like when reckoned against the relentless machinery of global capitalism. Truly, winning is everything because we literally can't imagine anything else more valuable:

> Neoliberalism retracts this "beyond" and eschews this "higher nature":
>> the normative reign of *homo oeconomicus* in every sphere means that there are no motivations, drives, or aspirations apart from economic ones, that there is nothing to being human apart from "mere life." Neoliberalism is the rationality through which capitalism finally swallows humanity: not only with its machinery of compulsory commodification and profit-driven expansion, but by its form of valuation. (Brown, 2015, p. 44; original emphasis)

What if people truly had the space to fail? What if there were alternatives to success and winning that didn't automatically and inexorably lead to failure? What if failure could be refigured as both a necessity and a prerequisite for not only success but also for the ethical, sane practice of life itself?

What if there were more to life than "*#winning!*"?

WHAT IS FAILURE? WINNERS, LOSERS & DIFFERENTIATION

Celebrities, politicians, and other public figures are as susceptible to failure as the rest of us, though when they fail it is quite often in a more spectacular fashion. Such is the nature of modern celebrity. In the summer of 2022, the American public gleefully picked apart the personal lives Johnny Depp and Amber Heard in daily dispatches from the courtroom (Roberts, 2022). With each fresh failure revealed through tearful testimony, we get another taste of the bittersweet fruit of *schadenfreude*.

For some lucky ones, failure even functions as a prerequisite for a mid-career revival or future success. Robert Downey, Jr. managed to reinvent himself from a coked-out has-been twenty years ago to a coveted spot atop the Marvel Pantheon. Michael Jordan's now-mythical failure to make the varsity team in high school—a story retold so often it has become woven into the fabric of the modern sports ethos—preceded his inexorable rise to basketball superstardom. Even Oprah Winfrey was fired from her first on-air gig as an evening news anchor (Zurawick, 2011), later becoming the world's most beloved talk show host and baroness of a billion-dollar media empire.

A key feature of this kind of failure is that it must be followed by a convincing narrative of self-overcoming and triumph through perseverance, like the gangly Abraham Lincoln and his undisputed place of honor in American political mythology. We can celebrate the failure(s) of those who ultimately go on to win and win big. There are others: Winona Ryder (from shoplifting strange things to reinventing herself in the Netflix hit *Stranger Things*), Britney Spears, Neil Patrick Harris, Michael Keaton, Eliot Spitzer, and Mark Sanford, just to name a few. Failure *of a certain kind* can almost always be forgiven and even forgotten with enough subsequent wins or even a single really big win.[5]

Duina (2011) calls them the "turnaround victors" (p. 101), a class of winners who lose initially, perhaps even losing consistently for a long time, as in the case of

---

5   This is a key distinction. Some failures, such as moral failings and some criminal activity, cannot be so easily forgiven, if forgiven at all. It seems highly unlikely, for instance, that Harvey Weinstein is poised for a late-career comeback, to take one example among others. Then again, public opinion has softened a bit on Bill Cosby in recent years, so one never truly knows (Deodhar, 2022).

a Lincoln or a young Stephen King, only to turn it around and win big in the end. Hollywood loves winners like these, both in fiction and in real life, because they make for such good stories. Movie audiences adore narratives where the downtrodden hero overcomes all odds. Every March, fans of college hoops fall in love all over again with a mid-major Cinderella team that improbably survives to play in the Final Four. Other types of winners in Duina's (2011) useful taxonomy of winners and losers include the *consistent victors* (those who always win—boring!), the *selective winners* (those who only win once or twice but win in a spectacularly magnificent way, thus never having to prove their status as definitive winners again), and finally, the *relentless minds* (those who keep losing but whose "unfailing spirits and determination in the face of repeat failure at achieving the desired results" makes them heroes of perseverance and, thus, winners in the minds of many) (p. 105).

Turnaround winners need little elaboration. These are the stories that capture our imaginations and fill our myths and legends. They are the cherished chestnuts with which we send our children off to their slumbers; together these are the stories that fuel the American Dream. The ragtag soldiers of the Continental Army, being led by General George Washington, defeating the British Empire's war machine in the American Revolution. Ulysses S. Grant pulling himself up from a broken-down alcoholic on the Missouri plains to a great Civil War general and, ultimately, to President of the United States after the war. Rosa Parks triumphing over the forces of racism by refusing to take a seat at the back of the bus and sparking the kindling of the nascent Civil Rights movement.

Former NFL quarterback Tom Brady is perhaps the best and most widely recognizable contemporary example of a consistent winner. Brady never seemed capable of losing, even when by all rights he probably should have, such as when he led the New England Patriots to a thrilling come-from-behind victory over the Atlanta Falcons in Super Bowl LI in 2017. Down 28 to 3 midways through the third quarter, Brady rallied his squad to an unprecedented 34–28 overtime victory.[6] It remains the biggest comeback in Super Bowl history (Edmonds, 2022). Even "Deflategate," the cheating scandal whereby members of the Patriot's team and coaching staff were accused of deflating opponent's footballs, didn't let the air out of Brady's legacy as a consistent winner. On the other hand, relentless minds can be a bit more challenging to identify for reasons that we will examine below. The late actor Christopher Reeve is one example of a relentless mind-type of winner. As Duina (2011) describes it:

> Reeve was once Superman. An accident confined him to a wheelchair, paralyzed, from 1995 to 2004. He could have

---

[6] Super Bowl LI (in February 2017) was the first and, at the time of this writing, only Super Bowl to be decided in overtime.

resigned himself to a secluded, depressive life of inaction and self-pity. Instead, he famously chose to "go forward," to live his life to the fullest, and in the process, to work hard to help those who suffer from paralysis. His mentality was that of a winner and we, the audience watching and hearing, undoubtedly viewed him as such—definitely. (p. 105).

This fascinating sociological taxonomy of winners and losers merits some elaboration. First, it is important to realize that our love of winning (and winners) and our contempt for losing (and losers) is not as simple as it might appear. For Duina (2011), as both spectators and competitors, whether in sports, the game of life, or some other competitive arena, winning in and of itself is not terribly interesting. Instead, certain factors have to be present—there is no great pleasure in watching a chess master put a kindergartener in check or an NBA star dunk on a high school player. Duina (2011) suggests that four elements must be present for competition to trigger the "effort-reward mentality" (p. 17) so central to American society and our well-documented love of winning[7]: (1) the promise of differentiation among participants and competitors, (2) uncertainty as to who will win and the ever-present possibility of failure (i.e., the risk involved in competing in the first place), (3) the safe distance that the spectator has from the event itself (no real harm can come from losing, in other words), and (4) there must be an element of schadenfreude (Duina's term is "sadism") in which we take pleasure in watching others struggle and potentially fail (pp. 20–34). "We are interested in the thrill and subliminal satisfaction that come from contemplating but then avoiding danger, the subtle pleasures we feel from seeing others suffer, and above all, *our desire to be different and define our own identity*" (Duina, 2011, p. 33; emphasis added).

This last characteristic of competition—the potential to distinguish ourselves from others—is perhaps the most essential because it has to do with competition as a practice of identity formation. Duina (2011) devotes an entire chapter to the thrill we get from seeking competition in order to set ourselves apart from our competitors and from the mass of humanity. This thrill is not merely connected to the inherent pleasure of winning, however, but also to having one's worldview legitimated through competition and through the identity-forming process of distinction and differentiation. "A central function of competition—a key raison d'être—is to *make distinctions*, to differentiate among people in a

---

7 According to the World Values Survey (https://www.worldvaluessurvey.org), an ongoing international research project that attempts to map and rank the "social, political, economic, religious and cultural values of people in the world," Americans consistently score at the top of surveys that examine attitudes surrounding how much stock we place in winners and in the act of winning.

normative (better versus worse, good versus bad, right versus wrong) manner" (Duina, 2011, p. 192; original emphasis). In other words, we compete so that we may draw even more firmly the distinctions between ourselves and others. Failure is essential insofar as it brings to life those all-important distinctions between "us and them." (Cue the Pink Floyd.)

Internet culture is obsessed with failure, especially the meme-laden, pre-mainstream, and often mean-spirited internet culture of roughly 2006 to 2012 (Phillips & Milner, 2021; Douglas, 2014). So-called "fail content" was a staple of message boards and meme channels like 4chan, where users reveled in the embarrassment and almost ritual humiliation of others (also known as "lulz") through memes, images, and inside jokes. On today's internet, such fail content still exists on social media sites like X (formerly Twitter) and TikTok, but the specific architecture of the web during this earlier era lent itself more readily to such crudely sketched, "stickly" images. Douglas (2014) calls the dominant aesthetic of this era of internet culture "Internet Ugly," a sloppy, amateur-driven visual aesthetic borne out of rapid-fire posts and the necessity of quickly producing content in order to participate (and win lulz) on rapidly evolving threads. As Douglas (2014) goes on to explain, on 4chan, for example, a meme incubator largely responsible for launching Internet Ugly, there simply isn't enough time for users to produce polished content and images:

> Every thread is deleted within days or sometimes minutes; these constantly disappearing pages encourage rapid iteration of ideas. Users frequently make quick-and-dirty cut-and-paste photo manipulation as conversational volleys. But these images are rarely sophisticated—polish your reply in Photoshop for an hour and the thread might be done before you are. (p. 315)

Over time, the Internet Ugly aesthetic developed from a glitchy, barebones necessity to a look that users intentionally and proudly cultivated as the aesthetic hallmark of online "fail culture." Adopting the Internet Ugly aesthetic signaled that one had "learned how to internet" and thus was on the right side of the us/them divide that powered internet culture's "obsession with failure generally" (Phillips & Milner, 2021, p. 59). Growing out of the subculture of online trolls, the injunction to "learn how to internet" was code for knowing:

> how to replicate or at least decode the internet culture aesthetic, to respond to memes 'correctly,' and, most important of all, to not take anything too seriously. The result was to cleave the *us* who knew how to internet, who got the jokes, who responded to things with a troll face, from the *them* who

didn't or couldn't or wouldn't. For internet people, feeling distressed online—because something someone saw something unseeable, because someone clicked a link they shouldn't have, because someone fed the trolls—was a self-inflicted wound. (Phillips & Milner, 2021, p. 58).

In wrapping up the discussion of competition as a ritualized way of articulating differences, Duina (2011) also notes how, in a curious (and faulty) logic of generalization, "we have a puzzling tendency to use the outcomes of competitive events to generalize about the competitors" (p. 48). Thus, successful athletes and coaches become CEOs and leaders of diverse organizations. We hang on Elon Musk's every tweet, extrapolating from his success at finally making an electric car people want to buy that he must also be a gourmet chef, an accomplished lover, an expert in education, or a social media tycoon (Dang & Roumeliotis, 2022). Warren Buffett, another of the world's richest men, is yet another example of someone who, because he has attained great success in one rather limited realm of human experience, we assume must be proficient in many others. Donald Trump, yet another rich man known mainly for cheating others in business and starring in his own reality TV show, is surely capable of leading the free world . . . right? Competition, in other words, is more than just a laboratory that produces winners and losers. Competition produces distinctions, identities, and legitimations. As we will see in the next section, this is hardly a new phenomenon, though contemporary neoliberalism has given it a few interesting twists.

AGONISM, *ARETE*, AND THE GREEKS

Ancient Greek culture provides a useful starting point for a discussion of the evolving nature of failure throughout history. In a masterful reading of the rich interplay between rhetoric and athletics in ancient Greece, Hawhee (2004) persuasively links the centrality of the agon, or the site(s) at which contests and victorious encounters took place, to the repeated production of *arete*, a word that is often simply translated in modern English as "virtue," but that more accurately refers to the complex interplay of forces that, for the Greeks, produced what we might think of as a repeated performance of virtuosity, skill, goodness (*agathos*), or glory (*kleos*).

Crucially, neither the agon nor the complex, repetitive production of arete were concerned solely or even primarily with victory, winning, or some other ends-driven outcome. To be sure, the promise of victory, of defeating one's enemy in battle or decisively pinning a wrestling opponent at the Olympic games, were a significant component of the agonistic encounter—encounters that, it should be mentioned, extended beyond athletic competition and martial combat to encompass rhetorical displays of cunning oratory and sophistic competition. However, as Hawhee (2004) repeatedly warns, to stop there would be to miss the larger and more compelling picture; the Greek term *athlios* was the one more closely related to the "explicit struggle for a prize" as the result of outcome-driven competition (p. 15). Agon, by contrast, with its etymological connections to the *agora*, or marketplace, served Greek culture as "the ancient gathering place *par excellence*," emphasizing "the event of the gathering itself—the contestive encounter rather than strictly the division between opposing sides" (Hawhee, 2004, pp. 15–16; original emphasis).

At the same time, it is the lure of potential victory in the context of the agon that gathers, structures, and enables the production of arete, which it should be pointed out, held a great deal of value in Greek society, particularly for male citizens (Hawhee, 2004). For the Greeks, arete was the driving force of agonistic encounters, the corporeal and discursive display of virtuosity that could only be repeatedly enacted—never finally attained—in the occasional space of the agon, whether athletic competition, oratorical performance, or martial showdown on the field of battle. Hawhee (2004) is careful to note the central role of repetition to the entire arete-producing enterprise. Since, for the Greeks, one's identity was functionally inseparable from one's actions, the agon played an all-important role in providing the stage on which these repeated enactments of arete could unfold in real time. In other words, Hawhee (2004) writes, for "the ancient Athenians, identity did not precede actions, and this applied to all aspects of one's life. That is, one could not just 'be' manly (*andreios*) and all that entails without displaying 'manliness' through manly acts of courage" (Hawhee, 2004, p. 18). In short, arete, in both its bodily and discursive forms, was a function of one's virtuous actions that could only be repeatedly demonstrated, never finally "won" once and for all.

By late Roman antiquity, as literacy and writing began to gradually supplant oratorical display, the suppler, more complex Greek notion of arete ossified into something closer to our own morality-tinged notions of virtue. At the same time, the all-important linkages between repeated enactment and the production of arete also hardened into a form more recognizable to the modern reader. Quintilian, writing in his *Institutio Oratorio*, demarcates good and bad writing throughout this classic rhetorical treatise by referring to the supposedly gendered qualities of each. Carr (2013), drawing on Brody's (1993) feminist history of writing advice and instruction, *Manly Writing*, persuasively makes the case that by the time of Quintilian, "a speaker's inability to display adequate skills in oration and argument represented the possibility of the speaker's 'fail[ure] to be manly, the possibility for an invasion of the male writer by the feminine'" (para.

15). Writing/oratory that is deemed bad, sloppy, or ineffective is, according to Quintilian, associated with the feminine, whereas good writing/oratory is "virtuous, clean, strong, and manly" (Carr, 2013, para. 15). We will see this connection between failure and unmanliness return again in the coming millennia and in the following sections of this chapter. Further, Carr notes that Quintilian believed that "men whose rhetoric was sloppy, showy, or deemed not 'good' were accused of producing *effeminate* rhetoric, the province of the eunuch, an 'unnatural' deceptive being robbed of its reproductive organs" (Carr, 2013, para. 15). Here, perhaps for the first time in such a modern form, we can see most clearly the links between masculinity and failure.

FAILURE IN THE MEDIEVAL UNIVERSITY

The long and fabled history of the modern research university in the West is replete with agonistic, male-centered struggles as ritual sites of failure and success or victory, largely because of the centrality of oral disputation (and hence, rhetoric) to the traditional curriculum. As Connors (1997) notes unequivocally, women have been excluded from the history of the university, in large measure, because they were barred from being rhetoricians and, in many cases, from speaking publicly in the first place. He writes:

> From 500 B.C. through 1840, women were definitively excluded from all that rhetoric implied in its disciplinary form. Rhetoric was the most purely male intellectual discipline that has existed in Western culture. Women were not merely discouraged from learning it, but were actively and persistently denied access to it, and thus the discipline coalesced around male behavior patterns. (Connors, 1997, pp. 28–29)

In Clark's (2006) comprehensive history of the modern research university, agonism looms large in the medieval practice of disputation (*disputatio*), which Clark (2006) identifies as one of two essential academic activities that structured academic life and secured the fortunes (or failures) of would-be scholars, masters, and doctors from the Scholasticism of the medieval era up to the proto-disciplinary era of the nineteenth century (pp. 68–69). (It will surely come as no surprise to most readers that the university's other essential activity during the previous millennium was the lecture, in all its droning pomp and glory.) Both the disputation and the lecture were oral practices *par excellence*, and they retain much of this character even up to the present day. Indeed, the history of the modern research university cannot be told without repeated reference to the gradual triumph of literacy over orality, or as Clark (2006) puts it, "the hegemony of the visible and legible over the oral" (p. 68). This gradual shift, of course, ties the evolution of the modern research university to the crucial distinction between orality and literacy that has shaped—at least according to some scholars and theorists—the last 2,000+ years of human knowledge and intellectual development (Ong, 1982/2002).

In the late Roman Code of Justinian (*Codex Justinianus*), which dates back to the mid-sixth century CE, the architects of the medieval university found justification for their argument that Roman law bestowed upon scholars the same privileges as crowned athletes. As Clark (2006) notes, the jurists Bartolus and Baldus "could easily liken academic training to athletic competition in imperial Rome because medieval disputation resembled a joust" (p. 74). In its earliest instantiations, the medieval disputation was a semi-ritualized display of oral dominance, one that was quite often cast in martial terms. As Clark (2006) notes, "a rhetoric and theater of warfare, combat, trial, and joust have been central to scholastic and academic practices since the twelfth century" (p. 75). Like the practice of law in medieval Europe, the practice of disputation in the early university was more concerned with ritualized displays of power, force, authority, and strength than with either the discovery of facts or the disinterested pursuit of original knowledge for its own sake. These concerns would come much later. But the disputation was central to academic life and career advancement; its basic tenets have survived to this day in the form of oral exams and the would-be doctoral candidate's final, ostensibly public, dissertation defense.

The disputation, in its most general form, resembled a courtroom, which only served to heighten its agonistic, "joust-like" qualities. There was the presider (*praeses*) or "judge," the respondent (*respondens*) or "defense," and the opponents (*opponentes*) or "plaintiff" (Clark, 2006, p. 76). The focus was on the form of the proceedings more so than on the content of the arguments. In the public disputation, the general public, as well as key university figures, academic officers, and even local nobility, could perform the role of the opponent; the presider was a member of the faculty, usually a master or doctor, who took his place at the *cathedra*, an ornate lectern located in a central location. Place and space were key elements of the proceedings, with nobles and academic officers in the audience taking their seats on elevated benches in such a way that preserved and displayed their status as "set off [or apart] from the general public" (Clark, 2006, p. 77). From the Middle Ages on, the disputation could be "formal or informal, public or private [and] might take place daily, nightly, weekly, monthly, quarterly, semiannually, or annually" (Clark, 2006, p. 76). As suggested by the ritual placing of key figures and participants in the disputation, the focus was squarely on maintaining existing and differential relations of power among the participants in a semi-ritualized setting.

In fact, the disputation was not conducted with the goal of producing new or original knowledge, at least not in the sense that we think of the term "original." Originality, in the medieval university, meant something more like "of or pertaining to the origin(s)" rather than its more modern connotations of innovation, academic discovery, and heretofore uncharted intellectual territory. Therefore, the primary focus of the disputation was not to break new intellectual ground but to reaffirm the canon and the canonical orthodoxy by ritualistically dispelling error and unorthodox knowledge while defending the honor of the canon. Clark (2006) puts it this way:

> The disputation was an oral event. It aimed not at the production of new knowledge but rather at the rehearsal of established doctrines. What was produced—oral argument— was consumed on the premises. The disputation did not accumulate and circulate truth. It, rather, disaccumulated or dismantled possible or imagined error. The roles instantiated differential relations of power and knowledge. Protected by a presider, a respondent learnt the dialectical arts needed to fend off erroneous arguments of opponents. One learnt, ultimately, how to defend the canonical as proclaimed in lecture. (p. 79)

AMERICAN STRIVERS: MASCULINITY AND SPECULATIVE CAPITALISM IN THE AGE OF "GO-AHEAD"

As Sandage (2005) argues in *Born Losers: A History of Failure in America*, a meticulously researched history of American losers both notable and obscure, "The American who fails is a prophet without honor in his own country" (p. 18). Indeed, since the early nineteenth century, failure in the American context has been squarely focused on one's own fluctuating fortunes, on the triumph or downfall of the individual striver. Crucially, the ability to succeed or the propensity to fail becomes an essential trait of individual identity in the American nineteenth century, a story that Sandage (2005) narrates (with receipts!) in this magisterial history. Culling material from across the historical record, including revealing snippets from debtors' journals and private diaries, *Hunt's Merchants' Magazine*, business records, contemporary advertisements, and the popular journalism and cultural commentary of the day (including such stalwarts as *Harper's* and the *Atlantic Monthly*), Sandage (2005) illustrates with copious detail how the "master plots and stock imagery of individual moral blame infused the culture of American capitalism" (p. 92). "In this way," Sandage (2005) writes, "failure proved the doctrine of *achieved identity*. 'Men succeed or fail . . . not from accident or external surroundings,' a Massachusetts newspaper reiterated in 1856, but from 'possessing or wanting the elements in themselves'" (p. 92; emphasis added).

Notably, failure was, from early on, located "in the man." It was, in other words, an internalized condition—an essential trait of the individual—and at the time, the popular discourse on failure in business and elsewhere in life treated it not unlike a disease or genetic predisposition (Sandage, 2005). In 1842, no less a commentator than Ralph Waldo Emerson wrote in his journal, "The merchant evidently believes the . . . proverb that nobody fails who ought not to fail. There is always a reason, *in the man*, for his good or bad fortune, and so in making money" (Gilman & Parsons, 1970, p. 295; emphasis added). This bit of Emersonian wisdom appears again and again in Sandage's (2005) historical overview, as the book painstakingly chronicles the gradual development of interiorized failure as a species of character *in the man*.

Take the word *loser*, for example. Sandage (2005) shows how a newspaper report on the 1820 Boston fire could refer to an innkeeper with great material losses as a loser in a neutral sense: "The keeper of the hotel *is a great loser*, particularly in furniture and liquors" (p. 131; emphasis added). This is not an image of the loser in the contemporary, post-Beck (1994) sense ("I'm a loser baby / So why don't you kill me?"), but in a neutral and more literal sense, referring simply to someone who has lost a great deal of material property and wealth. By mid-century, and accelerating in the bust-and-boom, "go ahead" decades following the Civil War through the Gilded Age, to be *a loser* ceased to be a one-off occurrence, something that happened to somebody, but had transformed into an interiority, a type, or essential quality. It was to be a "bad egg," a "good for nothing," or in the words of one credit agency report from 1852, "Broke & run away . . . not w[orth] the powder to kill him" (Sandage, 2005, p. 130).

Other entries were similarly colorful, as Sandage (2005) dutifully records: "Cannot be w[orth] anything tho has the strange faculty of being always in bus[iness] & yet doing nothing" (p. 149). Another entry reported, "We have no confidence in his success or bus[iness] ability," while yet another opined cheerily, "Bus[iness] on the increase & parties here who sell [to] him largely have confidence that he will finally succeed & become well off" (Sandage, 2005, p. 100). These notes and millions of others could be found in the 2,580 handwritten ledgers that Mercantile Agency clerks researched, scribed, and scrupulously maintained between 1841 and 1892 (Sandage, 2005, p. 128). Founded by Lewis Tappan in 1841, the Mercantile Agency was the nineteenth century's version of Equifax, Experian, and TransUnion, the holy trinity of modern credit reporting in the United States, all rolled into one. There were competitors, of course, but Tappan's Mercantile Agency was the first and arguably the most influential. Codifying confidence (or the lack thereof) in the service of credit capitalism, the Mercantile Agency sought to manage risk

> *by managing identity*: a matrix of past achievement, present assets, and future promise. Neither rating consumers nor granting credit, it graded commercial buyers for wary sellers. Lewis Tappan—an ardent social reformer—did in the marketplace what others did in asylums and prisons. He imposed discipline via surveillance: techniques and systems to monitor and classify people. Local informants quietly watched their neighbors and reported to the central office. . . . The marketplace now had a memory, an archive for permanent records of entire careers. (Sandage, 2005, pp. 100–102; emphasis added)

Moreover, Sandage (2005) is careful to show how nearly as far back as the dawn of the Republic, failure—whether to pay one's debts or remain solvent in business or make good on some other life-sustaining enterprise—contained within it a moral obligation as well as a financial one. Even in the years immediately following the Civil War, when modern contract law made it possible for a man to legally discharge his fiscal debts, the question of whether his moral debts could be so easily discharged remained.[8] As Sandage (2005) writes, "Ironically, a magnified sense of moral obligation as a thing apart, a truth immune to the legal fictions of the contract, laid the foundation for U.S. bankruptcy reform after the Civil War. The reason stayed '*in the man*,' but the remedy did not" (p. 66; original emphasis). To fail in business, even if one could discharge one's debts, did not automatically make good on the stiff moral penalty that remained firmly attached to the individual debtor.

The American "Go-Ahead" nineteenth century, with its devastating financial panics, banking collapses, credit crises, and fledgling bankruptcy reform, fused the practical republican ideals of manliness and moral virtue with the burgeoning market economy and the new entrepreneurial realities it engendered. Crucially, to fail in business was seen as both a moral failing and a failure of manhood. "To a nation on the verge of anointing individualism as its creed," Sandage (2005) writes, "The loser was simultaneously intolerable and indispensable. Failure was the worst that could happen to a striving American, yet it was the best proof that the republican founders had replaced destiny [i.e., one's station at birth] with merit. Rising from laborer to entrepreneur was the path to manhood" (p. 27). The phrase "go ahead," with its origins as a sailor's yell, came into vogue as a way

---

[8] Because of the historical context under discussion here, I am intentionally using masculine pronouns.

to capture the "go ahead spirit" of the mid- to late-nineteenth century. Sandage (2005) writes that it "named a kind of masculinity wherein some delivered while others 'miscarried.' Men failed because they lacked spunk" (p. 87).

Prior to this, before the advent of market capitalism and the accompanying celebration of the entrepreneurial self, *to fail* (or to be *a loser*) was an accident of fortune, a more or less random waylay on the highway of life that could happen to anyone. Similarly, in the early Republic, what we now think of as "success" was framed as "yeoman competency, which valued the maintenance of current status and plenitude more than the cultivation of risky ambitions" (Sandage, 2005, p. 81). Sandage (2005) notes how "The man with 'a competency' (in the language of the eighteenth and early nineteenth centuries) sustained his independence by land ownership and contentment, providing for his family today and squirreling away necessary resources against tomorrow's troubles (p. 81). However, by the end of the nineteenth century, the concepts of success and failure had evolved and complexified; success now meant a restless, relentless striving for more, the robust, energetic, and distinctly "American *go-aheadism*" of the era (Sandage, 2005, p. 84). Failure, by extension, had become a stigma and developed an interiority and depth all its own—a wanting or lacking "in the man." A "failure" no longer referred to an unfortunate event or set of circumstances, like highway robbery or a fluke illness, but referred instead to a *person*, one who was morally suspect and effeminate at worst, lazy and shiftless at best.

As the entrepreneurial subject has evolved alongside global, just-in-time capitalism and neoliberalism have turned individuals into always-on digital media companies, there are now perhaps more ways to fail—and fail in full view— than ever before. Meme culture, with its "Epic Fail," pays homage to our thinly cloaked obsession with failure, as does the rich patois of schadenfreude that has come to define reality TV and celebrity culture. However, even as neoliberalism has undoubtedly amplified, intensified, and infused our language of personal failure, it has predictably shrunk both our vistas for imagining success outside of the market-driven limits of neoliberalism and the "higher natures," as Brown (2005) puts it (p. 44), that make us human in the first place.

#WINNING: CHARLIE SHEEN, DONALD TRUMP AND THE REVIVAL OF FAILURE

It is entirely fitting that during and in the immediate aftermath of the Trump presidency, there would be a revival of interest in failure as an academic and theoretical concept. After all, without failure, there can be no winning, and if there's one thing Trump stood for, it was #winning. At a rally in 2016, then-candidate Trump famously claimed that if elected, "we're gonna win so much, you may even get tired of winning." His rallies, for years a notorious and inextricable part of the fabric of American politics, were far less about policy prescriptions or legislative goals than they were about the brute show of force through numbers—a red sea of MAGA hats and Punisher t-shirts. The message was nothing if not consistent: I will return the US to its winning ways.

As preoccupied as he appears to be with winning, Trump also (in)famously loves to call out "losers." In a September 2020 conversation with senior members of his staff, Trump reportedly referred to 1,800 WWI-era US marines buried in a military cemetery in France as losers, presumably because they were dead. (The fact that they died fighting for their country doesn't seem to impress Trump, either.) Goldberg (2020), writing in *The Atlantic*, suggests that Trump's "capacious definition of *sucker* [a synonym for *loser* in Trump-speak] includes those who lose their lives in service to their country, as well as those who are taken prisoner, or are wounded in battle."

He called John McCain a "loser" for getting captured in Vietnam and spending nearly six grueling years as a POW in North Vietnam. He referred to former president George H. W. Bush as a loser for getting shot down by Japanese soldiers during WWII. Before he was banned in early 2021, Trump repeatedly took to X (then Twitter) to call out those he saw as losers: political opponents, fellow Republicans, journalists, women he didn't like, the parents of Gold Star Army Captain and war hero Humayun Khan, and the list goes on. Confronted with the reality of his own loss of the presidency in 2020, Trump and his supporters haven't taken it well. He first doubled down on his phony claims that the election was somehow rigged before setting in motion an attempted coup on January 6, 2021. The rest is history.

Trump's definition of a loser is probably looser than most, but I would suggest that the former president's acerbic and totally unprecedented habit of deploying the "L-bomb" reflects, albeit in an exaggerated way, a key feature of American life and culture, one that must be considered in any exploration of failure. Charlie Sheen called our attention to it over a decade ago in a bizarre series of public spectacles. In this chapter, I simply call it *#winning* (pronounced "hashtag winning"). As Sitman (2019) writes:

> These [neoliberal] policies and others seem designed to sow paranoia and inflict pain, which is part of the point. The right benefits from people becoming more isolated, hunkered down, wary of others, and doubtful that a better future can be built. It is to such people that the reactionary message appeals: the best you can hope for is to hoard what you have, and attack the shadowy forces and alien others that you're told

imperil you and your livelihood. Solidarity and generosity are turned into risky wagers not worth taking.

What we may need now is a collective, societal understanding of failure that spreads the socio-economic effects of failure across society. One way to achieve this may be through universal basic income (UBI). By providing everyone with the basic necessities of life through one of the many popular universal income proposals now being considered in progressive US cities like Los Angeles, Denver, and even Birmingham, Alabama, citizens can reduce the individual shame and indignity late capitalism offers most people across society (DiBenedetto, 2022).

RE-ENVISIONING SUCCESS: THE NEOLIBERAL FAILURE OF IMAGINATION

The problem, as I have suggested in this brief history, may not lie so much with the ubiquity of failure but in our impoverished ideas about what constitutes *success* and a life well lived, or what philosophers used to call "the good life." Neoliberalism, as I have endeavored to show, has impoverished our imaginations. As I have argued elsewhere (Cook, 2013), it mocks both our attempts at collective action and our imaginings of a world beyond work and money with its relentless logic of individual achievement and its narrow focus on material wealth. Trump, with his crass and cruelty and insults and continuous crowing about #winning and Making America Great Again (MAGA), is the apotheosis of this neoliberal failure of imagination.

In closing, I want to suggest that the rise of running culture in North America and the multitudes it contains—sport, hobby, competition, festival atmosphere, community, social outlet, and more—may serve as an interesting counterpoint to neoliberal logics of success and failure. In the last several decades, running has gradually emerged in the United States and other developed countries as the sport of the masses. If horse racing is the sport of kings, then running is, as Bingham (2019) suggests, the sport of "kings, queens, and the people." Part of running's appeal lies in its simplicity, the fact that virtually anyone of sound body can do it. You don't need special equipment or an expensive gym membership or years of training and know-how. You don't even really need running shoes (Hopes, 2022), though I would personally recommend it. In the sport of running, everyone wins, and everyone cheers on everyone else. If a runner falls or injures themselves on the course, it is viewed not as a failure of that individual but as a failure of the support crew, volunteers, course marshal, and others to ensure the success and well-being of everyone involved. Well-managed races are a thing of beauty. The crowd comes together to support each other.

Similarly, the running community in North America is geared not so much toward the stark binary of winning and losing but toward mutual aid, support, collectivity, and enthusiasm for the practice itself. The focus is on being together, supporting each other, cheering on your buddies. The vast majority of regular runners—even competitive ones—never win any races; few even place in their age groups. But here is where winning doesn't equal the feeling of accomplishment and sheer joy that runners get when they finish their first race—whether a 5K fun run or a 26.2-mile marathon—is the point, not whether an individual crosses the finish line first or last. (Well, aside from the massive health benefits that running provides—a point on which nearly all exercise scientists and healthcare professionals agree [Lee et al., 2017; Willis, 2017].) In other words, the dynamics of failure, its consequences as well as its costs, are spread out across the racing community, from participants to volunteers to spectators to paid employees. You still have to pony up your $110 registration fee, of course, because . . . capitalism, but from that point on, the beating heart of race day is all about the feeling of community that inevitably arises from the undulating throng and the unmistakable sound of injection-molded foam rubber on pavement.

Now, don't get me wrong. I am not so naïve as to think that running is not a competitive sport—it is, and there are those elite runners who compete at the highest levels. But at the end of the day—or rather, at the start of race day—the world-class marathoners line up at the same starting line as the stooped middle-aged guy with the beer gut who signed up on a dare. It doesn't matter how fast you are or how slow you are. It doesn't matter what your body type is or how much you weigh (Runner's World, 2022). Running is egalitarian, yes, but it is more than that. It is a model for community that may help us re-think our values surrounding #winning and scarcity, success, and failure.

What would it take for academia to adopt a similar framework for understanding and working through the dynamics of failure and success? Higher education is, as many have indicated, as hierarchical an institution as it gets, where individual successes and failures mean everything—for faculty as well as students. As every professor knows, even a practice as banal as group work has a bad reputation in higher education, which suggests the extent of the focus on the individual and her ultimate success or failure (Lang, 2022). As I have argued in this chapter, there are powerful forces working against such a reconceptualization of individuals, forces that suture the techno-algorithmic to the socio-economic in ways that threaten any meaningful reversal of our current situation vis-à-vis failure and success. Appadurai and Alexander (2020) show how ubiquitous digital connectivity has transformed the decidedly nineteenth-century record-keeping of the old Mercantile Agency into something far more dangerous and penetrative. This, they argue, has led to a "tectonic shift in the classical idea of identity" (Appadurai & Alexander, 2020, p. 61). What they call "predatory dividuation" is the process by which individual human subjects are broken down "into a series of scores, ranks, features, attributes, and dimensions"—data that are "useful for the production of immense profit by the financial industries . . . [a] decomposition of the individual [that] is crucial for risk ratings, credit scores, consumer profiling, and for other operations on which contemporary finance depends" (Appadurai & Alexander, 2020, p. 61). Western modernity's idea of the sovereign individual, where "personality, agency, motivation, interest, and the body were encased in a single envelope"—has been supplanted by global capitalism's newfound ability, via digital technologies of control, to transform

> the nature of human subjectivity to make it easier to aggregate, recombine, monitor, predict, and exploit subjects for the purposes of financial markets, primarily by making scorable and rankable "dividuals" the sources of debt. To incur debt, you need no special ethical, biological, or racial capacities. You need to be a debt-worthy dividual. (Appadurai & Alexander, 2020)

They go on to analyze Uber as an example of a company that exploits this new logic of the "dividual" to blur the lines between human drivers and bots, further cementing the illusory "horizon of endless choice" that Appadurai and Alexander (2020) see as so dangerous to classical liberalism's conception of the individual human subject (p. 124).

In closing, I am reminded of a famous and highly-meme-able quote attributed to former president John F. Kennedy: "One person can make a difference, but everyone should try." This is the way. It is only through collective action that individuals can come together to change the world, to cast off oppressive systems, to subvert the suffocating logic of neoliberalism, and to complexify the simplistic binary of success and failure.

REFERENCES

Aaron, H. J. (2020, June 23). The social safety net: The gaps that COVID-19 spotlights. *Brookings*. https://www.brookings.edu/blog/up-front/2020/06/23/the-social-safety-net-the-gaps-that-covid-19-spotlights/.
Ahmed, S. (2017). *Living a feminist life*. Duke University Press.
Appadurai, A. & Alexander, N. (2020). *Failure*. Polity.
Beck. (1994). *Mellow gold* [Album]. DGC Records.
Bingham, E. (2019, January 16). Why running is the sport of kings, queens, and the people. *Stuff*. https://www.stuff.co.nz/life-style/well-good/teach-me/109906347/why-running-is-the-sport-of-kings-queens-and-the-people.

Brody, M. (1993). *Manly writing*. Southern Illinois University Press.
Brown, W. (2015). *Undoing the demos: Neoliberalism's stealth revolution*. Zone Books.
Burger, E. (2012, August 21). Teaching to fail. *Inside Higher Education*. https://www.insidehighered.com/views/2012/08/21/essay-importance-teaching-failure.
Carr, A. D. (2013). In support of failure. *Composition Forum, 27*. https://compositionforum.com/issue/27/failure.php.
Carr, A. D. (2017). Failure is not an option. In C. Ball & D. Loewe (Eds.), *Bad ideas about writing* (pp. 76–81). University of West Virginia Libraries Digital Publishing Institute.
Carr, A. D. & Micciche, L. R. (Eds.). (2020a). *Failure pedagogies: Learning and unlearning what it means to fail*. Peter Lang.
Carr, A. D. & Micciche, L. R. (2020b). Introduction: Failure's sweat. In A. D. Carr & L. R. Micciche (Eds.), *Failure pedagogies: Learning and unlearning what it means to fail* (pp. 1–7). Peter Lang.
Clark, W. (2006). *Academic charisma and the origins of the research university*. University of Chicago Press.
Connors, R. J. (1997). *Composition-rhetoric: Backgrounds, theory, pedagogy*. University of Pittsburgh Press.
Cook, P. (2013). Survival guide advice and the spirit of academic entrepreneurship: Why graduate students will never just take your word for it. *Workplace, 22*, 25–39. https://doi.org/10.14288/workplace.v0i22.184425.
Cornwall, G. (2022, May 1). Sprinting upstream: The incredible pressure faced by college-bound high schoolers. *Salon*. https://www.salon.com/2022/05/01/sprinting-upstream-the-incredible-pressure-faced-by-college-bound-high-schoolers/.
Dang, S. & Roumeliotis, G. (2022, October 28). Musk begins his Twitter ownership with firings, declares "the bird is freed." *Reuters*. https://www.reuters.com/markets/deals/elon-musk-completes-44-bln-acquisition-twitter-2022-10-28/.
Davidson, C. N. (2022). *The new education: How to revolutionize the university to prepare students for a world in flux*. Basic Books. (Original work published 2017)
Deodhar, N. (2022, February 3). We need to talk about Cosby throws light on how complicated legacies should be sensitively handled. *Firstpost*. https://www.firstpost.com/entertainment/we-need-to-talk-about-cosby-throws-light-on-how-complicated-legacies-should-be-sensitively-handled-10344161.html.
DiBenedetto, C. (2022, September 18). Every US city testing free money programs. *Mashable*. https://mashable.com/article/cities-with-universal-basic-income-guaranteed-income-programs.
Douglas, N. (2014). It's supposed to look like shit: The internet ugly aesthetic. *Journal of Visual Culture, 13*(3), 314–339. https://doi.org/10.1177/1470412914544516.
Duina, F. (2011). *Winning: Reflections on an American obsession*. Princeton University Press.
Edmonds, C. (2022, February 11). Biggest comebacks in Super Bowl history. *NBC Philadelphia*. https://www.nbcphiladelphia.com/news/sports/super-bowl-2022/biggest-comebacks-in-super-bowl-history/3143254/.
Ehrenreich, B. (1989). *Fear of falling: The inner life of the middle class*. Harper Perennial.

Feigenbaum, P. (2021). Welcome to "Failure Club": Supporting intrinsic motivation, sort of, in college writing. *Pedagogy, 21*(3), 403–426. https://doi.org/10.1215/15314200-9132039.

Fischman, W. & Gardner, H. (2022). *The real world of college: What higher education is and what it can be.* MIT Press.

Foucault, M. (2003). The birth of biopolitics. In P. Rabinow & N. Rose (Eds.), *The essential Foucault* (pp. 202–207). New Press. (Original work published 1979)

Gilman, W. H. & Parsons, J. E. (Eds.). (1970). *Journals and miscellaneous notebooks of Ralph Waldo Emerson* (Vol. 8). Belknap Press of Harvard University Press.

Goldberg, J. (2020, September 3). Trump: Americans who died in war are "losers" and "suckers." *The Atlantic.* https://www.theatlantic.com/politics/archive/2020/09/trump-americans-who-died-at-war-are-losers-and-suckers/615997/.

Hallmark, T. (2018, February 11). When 'failure is OK' is not OK. *Chronicle of Higher Education.* https://www.chronicle.com/article/when-failure-is-ok-is-not-ok/.

Hawhee, D. (2004). *Bodily arts: Rhetoric and athletics in ancient Greece.* University of Texas Press.

Hopes, S. (2022, September 2). Is barefoot running better for you? *LiveScience.* https://www.livescience.com/barefoot-running-better-for-you.

Kapur, M. (2015). Learning from productive failure. *Learning: Research and Practice, 1*(15), 51–65, https://doi.org/10.1080/23735082.2015.1002195.

Lang, J. M. (2022). Why students hate group projects (and how to change that). *Chronicle of Higher Education.* https://www.chronicle.com/article/why-students-hate-group-projects-and-how-to-change-that?sra=true.

Lee, D., et al. (2017). Running as a key lifestyle medicine for longevity. *Progress in Cardiovascular Diseases, 60*(1), 45–55. https://doi.org/10.1016/j.pcad.2017.03.005.

Luce, E. (2018). *The retreat of Western liberalism.* Atlantic Monthly Press.

McMurtrie, B. (2022, April 11). 'It feels like I'm pouring energy into a void': Faculty members share their thoughts on trying to reach disconnected students. *Chronicle of Higher Education.* https://www.chronicle.com/article/it-feels-like-im-pouring-energy-into-a-void.

Medina, J., Benner, K. & Taylor, K. (2019, March 12). Actresses, business leaders and other wealthy parents charged in US college entry fraud. *New York Times.* https://www.nytimes.com/2019/03/12/us/college-admissions-cheating-scandal.html.

Mineo, L. (2021, June 3). Racial wealth gap may be a key to other inequities. *The Harvard Gazette.* https://news.harvard.edu/gazette/story/2021/06/racial-wealth-gap-may-be-a-key-to-other-inequities/.

Odell, J. (2019, May 20). *How to do nothing: Resisting the attention economy.* Melville House.

Ong, W. J. (2002). *Orality and literacy: The technologizing of the word.* Routledge. (Original work published 1982)

Passy, J. (2019). Millions of Americans are one paycheck away from 'financial disaster.' *MarketWatch.* https://www.marketwatch.com/story/half-of-americans-are-just-one-paycheck-away-from-financial-disaster-2019-05-16?mod=personal-finance.

Phillips, W. & Milner, R. M. (2021). *You are here: A field guide for navigating polarized speech, conspiracy theories & our polluted media landscape.* MIT Press.

Rickly, R. (2017, April). Failing forward: Training graduate students for research —An Introduction to the Special Issue. *Journal of Technical Writing and Communication, 47*(2), 119–129. https://doi.org/10.1177/0047281617692074.

Roberts, S. (2022, May 13). The empty center of the Johnny Depp and Amber Heard trial. *Defector.* https://defector.com/the-empty-center-of-the-johnny-depp-and-amber-heard-trial/.

Runner's World. (2022, January 4). Why running is for everyone: Our message and mission. https://www.runnersworld.com/uk/news/a37867676/body-image/.

Sagan, A. (2016, March 27). Librarians fight precarious work's creep into white collar jobs. *The Daily Courier.* https://www.kelownadailycourier.ca/business_news/national_business/article_0b5bea1c-67af-587c-a948-c68eb53de0f0.html.

Sandage, S. (2005). *Born losers: A history of failure in America.* Harvard University Press.

Sitaraman, G. (2019, December 24). *After neoliberalism.* The Nation. https://www.thenation.com/article/archive/neoliberalism-policies-nationalism/.

Sitman, M. (2019, July 25). Anti-social conservatives. *Gawker.* https://www.gawker.com/politics/anti-social-conservatives.

Smith, K. (2010). *Mess: The manual of accidents and mistakes.* Penguin.

Thomason, A., Gluckman, N. & Ellis, L. (2020, March 12). One year after college-admissions scandal, 3 questions about what (if anything) has changed. *Chronicle of Higher Education.* https://www.chronicle.com/article/one-year-after-college-admissions-scandal-3-questions-about-what-if-anything-has-changed/.

Willis, J. (2017, May 1). Science: Running is better than every other exercise at making you live longer. *GQ.* https://www.gq.com/story/running-is-good.

Zurawik, D. (2011, May 18). Oprah—Built in Baltimore. *The Baltimore Sun Magazine.* https://www.baltimoresun.com/entertainment/bs-xpm-2011-05-18-bs-sm-oprahs-baltimore-20110522-story.html.

CHAPTER 2.

COUNTERPOINT: WHY NOT INTELLECTUAL RISK?

Alexis Teagarden
University of Massachusetts Dartmouth

Justin Mando
Millersville University of Pennsylvania

Carolyn Commer
Virginia Tech

What is the point of failure? Lauded by some scholars as a necessary aspect of writing—and, more broadly, learning—other researchers treat failure as a problem to be reflected on in order to avoid repeating.[1] In classroom practice, meanings also diverge. Interviews with writing faculty led Thoune (2020) to argue instructors see the writing process as "dotted with failure" (p. 59) and "premised on the acknowledgment and anticipation of failure as part of how writing works" (p. 54). Phillips and Giordano (2020), by contrast, speak of students at open-access campuses who "come to college conceptualizing writing as a series of inherent failures or believing academic failure is inevitable" (p. 155). In both, failure is a series of events and an assumed outcome. Yet the meaning is diametrically opposed: Failure represents the optimism of a fully engaged learning process and the pessimism of an already foreclosed learning opportunity.

Scholars of failure further complicate the picture. Barrón and Gruber's (2020) joint reflection describes five "constructs of failure" they encountered over their academic career:

> The most negative ones emphasize the unsuccessful performance as students, teachers and researchers; the positive ones encourage us to see failure as always leading to new information as well as new actions and behaviors. We have been told that failure is inevitable in our attempts to succeed, and

---
[1] We wish to acknowledge Ana Cooke's contributions to the conception of intellectual risk-taking that helped develop this chapter and note that her insight influenced all our thinking on failure and risk-taking.

DOI: https://doi.org/10.37514/PER-B.2024.2494.2.02

> because we are classified as faculty of color and international faculty, we are encouraged to see failure as a possible site of resistance in our attempt to subvert normative behavior. (p. 83)

Failure in the academic realm thus points in many directions. It can (1) undermine one's professional self, (2) provide important information, (3) suggest new ways of working and being, (4) form part of the learning process, and also (5) create opportunities to challenge norms. While some of these constructs can peacefully coexist, others work at cross purposes. Such varying definitions create ambiguity about failure's meaning, value, and role. But disparate views of failing have long characterized the academic conversation. Perhaps this explains why *Naming What We Know* includes a section on failure but hedges the title: "Failure *can* be an important part of writing development" (Carr & Brooke, 2015, p. 62, emphasis added).

Recent scholarship on failure has recognized its many inherent issues; ambivalence, for example, underpins the preface (Hay, 2020), introduction (Carr & Micciche, 2020), and afterward (Inoue, 2020) of the edited collection *Failure Pedagogies*. Yet failure maintains its allure. Perhaps this is because most scholars and teachers of writing believe what *Writing on the Edge* ran as the title quote for an interview with William E. Coles: "Failure is the way we learn" (Boe & Schroeder, 2002, p. 7). Conversations about failure have thus repeatedly recognized it as an important means of learning and as the end result of not learning enough. Failure's paradox—coupled with its stakes: personal, social, and academic—explains some of the ambivalence in the scholarly literature. But it does not illuminate a path to meaningful classroom implementation. What are we meant to teach students about failure, and how? The same holds for scholars interested in failure-focused projects. Which kind of failure merits attention, and by what methods do we explore it?

Previous projects on failure literature have noted its ambiguities and divergences; Carr and Micciche's (2020) pluralized title *Failure Pedagogies*, for example, foregrounds multiplicity. But the causes and consequences of failure's ambiguous meaning have received limited attention. Specifically, we contend that calls in Writing Studies to teach and study failure elide a set of competing values and concomitant agendas. Together, these varying conceptions of failure create a rich inquiry into a complex concept, but the differences are not often acknowledged—to the detriment of instructors attempting to engage with failure pedagogies and researchers interested in advancing this line of scholarship. Better recognition of conflicting views might produce more pointed research and provide a better guide to teachers looking to incorporate aspects of failure pedagogy.

We base our argument on a review of 24 journal articles, chapters, and books published between 1996–2023 from scholars in the general field of Rhetoric, Composition, and Writing Studies (RCWS) and focused on projects that position failure as an animating pedagogical purpose. Among them, we found we could separate out three strands of purpose: Scholars and teachers of writing take up failure in order to (1) inform practice by retrospection, (2) transform character by affective experience, or (3) form and reform plans by illuminating constraints and desires. Grouped this way, the shared traits of each strand align with the classical branches of oratory and their orientation toward time: the forensic (focused on the past), the epideictic (focused on the present), and the deliberative (focused on the future).

Forensic case studies of past failures or epideictic calls for re-imagining failure appear to dominate discussions; there has been less attention to the deliberative potential of failure. At first glance, this makes sense. How could failure, a thing that has to happen, be studied from a future-oriented perspective? However, we find clarity about the deliberative approach when we consider how the potential for failure may help students deliberate about future action. When we discuss the potential for failure, we are really talking about *risk*, and when we locate this risk in the classroom and relate it to learning goals, we arrive at *intellectual risk*.

In what follows, we present the conversation about the pedagogical role of failure through this division of the forensic, epideictic, and deliberative strands. Then, we offer a counterpoint: If we want students to truly learn from failure, we should turn our attention to intellectual risk-taking. Intellectual risk-taking, we argue, has the greatest potential to help student writers weigh multiple options, reconsider dominant ideals of "success," and engage with others in deliberation that will help them learn.

THE FORENSIC STRAND OF FAILURE STUDIES (LEARN FROM IT)

Forensic studies examine past instances of failure, asking what happened and who or what is at fault. Such work aims to analyze past instances of failure in order to understand what went wrong; Segal's (1996) "Pedagogies of Decentering and a Discourse of Failure" exemplifies this strand. Segal's examination of failure narratives, for instance, in part identifies four types of accusations: failure caused by the students, the teacher, the institution, or the pedagogical theory. Inoue's (2014) "Theorizing Failure in Writing Assessment" offers a more recent example. By examining writing assessment scholarship, he argues that standard constructions of failure themselves fail to support student learning. Work in the forensic strand also looks at more specific instances of failure. Alvarez (2001) mirrors Segal's study at a more local level by asking her high school students to develop narratives explaining why they or their classmates had previously failed a course; the results prompt her to overhaul her curriculum. Lehn (2020) and D'Agostino (this volume) both turn inward, considering moments of failure in teaching and dissertating, respectively. Regardless of the scope, for forensic scholarship, past failures allow us to reflect on what went wrong and draw lessons from it.

However, underlying these forensic studies are two debatable assumptions worth considering: (1) failure is inherently a problem to overcome, and (2) reflecting on past failures can help us develop skills to succeed next time or at least better address failure's consequences.

The first assumption treats failure as something gone wrong. As the examples above suggest, the failures taken up by the forensic strand are undeniable issues. Lehn (2020), for instance, defines failure as "moments when some sort of harm may have occurred or was mismanaged in a classroom" (p. 142). Pantelides (2020) argues:

> Plagiarism accusations can lead to identity trauma in which students are forced to reckon with a vision of themselves that they don't recognize, that of failure, and this revisioning of their identity and the attendant fear has long-term impact on their relationships. (p. 40)

Inoue (2014) further generalizes the harm caused by continuing failed practices; they create "psychological consequences for all students in the system that negatively affect their learning" (p. 336). For the forensic camp, failure is a problem to be reckoned with, not a state to desire.

The second assumption is that attention to past failures can help us find a path to success. Indeed, as Segal (1996) argues, reflection on failure is important because it helps us develop "productive strategies of amelioration" (p. 189). Thus, this strand focuses on failures in order to generate effective responses. Some work identifies failures in Writing Studies theory in order to promote what they see as better practices (e.g., Alford, 2020; Inoue, 2014). Others attend to failures at the institutional level. Pantelides (2020) interviews students charged with academic integrity violations to argue our current institutional approach to plagiarism is a failure and needs redress. Cox (2011) interviews a more general sample of community college students, concluding that faculty must address the "student fear factor" that often arises from and perpetuates failure. In this volume, D'Agostino recommends improvements to departmental dissertation processes in light of his own initial failure. Wood, building on Segal's work, questions common approaches to providing feedback in order to find better ways to "talk about failure with students." Failures at the individual level also inspire forensic projects. Lehn (2020) and Alvarez (2001) interrogate their own classroom failures to improve their praxis. Bartkevicius (2023) makes direct the forensic connection between the practices of teaching and writing: "Teaching, like writing, involves rough drafts (little failures) and revisions" (p. 117).

For writing instructors, the forensic approach, especially treating drafts as "little failures," is likely the most familiar. Carr (2013) offers an accurate description of this strand's approach, even as she disagrees with it: "In this model, failure indicates that students have missed the signposts and wandered off into the wilderness" (n.p.). Thoune's (2020) faculty interview data similarly demonstrates a broader commitment among writing faculty to the view of failures as teachable moments: "Instructors need students to fail so that they can provide the kind of feedback that leads to learning" (p. 59). Translating this failure perspective into classroom practice means helping students identify and analyze past instances of failure and then use that information to improve their work. Teachers need to show students how to "fail forward," argue Rickly and Cook (2017), drawing on John C. Maxwell's theory to "use [failure] as a lesson and a stepping stone" (p. 127). Bartkevicius (2023), in reflecting on Richard Lloyd-Jones's pedagogy, recalls that in his class, "Failure was welcome, as long as we explored, in writing, what had gone wrong and what we could learn from where the writing had taken us" (p. 115). Returning to undergrads, Inoue (2019) shared teaching materials built on similar reasoning: "We have to embrace our failures, because they show us the places we can improve, learn, get better" (p. 330). Alford (2020) describes a specific classroom instantiation; she focuses her writing conference conversations around students' use of clichés. Clichés, for Alford, point to important but underdeveloped elements of the argument; they are places in writing that can spark important revision even though, in her example, a student ultimately cut the clichés from the final draft. Here again, "little failures" provide important information about what went wrong or what does not work, allowing writers to remedy problems.

For the forensic camp, failure is understood as a marker or a means to an end but not an end in itself. Thus, the uniting purpose of this strand is amelioration: to improve theory and practice by studying what does not work. Embedded in this view, we note, is often another assumption: that "success" (however defined) is the goal. This assumption is directly challenged by the epideictic strand.

THE EPIDEICTIC STRAND OF FAILURE STUDIES (LIVE IN IT)

In contrast to the forensic view of failure as a rendered past judgment, the literature we classify as "epideictic" draws from the classical trope of praise and blame to reframe failure as an affective experience—one that is valuable as an end in itself. For example, Carr (2013) describes failure as "a deeply felt, transformative process" (n.p.). Her work illustrates an early focus in this strand, how failure can 'afflict the comfortable' by shaking complacent students out of channeled success and showing them a wider landscape of possibilities. She recounts her first real experience with failure: "Until then—" she acknowledges, "and, I say this knowing full well the kind of naïve, irritating student it makes me sound like—I found writing to be effortless" (n.p.). Her personal experience illustrates the larger pedagogical purpose underwriting much work in this epideictic strand, a concern that students can succeed without friction and thus never have cause to develop skepticism of the systems that guide their education.

To counter or redefine dominant ideals of "success," a shared emphasis in this strand is how students should *feel* in the moment of experiencing failure. Gross and Alexander (2016) argue "failure and negative emotions are an ineradicable and sometimes crucial component of our educational lives" (p. 288) and point to queer theorists who show that "unhappiness, dissatisfaction, and even failure might serve as entry points to critique the power structures and normalizing discourses that direct our lives and efforts along certain lines" (p. 288). Myers (2011) likewise celebrates the classical figure of Metanoia for symbolizing "an important form of reflection in which the emotional impact of a missed opportunity motivates a transformation of thought" (p. 11) and, in her later work, gives voice to the premise: "Engaging the emotion that surfaces in the middle of failure can uncover the stories we are telling ourselves about how and why we and others failed, and we can begin to shape new questions and responses" (Myers, 2019, p. 57). In their *Failing Sideways: Queer Possibilities for Writing Assessment*, West-Puckett, Caswell and Banks (2023) make a case for the "productive potential in the failure-shame entanglements of writing assessment" (p. 73). All of these advocates define failure as an affective experience with the desirable potential to prompt transformation.

This strand positions the primary focus of writing pedagogy as the cultivation of specific kinds of dispositions, in contrast to the forensic approach's interest in ameliorating problems or developing problem-solving skills. And the focus on disposition ties back to the thread's foundational texts: Halberstam's (2011) *The Queer Art of Failure* and pedagogical arguments made by education scholar Bain (2012). Bain, in turn, draws heavily from Dweck's work in psychology on fixed and malleable intelligence—all works that prioritize the development of specific ways of thinking and being. Thus, for the epideictic strand, failure is about more than seeing ways to improve drafts, syllabi, and research plans. The pedagogical imperative is to create critical awareness and a disposition for change; failure is a means of seeing the world and oneself differently.

Seeing differently, therefore, becomes a guiding metaphor for the epideictic strand. Carr (2013), again, ultimately argues that the experience of failure "helps us see that there are other ways of moving through the world, alternative ways of coming to know lived experience" (n.p.). Beare (2018) frames his rejections from graduate school as akin to "discovering that half of the map had been erased, I felt disoriented and confused" (p. 258) but ultimately that "the removal of one route of opportunity makes room for the consideration of multiple alternative options" (p. 259). West-Puckett et al. (2023) ask readers to recognize failure "not as the pop-psychology model of failing forward or the success-framed model of failing backward (down) but as lateral moves that create different (im)possibilities" (p. 24). The spatial metaphor dovetails with another shared premise, that the experience of failing serves us best when experienced in the eternal present, hence Carr's (2013) language of "dwelling in failure" (n.p.). West-Puckett et al. (2023) "wonder why we focus so much on the future, often at the expense of the present" (p. 92). Others in this strand testify to the power of inhabiting failure. Beare (2018) argues that his first failed applications to doctoral programs "afforded the space and time to think" (p. 259). Myers's (2019) "Unspeakable Failures," while tempering her earlier embrace of failing, still draws on Ahmed's work to argue we should "focus on stopping" rather than pushing through failure (p. 57). Wandering in the wilderness, even stopping there, is a valuable experience for the epideictic camp, not a mistake to correct as with the forensic strand.

Not every experience of failure proves enlightening, as the epideictic strand itself acknowledges. Bain (2012), whose theory of learning grounds much work in this strand, acknowledges how failure can dampen educational efforts rather than spark them. He recounts a hypothetical scenario about Karolyn, who enters college believing herself a smart, capable student, a view of self undermined by consistent failure in her intro math class: "In the inner recesses of her mind, in those dark places where feelings and thoughts mingle like dance couples, she began to explore a new self. Maybe that self wasn't as smart as she had thought," (Bain, 2012, p. 103). Karolyn, in this story, retreats from all academic challenges. Faced with failure, Karolyn shuts down. Bain's hypothetical example finds real counterparts in studies on how students respond to failing (Pantelides, 2020; Cox, 2011). And the epideictic thread shows increasing attention to the consequences of advocating failure (see, e.g., Myers, 2019; Carr & Micciche, 2020). Rather than rehabilitating students stuck in an impoverished view of success, failure can debilitate students, especially students already marginalized by U.S. educational systems. Failure might be a way to learn, but it does not guarantee learning; it might prompt transformation, but it does not promise a good one.

In short, the epideictic strand unifies around the promise of failing as a means of transformative learning (that is an end unto itself), though proponents differ on the perils involved. The emphasis on dwelling in failure rather than moving past it delineates epideictic work from forensic and serves to illustrate the fundamentally different views of failing that circulate within failure studies scholarship.

THE DELIBERATIVE STRAND OF FAILURE STUDIES (PLAN FOR IT)

We describe the third strand we find in the failure literature as "deliberative" because this scholarship focuses on the types of deliberative processes students must go through in order to navigate potential failure. Unlike forensic studies of failure that reflect on past examples or epideictic calls to embrace the transformative power of failure, deliberative studies look to the future and emphasize action—the role of "navigating" choices, weighing multiple options, and considering context, purpose, and audience.

The deliberative strand tends to take a strong stance against unreflective calls for failure. For example, Johnson and Sheehan (2020) begin by agreeing with much of the epideictic strand's larger mission, including that everyone should question the entwined social scripts for success and happiness. But they ultimately reject the universal applicability of embracing failure. They both draw inspiration from and critique Halberstam (2011): "If we demand students fail and feel bad while doing it, what damage are we fostering in our classrooms?" (p. 130). They acknowledge failure's potential for learning but also note the epideictic strand's limited attention to failure's costs, asking, "Who has the privilege to fail?" (p. 133). Within this collection, Tellez-Trujillo similarly argues, "It is imperative to remain considerate of student vulnerabilities," building from the premise that "no one emerges from adversity unscathed, if they emerge at all." Thus, Tellez-Trujillo also tempers epideictic advocacy, accepting Carr's (2013) view of failure as a transformative place but rejecting the goal of "dwelling" in it; for Tellez-Trujillo (this volume), failure is not a core identity but rather a space to strategically "enter and emerge from." For these authors, a classroom emphasis on failure requires attention to its ethical dimensions and material consequences. A uniform insistence on failing ignores them and thus proves an incomplete pedagogical guide.

Because of concerns about the universal applicability of the term "failure," the deliberative strand also tends to employ the argument strategy of dissociation in order to distinguish harmful from beneficial types of failure and responses to it. For example, Feigenbaum (2021) argues that we should promote "generative failure" instead of assessment-driven "stigmatized failure" (p. 14). Feigenbaum argues that students will embrace generative failure only after instructors overcome the fear that stigmatizes failure and that one way to do so is "by interrogating failure's de facto rootedness in an ethos of competitive individualism and envisioning an alternative ethos grounded in communalism" (p. 15). In parallel, Tellez-Trujillo unsettles a cultural assumption that overcoming adversity is an independent effort by countering the typical view of individual resilience with the communal paradigm of feminist resilience.

Finally, we find that this strand of scholarship tends to emphasize students' situated process of decision-making. Enacting the deliberative approaches in the classroom does not treat failure as an ideal way of being but rather as a potential outcome of human actions, one that should factor into decision-making. For example, Feigenbaum (2021) argues "teachers must help students negotiate [failure] paradigm dissonance" because "students frequently experience failure as a source of fear and anxiety that impedes risk-taking and experimentation" (pp. 13–14). Trujillo-Tellez (this volume) advocates for writing assignments that help "students take an agented position" and encourage "planning for more purposeful failures," an approach she defines as both resilience and risk-taking. In parallel, Johnson and Sheehan (2020) describe their approach as "navigation . . . a material-discursive practice that acknowledges the labor of strategizing, weighing expectation against personal desire" (p. 137). With this emphasis on the activity of deliberate decision-making, Johnson and Sheehan's chapter concludes by asking readers to "recognize the risk and complexity of making those choices" (p. 138). By turning the conversation from experienced to anticipated failures, this strand shifts focus from the products of failure to the process of taking intellectual risks—and how teachers might ethically and effectively help students navigate the process.

POINT OF ORDER: FROM FAILURE TO RISK

The deliberative strand aligns with an approach we have developed in our previous scholarship on intellectual risk-taking. In a 2018 *Composition Studies* article, we proposed a pedagogical approach to intellectual risk-taking that was also framed as an issue of "navigating tensions" (Teagarden et al., 2018). We defined taking an intellectual risk as an option with stakes attached, ones felt by the student. Intellectual risk-taking, we argued, can only occur when a student faces a choice among at least two options related to learning, where at least one of the options has consequences, ones that the student—not the instructor, not the audience—recognizes as meaningful. Students must then weigh the potential positive outcomes against the negative ones, such as being perceived as less competent, receiving public criticism, or losing an aspect of one's social identity (Beghetto, 2009; Foster, 2015; Haswell et al., 2009). Necessarily, these deliberations over intellectual risk occur throughout the writing process.

In a follow-up article in *Rhetoric Review*, we further theorize intellectual risk-taking as a *rhetorical process*, i.e., situated, responsive to an exigence, and addressed to an audience (Commer et al., 2024). The consequences of a student's choice arise from audience response—be it that of the instructor, an imagined audience, specific classmates, or one's self. We argued:

> Intellectual risk-taking is an act of responding to a *kairos* (Dufourmantelle) or opportune moment in the writing process that "provokes a deliberative reaction" (Weil) and has an outcome—insofar as it may result in loss or failure—that holds meaningful "stakes" for the writer taking the risk (Johnstone, 1991, p. 5)

Our definition of intellectual risk suggests a pedagogy that foregrounds decision-making, which is active, done within a community, and responsive to communal, as well as individual, values. It emphasizes the uncertainty that planning for the future entails and how such plans should then always grapple with potential failure and consequences for self and others. Our approach ultimately values the deliberation undertaken over the plan developed or its outcome. Like Johnson and Sheehan (2020), we agree that while writing instructors can help students recognize options and their potential consequences, it is the individual student who ultimately determines what options count as risky as well as whether such risks are worth taking. We, therefore, see intellectual risk-taking as a rhetorical form of self-deliberation.

This approach to possible failure (which we view as an inherent element of "intellectual risk") focuses on fostering student agency, which has implications for a social justice mission for writing studies. For example, Johnson and Sheehan (2020) argue that researchers and teachers should be "oriented to social justice" and, in doing so, should value the intellectual labor and risks involved in navigating pathways between one's desires and one's constraints. This echoes an argument put forward by Canagarajah and Lee (2013) in the edited collection *Academic Risk-Taking*. Canagarajah and Lee also advance social justice goals; they argue for more inclusive norms in academic publishing. They claim the field can better accomplish such work if we "train novice scholars to negotiate with the multiple parties and texts involved in the publishing process" (Canagarajah & Lee, 2013, p. 94). For both Canagarajah and Lee and Johnson and Sheehan, writers' "desires" are curtailed by systematic norms and outside expectations. Both sets of authors maintain that the collision of desires and constraints requires writers to make choices, and both argue for valuing the decision-making process rather than just the products such decisions yield. And while both chapters engage with failure, they each ultimately shift focus from failure to intellectual risk, proposing we teach students how to deliberate about risky choices, like those where failure is a possible outcome.

Turning from failure to risks calls us back to Coles' argument from our opening (Boe & Schroeder, 2002). In our eyes, Coles identifies the reason so many instructors feel compelled to foreground failure: "Failure is the way we learn." We argue, however, this claim does not reckon with the full, paradoxical truth Feigenbaum (2021) describes: Failure is the way we learn, but failure is also the mark of not having learned. Yet our introduction cuts Coles' statement short, and reading further finds him suggesting a way out of failure's problematic paradox. Immediately after claiming failure is the way we learn, Coles clarifies his stance:

> WOE: Is it accurate to say about a writing course that a certain amount of initial failure is not only inevitable but also desirable?
> COLES: I think it is, yes, in several ways, and for that reason ought to be considered as something other than failure. It ought to be named and planned for, built into a course and then capitalized on. (Boe & Shroeder, 2002, p. 12)

Coles' emphasis on "initial failures" departs from Johnson and Sheehan, as they maintain the value of failure as a sometimes worthy end. But Coles, like Johnson and Sheehan and like Canagarajah and Lee, argues for attending to the way failure can, even should, happen within an intellectual project. This approach calls for an instructional design that promotes the "in-process" not-always-successful work as future-oriented "navigation" (Johnson & Sheehan, 2020; Teagarden et al., 2018) or "negotiation" (Canagarajah & Lee, 2013). Either term prompts forward-looking considerations of risk rather than backward-facing experiences of failure, and each opens up a deliberative approach to the question of future potential failures. In general, we believe that most teachers who are proponents of failure pedagogies agree with Coles that failure is valuable because it is a powerful means to accomplish writing class goals. Even the strongest advocates value failure for what it engenders. For example, when Carr (2017) writes, "Failure is integral to learning and development" (p. 79), she makes learning and development, not failure itself, the goal. Failure is a means of learning, we grant, but so too is intellectual risk-taking.

We believe that the advantage of focusing on "intellectual risk-taking" in the classroom (instead of focusing on failure) is that it can offer a more positive learning goal for students. Outside the field of RCWS, educational psychologists Abercrombie et al. (2022) similarly argue that intellectual risk-taking is "broader than a response to failure, and includes a positively valenced, generative learning dimension," emphasizing intellectual risk-taking can foster "actions that are more exploratory than reactive" (p. 7). More specifically, our review has shown how intellectual risk inherently overlaps with deliberative failure projects while emphasizing generative rather than stigmatized framings. But we also see opportunities for an intellectual risk focus to advance the forensic and epideictic missions, without requiring instructors to first overcome students' negative associations of failure or to build artificial experiences with failure into a curriculum. We thus argue intellectual risk is a more helpful concept than failure, offering greater classroom affordances while less ethically fraught and with fewer rhetorical burdens.

What Intellectual Risk Offers the Forensic Perspective

Foregrounding intellectual risk instead of failure offers potential for the overall mission of the forensic strand. We grant that a forensic approach to failure offers inventional capacity, as most scholars, teachers, and students can point to times where something did not work. But the backwards-facing focus is also a limitation. Such work can only be done on what is already complete, on a failure already rendered. Students can mine their past experiences for lessons but this approach gives no guidance on how to prospect for future options.

Students, moreover, often do not intuitively understand their decision-making as writers, which limits the utility of starting with a past failure. If students do not recognize points of agency, then they will struggle to see how their choices could have contributed to a failed attempt. This undercuts the efficacy of reflection as a process of information-seeking. Moreover, as the epideictic and deliberative strands argue, most students come predisposed to define failures in terms of other people's judgments or preexisting social scripts rather than develop their own sense of what worked, what did not, or even what constituted failure and success in the first place. Since the forensic strand tends to accept failures as externally defined, this approach could end up reifying students' beliefs rather than equipping them to generate their own definitions of success.

Intellectual risk, in contrast, emphasizes contingency, where some choices can be wise but ultimately unsuccessful. This can help students understand failure as not always the result of mistakes or errors but rather a part of making choices in the face of uncertainty. An intellectual risk framing can thus make failure more an exploration of the contingent factors of a situation that resulted in failure rather than a hunt for mistakes or a performance of self-chastisement.

In asking students to evaluate potential risks ahead of time, if and when they fail, students might also be better prepared to identify decision points and reflect more systematically. For just as forensic investigators at a crime scene must piece together evidence to establish a logical chain of causation, so must writing students plot the winding route to "failure" if they are to learn from it.

This involves detective work. They must uncover and sequence class notes, highlighted readings, discarded outlines, feedback from instructors, conversations with classmates, circumstantial situations, rough drafts, and false leads. Then, they must decide where to place the blame. The process can be made easier if we prime students to track risky decisions well before they have potentially failed.

Rather than foregoing discussions of failure, foregrounding intellectual risk lays the foundation for purposeful considerations of unsuccessful attempts. A rhetorical approach to intellectual risk-taking provides students a bread-crumb trail to follow back to those forking paths—to repeat Holmes and Wittman's (2020) allusion—allowing students to reflect on specific choices among the available means of persuasion. And so, an intellectual risk approach maintains the value of reflecting on past failures while emphasizing path-finding. It backgrounds the rendered judgments of others while still foregrounding a core mission we see underpinning the forensic strand: promoting student, teacher, and researcher agency while acknowledging situational constraints. In short, the lens of intellectual risk-taking creates opportunities to look backward and forward, learning about what works from past failures (and successes) as well as imagining how choices might play out with work-in-progress.

What Intellectual Risk Offers the Epideictic Strand

Relocating from failure to risk might be a temporal shift for the forensic strand, but what intellectual risk-taking offers the epideictic perspective is more of a dispositional shift. We start by noting the high stakes involved in advocating for failure, as defined by members of the epideictic strand. Much of the epideictic literature describes the negative consequences, especially in terms of emotional states, that accompany failure. These accounts serve as a useful check, reminding readers that not everyone—perhaps hardly anyone—likes failing or being subject to failure. West-Puckett et al. (2023) acknowledge that their enactment of failure entails risk-taking: "Queer assessment killjoys stray from well-worn pathways that iteratively move toward success; they risk the attainment of material and social rewards in order to pursue different trajectories and horizons" (p. 85). Overall, this strand claims failure's potential overrules possible downsides; we, like the deliberative strand, see the destructive potential as a serious limitation to epideictic aims.

Feigenbaum's (2021) generative failure is one approach that suggests we can experience failure without being penalized so severely. But if we minimize the stakes of failure, can we still produce the crucial kind of experience? Can exercises that prompt generative failure take students into the affective dimensions that will lead to the most substantial insight? Carr (2013) does not believe so. She says, "I'm not especially interested in failure that doesn't involve feelings of shame" (n.p.).

She is drawn to the "double movement" of failure that, through pain, helps us transform our view of ourselves both as individual beings and beings in relation to others. West-Puckett et al. (2023) build on this view, positing: "Shame is a faithful traveling companion to those who search together for failure. Without it, however, we can't know the flip side of shame, which is pride" (85). They thus advocate failure's role in creating powerful affective states, both negative and positive.

But we argue failure is not the only entry point to emotionally powerful experiences. Like failure, risk is as much an affective state as it is an external measure, and it can prompt students to experience the emotional catalyst of being drawn both "toward painful individuation, [and] toward uncontrollable relationality" (Carr, 2013, n.p.). Identifying intellectual risks, after all, requires individual judgment, but one that is socially situated and where others' judgments contribute to the evaluation of risk and reward and potentially form some of the positive and negative outcomes. Recognizing risky options can lead students into negative emotional states, in part because of unwelcome comparisons to others. Consider how Lee's "perception of risk led her to isolate herself during the writing process" and that "Ena's perceptions of her article as risky . . . and her fears of appearing too demanding and entitled as a novice scholar, however, prevented her from confidently asserting herself to the gatekeepers" (Canagarajah & Lee, 2013, p. 93). Cox (2011) finds a similar pattern among undergraduate students:

> For Ashley, the underlying fear involved being exposed—in front of the teacher and her peers—as too stupid for college classes. "I don't want to be the stupid kid in class, where everyone else is raising their hand, and I'm the only one not. And I know it's not going to be like that, but it's one of my biggest fears." (p. 34)

The feeling of risk, just like the experience of failure, can engender powerful, negative-affect states; both failure and risk can inspire students to question themselves and their situations. But dwelling in failure does not necessarily lead to good outcomes. Lee writes "Even now, years after the experience, I find myself almost back at the paralysis stage" (Canagarajah & Lee, 2013, p. 85). And Cox summarizes Ashley's experience as "scaling down" her educational plans despite her excellent high school performance. Both students withdraw for fear of failure, which then causes a more consequential failure. Yet the resulting state is one of continued anxiety.

Thus, focusing on failure cannot guarantee positive transformation. But by shifting emphasis to intellectual risk-taking, those interested in the epideictic project move from "dwelling in failure" to "dwelling in possibility," the Emily Dickinson line that *Failure Pedagogies* contributors Holmes and Wittman (2020) advocate. Pushing students to imagine possibilities can serve to spark the same critical reassessments that much of the epideictic strand sees happen with failure. But it also emphasizes student agency over their decisions—from what to write to how to be. Rather than embracing failure, teaching students how to navigate risk can call forth powerful affective states like uncertainty and discomfort while also fostering in students the deliberative skills and disposition of agency to make navigating such choices more possible.

RISK AND FAILURE: COUNTERPOINTS/COUNTERPARTS

Our three-strand model of failure offers readers a new way to understand the conversation about pedagogical interpretations of failure's purpose in the writing classroom. In making our case, we also present intellectual risk-taking as a counter to failure. Thus, we offer our review to identify the emerging differences in failure pedagogies, and we further argue that writing teachers should embrace the pedagogical potential of intellectual risk-taking on three grounds.

First, we argue that the concepts of failure and risk-taking are already often intertwined in scholarship, so understanding intellectual risk-taking is key for understanding failure. We have shown how deliberative approaches tend to move from failure to risk-taking, suggesting their interconnected nature. Forensic and epideictic arguments for failure also acknowledge the importance of risk-taking; for example, Inoue (2019) follows the forensic strand, and he exhorts his students "to take risks, in short to fail and learn from that failing" (p. 145). Bartkevicius (2023) titles her forensic chapter "On Failure: Notes Toward a Pedagogy of Risk." From the epideictic strand, West-Puckett et al. (2023) title their opening chapter "Risking Failure." And Carr (2013) recommends assignments based on the idea that "risk-taking and failure foster imagination" and says of her own experience that "identifying as a failure" has made her, among other benefits "less risk-averse" (n.p.). So, while we argue writing instructors would be better served by foregrounding the goal of intellectual risk-taking instead of failure, we view this as a way of pursuing similar goals and enacting the same values; risk and failure are better understood as counterparts than counterpoints.

Second, we argue that starting with intellectual risk-taking creates the capacity to meaningfully engage with failure—if and when it occurs—later in the course. Instructors interested in the learning potential of failure can thus develop classes where intellectual risk serves as students' initial encounter with this larger learning cycle. This design sidesteps the stigmatized baggage associated with failure so instructors can foster the engagement, trust, and deliberative skills necessary to take on the more fraught task of learning through failure.

Third, and finally, we argue, in agreement with Abercrombie et al. (2022), that intellectual risk-taking offers a positive learning framework that is "more exploratory than reactive" (p. 7). In other words, rather than focus on how to help students process or deal with failure after it happens, intellectual risk-taking encourages students to recognize the benefits of seeking and trying out new things. In this way, intellectual risk-taking encourages an exploratory approach to inquiry and to writing.

In making this argument, we recognize that shifting the scholarly conversation from failure to intellectual risk-taking could appear to be just a switch of key terms; emphasizing intellectual risk-taking will not guarantee that students actually take intellectual risks or learn differently from failure. Additionally, we acknowledge those who might question: "How is intellectual risk-taking really any different from Feigenbaum's generative failure?" We take these rivals seriously. However, our point is not that one term is inherently better than another but that intellectual risk-taking—as the rhetorical practice we have defined—invites deliberation and a pedagogical approach to inquiry that many theories of failure do not.

Thus, we argue writing teachers interested in the learning potential of failure may be better served by explicitly teaching students a rhetorical approach to intellectual risk-taking that encourages deliberating over the outcomes and stakes of risky choices, making strategic decisions, and reflecting on their outcomes, failed or otherwise. By embracing the deliberative cycle initiated when a writer recognizes an intellectual risk, writing instructors may support the dispositions and practices that help students face risks as well as negotiate the relational, contextual, and institutional dimensions of failure and failing.

REFERENCES

Abercrombie, S., Carbonneau, K. J. & Hushman, C. J. (2022). (Re)Examining academic risk taking: Conceptual structure, antecedents, and relationship to productive failure. *Contemporary Educational Psychology, 68*, Article 102029. https://doi.org/10.1016/j.cedpsych.2021.102029.

Alford, C. (2020). When one door closes, another opens; Or, appreciating clichés. In A. D. Carr & L. R. Micciche (Eds.), *Failure pedagogies: Learning and unlearning what it means to fail* (pp. 11–23). Peter Lang.

Alvarez, D. (2001). Why students fail. *Journal of Teaching Writing, 19*(1–2), 76–93.

Bain, K. (2012). *What the best college students do*. Harvard University Press.

Bartkevicius, J. (2023). On failure: Notes toward a pedagogy of risk. In D. Hesse & L. Julier (Eds.), *Nonfiction, the teaching of writing, and the influence of Richard Lloyd-Jones* (pp. 113–121). The WAC Clearinghouse; University Press of Colorado. https://doi.org/10.37514/PRA-B.2023.2005.2.09.

Barrón, N. G. & Gruber, S. (2020). Redefining failure: Controlling a sense of self. In A. D. Carr & L. R. Micciche (Eds.), *Failure pedagogies: Learning and unlearning what it means to fail* (pp. 83–95). Peter Lang.

Beare, Z. (2018). The strange practices of serendipitous failure: Considering metanoia as an alternative to kairos. In M. D. Goggin & P. N. Goggin (Eds.), *Serendipity in rhetoric, writing, and literacy research* (pp. 257–266). Utah State University Press. https://doi.org/10.7330/9781607327394.c020.

Beghetto, R. A. (2009). Correlates of intellectual risk taking in elementary school science. *Journal of Research in Science Teaching, 46*(2), 210–223. https://doi.org/10.1002/tea.20270.

Boe, J. & Schroeder, E. (2002). "Failure is the way we learn": An interview with William E. Coles, Jr. *Writing on the Edge, 13*(1), 6–22.

Canagarajah, S. & Lee, E. (2013). Negotiating alternative discourses in academic writing and publishing: Risks with hybridity. In L. Thesen & L. Cooper (Eds.), *Risk in academic writing: Postgraduate students, their teachers and the making of knowledge* (pp. 59–99). Multilingual Matters. https://doi.org/10.21832/9781783091065.

Carr, A. D. (2013). In support of failure. *Composition Forum, 27*. https://compositionforum.com/issue/27/failure.php.

Carr, A. D. (2017). Failure is not an option. In C. E. Ball & D. M. Loewe (Eds.), *Bad ideas about writing* (pp. 76–81). West Virginia University Libraries Digital Publishing Institute. https://textbooks.lib.wvu.edu/badideas/index.html.

Carr, A. D. & Brooke, C. (2015). Failure can be an important part of writing development. In L. Adler-Kassner & E. Wardle (Eds.), *Naming what we know: Threshold concepts of writing studies* (pp. 62–42). Utah State University Press.

Carr, A. D. & Micciche, L. R. (2020). Introduction: Failure's sweat. In A. D. Carr & L. R. Micciche (Eds.), *Failure pedagogies: Learning and unlearning what it means to fail* (pp. 1–7). Peter Lang.

Commer, C., Cooke, A., Mando, J. & Teagarden, A. (2024). (Re)locating the rhetorical commonplaces of failure and risk-taking. *Rhetoric Review, 43*(1), 78–94. https://doi.org/10.1080/07350198.2023.2286143.

Cox, R. D. (2011). *The college fear factor: How students and professors misunderstand one another.* Harvard University Press.

Feigenbaum, P. (2021). Telling students it's OK to fail, but showing them it isn't: Dissonant paradigms of failure in higher education. *Teaching & Learning Inquiry, 9*(1), 13–27. https://doi.org/10.20343/teachlearninqu.9.1.3.

Foster, D. (2015). Private journals versus public blogs: The impact of peer readership on low-stakes reflective writing. *Teaching Sociology, 43*(2), 104–114. https://doi.org/10.1177/0092055X14568204.

Gross, D. M. & Alexander, J. (2016). Frameworks for failure. *Pedagogy: Critical Approaches to Teaching Literature, Language, Composition, and Culture, 16*(2), 273–295. https://doi.org/10.1215/15314200-3435884.

Halberstam, J. (2011). *The queer art of failure.* Duke University Press.

Haswell, J., Haswell, R. & Blalock, G. (2009). Hospitality in college composition courses. *College Composition and Communication 60*(4), 707–727.

Hay, C. (2020). Foreword: Failure, fear, and alternate routes. In A. D. Carr & L. R. Micciche (Eds.), *Failure pedagogies: Learning and unlearning what it means to fail* (xi-xv). Peter Lang.

Holmes, A. N. & Wittman, K. (2020). The costs of clarity. In A. D. Carr & L. R. Micciche (Eds.), *Failure pedagogies: learning and unlearning what it means to fail* (pp. 25–37). Peter Lang.

Inoue, A. B. (2014). Theorizing failure in US writing assessments. *Research in the Teaching of English, 48*(3), 330–352.

Inoue, A. B. (2019). *Labor-based grading contracts: Building equity and inclusion in the compassionate writing classroom* (2nd ed.). The WAC Clearinghouse; University Press of Colorado. https://doi.org/10.37514/PER-B.2022.1824.

Inoue, A. B. (2020). Afterword: Failure and letting go. In A. D. Carr & L. R. Micciche (Eds.), *Failure pedagogies: Learning and unlearning what it means to fail* (pp. 259–263). Peter Lang.

Johnson, G. P. & Sheehan, R. (2020). The uses of queer failure: Navigating the pedagogical mandate of happiness. In A. D. Carr & L. R. Micciche (Eds.), *Failure pedagogies: Learning and unlearning what it means to fail* (pp. 127–140). Peter Lang.

Johnstone, H.W., Jr. (1991). Philosophy and argument. University Park: Pennsylvania State University Press.

Lehn, J. (2020). Committing to failure: Critical pedagogy and failure in classroom teaching. In A. D. Carr & L. R. Micciche (Eds.), *Failure pedagogies: Learning and unlearning what it means to fail* (pp. 141–152). Peter Lang.

Myers, K. A. (2011). Metanoia and the transformation of opportunity. *Rhetoric Society Quarterly, 41*(1), 1–18. https://doi.org/10.1080/02773945.2010.533146.

Myers, K. A. (2019). Unspeakable failures. *Composition Studies, 47*(2), 48–67.

Pantelides, K. (2020). After the accusation: The lasting impact of plagiarism trauma on student writing behaviors. In A. D. Carr & L. R. Micciche (Eds.), *Failure pedagogies: Learning and unlearning what it means to fail* (pp. 39–52). Peter Lang.

Phillips, C. & Giordano, J. B. (2020). Messy processes into and out of failure: Professional identities and open-access writers. In A. D. Carr & L. R. Micciche (Eds.), *Failure pedagogies: Learning and unlearning what it means to fail* (pp. 153–162). Peter Lang.

Rickly, R. & Cook, K. C. (2017). Failing forward: Training graduate students for research—An introduction to the special issue. *Journal of Technical Writing and Communication, 47*(2), 119–129.

Segal, J. Z. (1996). Pedagogies of decentering and a discourse of failure. *Rhetoric Review, 15*(1), 174–191.

Teagarden, A., Commer, C., Cooke, A. & Mando, J. (2018). Intellectual risk in the writing classroom: Navigating tensions in educational values and classroom practice. *Composition Studies, 46*(2), 116–238.

Thoune, D. L. (2020). Failure potential: Using failure as feedback. In A. D. Carr & L. R. Micciche (Eds.), *Failure pedagogies: Learning and unlearning what it means to fail* (pp. 53–62). Peter Lang.

West-Puckett, S., Caswell, N. I. & Banks, W. P. (2023). *Failing sideways: Queer possibilities for writing assessment*. Utah State University Press.

CHAPTER 3.
THEORIZING FAILURE THROUGH TEACHER RESPONSE

Shane A. Wood
University of Central Florida

> Failure in writing classrooms may very well be one of the most important yet undertheorized concepts in composition studies.
> – Asao B. Inoue

> When we think about re-conceptualizing failure, we have to think not only about the personal realm but also about the sociocultural context in which failure is embedded and throughout which it circulates.
> – Allison D. Carr, "In Support of Failure"

As teachers, we've probably had a conversation with a colleague, advisor, or administrator about a student failing. More often than not, conversations around failure in education place blame on students as opposed to inequitable systems or classroom practices. I would argue that the student is rarely, if ever, the *issue* when it comes to failure in writing classrooms. Students are often marked as "failures" based on how they use language. Writing assessments are designed to offer feedback on the language choices students make in writing. Students are usually penalized by narrow interpretations and judgments of language despite organizational commitments to students' rights to their languages (see "Students' Rights to Their Own Language," 1974). Grades are tools of measurement placed on student writing to demonstrate success or failure. Success and failure in writing are associated with some idea of a "standard." Writing assessment becomes a "yardstick model" where students' languages are measured against standardized English, "a fixed ideal of writing" (Inoue, 2014, p. 333). Teacher response becomes a justification for the letter grade, or at the very least, used to interpret letter grades in traditional writing assessment, whether the teacher wants them to be or not.

While research in writing studies has taken up failure (Carr & Micciche, 2020), and while education studies and writing scholarship have taken up failure through grading and assessment (Schneider & Hutt, 2023; West-Puckett et al., 2023; Blum, 2020; Inoue, 2014; Inoue, 2015; Johnson, 2021), teacher response has received less attention in recent scholarship around failure. A basic keyword search for "failure" in the *Journal of Response to Writing* leads to twenty-two results. Most are connected to grades or grading. None theorize failure through response. I find this absence in scholarship surprising for several reasons. It feels like now is a good opportunity to critically examine different aspects of classroom assessment, including teacher response. I feel like now is the time to re-emphasize response and why we respond while simultaneously questioning the status quo. It feels like now is the time to double down on the importance of response, arguably the most important part of teaching writing, while critiquing inequitable systems of assessment.

Grades aren't always the issue. A student might receive a "good" grade and still receive feedback that makes them feel detached and indifferent about their writing. A student can perceive a marginal comment as negative regardless of a "good" grade. If I'm being honest, I feel like my students have more visceral reactions and memories around teacher response than they do grades. Students' lack of interest in writing when they get to first-year composition seems to come from what they've been asked to write about (e.g., assignments) and how they've received feedback in the past (e.g., teacher response). Students seem to carry with them memories of feedback that have generated emotional responses, which have caused harm or, at the very least, caused them to disassociate from the writing process. Writing is no longer fun. There's no creativity, risk-taking, curiosity, child-like joy when it comes to engaging in writing. In part because of the systems, standards, and conditions that surround the teaching of writing. But I also think there's something to be said about how teachers respond to student writing.

Students tend to remember comments that made them feel like failure. When I ask my students to reflect on previous writing experiences in school, they rarely, if ever, talk about grades. Instead, they share stories about how the response made them feel. They talk about receiving red marks on their writing, or a comment in the margins that made them feel inadequate, or an end comment that was confusing.

Maybe these reactions toward response are memorable because feedback feels more personal than a letter grade. A letter grade is a symbol. Feedback is language—words, ideas, thoughts, feelings—in response to how someone chooses to use language. Maybe a marginal comment stands out not just because it makes visible an audience but because it intervenes on a specific idea a student was willing to share with us. We know writing is interconnected with identity. There's vulnerability and power in writing. The same can be said for feedback.

I've been drawn to how teacher response might fail for a while now. I've been interested in how response might fail in/through its production, circulation, and reception since I wrote about it in my thesis ten years ago. I remember reading Allison D. Carr's (2013) "In Support of Failure" and making connections between her good work and research on writing assessment and teacher response. Carr's description of failure as an "affect-bearing concept" and how failure *feels* and what that feeling *does* were significant to my understandings of failure through teacher response. In this chapter, I recommend we theorize, examine, and engage in conversations around how teacher response might *fail* and how we can address that failure with students in writing classrooms.

FROM GRADES TO (RE)EXAMINING RESPONSE

Higher education has a long, complicated history in the United States. Colleges were designed to exclude students based on race, gender, disability, and socioeconomic status. Universities were created to privilege white, abled-bodied upper-class men. Admission and grading are examples of institutional tools that have been used to exclude students going back to Harvard in 1636. But we only have to look back sixty years to see how admission standards were still being used to keep students like James Meredith out of the university. Meredith became the first Black student to attend the University of Mississippi in 1962 (after being denied admission). Exclusionary institutional practices designed to keep some students out are still with us. Look no further than recent attacks on diversity, equity, and inclusion in states like Texas and Florida.

I'm wary of how secondary and post-secondary institutions celebrate national rankings, state rankings, acceptance rates and standards, ACT/SAT scores, GPA scores, retention, AP classes. What's this saying? Isn't this an old narrative repackaged with different words? While institutions advertise these as measurements and markers of "success," I see them as modern-day markers of exclusion. These tools won't go away in higher education either. They might evolve and be refashioned, but they won't disappear. Education is built on the dichotomy of success and failure. Success is good. Failure is bad. Grades and traditional writing assessment practices reinforce that. Students are taught *not to fail* as opposed to seeing failure as *necessary for learning*. In kindergarten, students are rewarded (or punished) by gold stars, stickers, and grades.

Grades are powerful institutional tools that have been carefully integrated into various aspects of higher education. They complement the consumeristic and capitalistic nature of higher education in the United States. Grades function as a technology of surveillance (Johnson, 2021). They serve the university and reinforce hierarchies. Students are "allowed into" a major or class based on GPA and prerequisites. Scholarships are "given" or "taken away" based on grades. Schools threaten students with expulsion for poor performance as if receiving an F letter grade isn't devastating enough to morale. Institutions have created a system where students desire grades, and teachers are required to give them. Writing teachers have to provide a final letter grade whether we want to or not.

Alternative writing assessment practices, like grading contracts and ungrading, have become more popular over the last decade in writing studies. But the truth is, we're *still* grading (Fernandes et al., 2023). Maggie Fernandes, Emily Brier, and Megan McIntyre (2023) argue against using "the language of ungrading" altogether because it "misrepresents how students experience our courses" and "flattens the critiques of normative and oppressive writing assessment" (p. 148–149). We need to be honest with our students about classroom assessment. Grades are a part of writing classrooms. Teachers give grades, eventually. We should critique the problematic nature and institutional power of grades while also acknowledging how students might desire grades (Inman & Powell, 2018). There's no easy answer when it comes to writing assessment. In writing classrooms, grades tend to be used to judge language by a standard. Traditional grading based on writing "quality" often encourages students to adopt "standardized" English. Standardized English has been socially and culturally constructed to mean "good" writing in the United States. Students are disproportionately affected by these norms, especially marginalized students.

Some teachers might say grades are a form of feedback. While I understand that grades might communicate progress (or lack thereof), I would argue that teacher response should be separated from grading altogether in traditional and alternative writing assessment ecologies. I acknowledge this might be difficult, given the institution's fixation on grades and how students are conditioned to value them. It requires conversations with students about the purpose of teacher response. It might mean delaying the distribution of a letter grade until after students have reflected on feedback. This might seem too idealistic. I want to acknowledge teachers in precarious positions that might make this more difficult. There are already time constraints and institutional inequities being an adjunct, graduate teaching assistant, and non-tenure track faculty. I'm cognizant of 4/4 and 5/5 teaching loads every semester. Feedback takes a lot of time, and when you're teaching 100–125 students each semester, there's not a lot of time to give.

I also want to recognize that students are in a precarious position. It's difficult to persuade students in sixteen weeks not to desire grades after always receiving them and still receiving them in other classes. Students have a history with grades and feedback being produced and distributed at the same time, sometimes on the same page. It's safe to assume that decoupling the interconnectivity of grades and response might be challenging for teachers and students. Teacher response sits in a gray area between teacher and student, rubric and grade, institution and classroom. Unlike grades, which are mostly concrete and stable (A: 90–100; B: 80–89; C: 70–79; D: 60–69; F: 59 and below), feedback is fluid and dynamic. It's clear that feedback is also more student-centered in that it provides individualized direction to student writing. Feedback informs and guides the writer. When teachers respond to students, they're not just responding to writing; they're responding to a *writer*.

In this chapter, I offer a rendering of an ecology of response that indicates how feedback doesn't work in isolation but rather is informed and situated within and between various systems, activities, and structures. I do this so we might consider different points of origin failure can take through teacher response. It's important not to oversimplify teacher response or failure. Teacher response doesn't just fail because a teacher said something wrong, for example. I believe it's more nuanced than that. I introduce *feedback failure theory* to help us investigate teacher response more closely. Feedback failure theory looks closely at *production* and *perception*, or how teacher response gets produced and perceived. My hope is to peel back the layers of how response might fail or pinpoint moments where failure becomes embodied through feedback. I conclude with a description of a pedagogical practice that allows teachers and students to focus on how feedback somehow misses the mark, or fails, at least some of the time. Doing so resists ideas that attach failure to students and/or student writing. My hope is to alleviate the pressures and burdens students carry when it comes to writing and assessment and to create opportunities for more productive conversations to happen around feedback and failure.

ECOLOGY OF TEACHER RESPONSE

There's a rich history in writing studies on the purposes of teacher response (Sommers, 1982; Knoblauch & Brannon, 1982; Anson, 1989; Straub, 1996). One throughline in this scholarship is that teacher response should support student agency and encourage students to further engage in the writing process. Nancy Sommers (2013) calls feedback the "most enduring form of communication" teachers have with students (xi). Responding to writing is personal, Chris Anson (1989) acknowledges that feedback is "often difficult and tense" (p. 2). Different moments in the writing process call for different kinds of responses. David Green Jr. (2016) shares, "The evaluation of student writing, thus, is a complex negotiation driven by institutional context and teacher knowledge, both of which are reinforced by the curricula and evaluative materials developed and implemented by writing programs" (152). There are different stakeholders and objectives that inform writing courses, pedagogies, student learning outcomes, assignments, and assessments.

There are larger institutional aims and even state policies that shape first-year writing classes. Most first-year writing classes, for instance, are tied to general education curriculum and/or general education programs. General education curriculum often identifies specific outcomes first-year writing courses need to meet to fulfill university requirements (e.g., writing communication). Any examination of teacher response shouldn't *just* focus on the act of providing feedback to student writing. There's too much informing that interaction, too much between that act of communication. Each local context consists of different systems, structures, policies, assignments, expectations, goals, and outcomes.

I say this to emphasize how teacher response is locally situated and never in isolation. Anson (2000) challenges teachers to become more "reflective of the conditions, nature, and sources of their response to error in students' texts" (p. 17). How do we increase our awareness of institutional conditions, systems, and structures? How do we become more reflective of how cultural and social biases might shape response practices? How do we reconcile programmatic outcomes and policies with our own pedagogies and values when it comes to providing feedback?

To me, this starts with an understanding of an *ecology of teacher response* see Figure 3.1, which helps demonstrate some of the elements and forces in the ecology of response). Mya Poe, Asao B. Inoue, and Norbert Elliot (2019) write:

> We insist that writing assessment must be understood within an ecological framework. Because our metaphors structure our conceptual systems, ecological realities and the rhetorical framework used to describe them are necessary to displace elementalist notions of process and product. (p. 4)

We should map institutional norms and conditions and acknowledge policies and practices that shape response genres, such as marginal comments and end comments. Most importantly, we should take into account students' histories and memories with different response genres. Through mapping an ecology of teacher response and listening to our students, we can think more critically about how teacher response might fail or how failure might be embodied through teacher response. We can investigate how feedback is situated in classrooms and institutions that already fail students because judgments of language are never neutral.

Genres are ideological (Devitt, 2004). Response genres, like marginal comments, carry meaning and value to student writing—they offer ways of knowing, seeing, understanding, revising. These genres of response circulate in a much larger activity system. There's a recurring situation that facilitates teacher response: Teachers assign writing, students write, and teachers provide feedback. This situation occurs across writing classrooms.

Figure 3.1. Ecology of teacher response.

Theorizing Failure Through Teacher Response

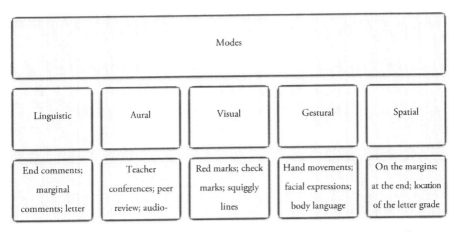

Figure 3.2. Modes and examples of response.

In addition to acknowledging how these elements inform response through its production, distribution, circulation, interpretation, and interaction with students, feedback needs to be understood through its modalities as well. Modes and mediums, of course, are never neutral. Power is situated in the tools and technologies we use to respond to student writing and is laced with values and beliefs that advantage some students and disadvantage others. For example, consider how recording audio feedback on Canvas or Blackboard without a transcript to supplement the audio is less accessible for students with auditory processing disabilities. The technology affects the production, perception, and meaning-making of the teacher's response.

Figure 3.2 helps situate how teacher response can be distributed through various modes of communication. It ties the five modes from the New London Group to specific examples of feedback. Of course, teacher response takes different forms and tones, as well.

For example, some responses might be informal, whereas others might be more formal. Some might be constructive or formative or summative. Some are from peer-to-peer, while others are teacher-to-student. Teachers can use multiple forms of feedback—end comments and marginal comments, for example—on any given assignment. Response scholarship has characterized feedback in several ways: Directive, facilitative, authoritative, collaborative, intentional, reflective, reader-based, student-centered.

Response comes at various stages of the writing process, too. For example, feedback on an earlier draft of student writing might ask for substantial content-based changes, whereas feedback on a later draft might be more concerned with stylistic elements of writing. Sommers (1982) suggests that it's "necessary for us to offer assistance to student writers when they are in the process of composing a text," and without feedback, "students assume that their writing has communicated their meaning and perceive no need for revising the substance of their text" (p. 149). C. H. Knoblauch and Lil Brannon (1981) write that response is designed to "dramatize the presence of a reader who depends on the writer's choices in order to perceive the intent of the discourse" (p. 1). Teacher response draws attention to the writing process and increases awareness of possible concerns within writing, like issues with organization, development, and focus. I feel like we should consider not only what teacher response does or when and where response happens in the writing process but also what's less visible through teacher response. It's important to examine what informs response and how response comes to be, why some modes might be more advantageous than others, and how to communicate these ecological nuances with students.

After all, when a teacher responds, they make their voice visible on the page. It's seen. It's heard. It's felt by students. If the text is a representation of the student, feedback reflects the teacher. But what about the things that shape that voice in the margins? Teacher response most certainly represents how a teacher experiences a text. But it does more than offer insight on an experience. Teacher response communicates values and beliefs about how a student chooses to language. Our readings and responses to student writing are shaped by who we are, where we are, our attitudes on language (Young, 2010), perceptions on error (Williams, 1981), thoughts about rhetorical moves in writing, our histories and memories with language, including how we've been trained to read and respond to student writing and how we've received feedback in the past on our own writing. Those are a few things that inform our reading and understanding and how we respond to student writing.

As much as we might attempt to decentralize our presence in the classroom through certain pedagogies (e.g., critical, collaborative), it's difficult to deconstruct ourselves with teacher response. Students have complicated histories with feedback that asserted and reaffirmed how much our perspective matters as teachers, especially when it comes to judging language and grading writing. We can deemphasize the letter grade through alternative classroom assessments. It seems counterproductive to deemphasize feedback. Response has always been valuable to teaching writing because it offers an opportunity to promote and encourage student agency. Feedback can support students' ability to make decisions about their writing: "To deny students any attributes of agency in making such choices is to deny them any right or responsibility for such choices, and so to discourage their investment in their writing" (Horner, 1992, p. 189). Later in this chapter, I describe an activity rooted in student agency and negotiation centered on teacher response.

In its simplest form, feedback, as defined by Darci L. Thoune (2020), "references the information you receive on a performance, activity, or action" (p.

53–54). We might consider how our response practices ought to complement our assessment values and ecologies (Wood, 2020). In some ways, this invites teachers to consider not only how their assessments align but also how response genres might fail students: "Genres have the power to help or hurt human interaction, to ease communication or to deceive, to enable someone to speak or to discourage someone from saying something different" (Devitt, 2004, p. 1). I think we need a pedagogy of response to help us investigate and better understand the nuances of response and failure. Something that can help us talk about teacher response and failure with students.

A PEDAGOGY OF TEACHER RESPONSE IN FIRST-YEAR WRITING

Perhaps the easiest thing to do might be to think about teacher response as complementary to pedagogy and to see whether response is *failing* to confirm what we believe to be true about writing and the teaching of writing. It might be beneficial to think about how response either complements or contradicts pedagogical values as we consider the ecology of teacher response (see Figure 3.1). For example, what does it look like to embody antiracism through responding to student writing if a teacher draws from social justice-oriented pedagogies? What does it look like to complement antiracist writing assessment ecologies with teacher response? Or what does it mean to enact response through disability studies and universal design for learning? At the heart of these questions is this: How do our pedagogies account for response, or vice versa? It seems like our pedagogical values should indeed influence the ways we respond to student writing.

A pedagogy of teacher response feels productive in helping us understand these nuances, especially since we spend so much time responding to student writing. Likewise, a framework that helps us associate failure not with students but with the production and perception of teacher response feels useful. Conversations with students about how we're always learning and growing as teachers from failure seem important. Judy Segal (1996) suggests that we need "accounts of failure, particularly accounts which might be theorized" (p. 189). In "Pedagogies of Decentering and a Discourse of Failure," Segal forms a taxonomy of responses to failure by theorizing her failed decentered classroom, and she concludes that "to complement accounts of success, which *are* available, we need accounts of failure, particularly accounts which might be theorized to be productive of strategies of amelioration" (p. 189). Like Segal notes, I think we need accounts of failure. In particular, I think we need to share when and how failure might exist through teacher response, and we need to demonstrate healthy dialogues about it. Productive conversations that help us understand failure, not run from it.

It seems valuable to connect feedback and failure, given students' experiences and attitudes with writing: "Many first-year college writers have a fear of writing, a fear of failure" (Price, 1997, p. 1). It might help to remember that many first-year writing students are unfamiliar with systems and structures of higher education. This is a new, unfamiliar space. More traditional first-year students are attempting to adjust to a context much different than K-12. There's not as much in-class time and definitely less familiarity with their teachers and peers. Meanwhile, adult learners in first-year composition have their own challenges to overcome. While adapting to this environment, students usually take first-year writing during their first semester in college. Carol Price, echoing Kenneth Bruffee's (1980) assertion that language is tied to identity, writes that students "are afraid to try to put their thoughts onto paper and expose their inadequacies" (p. 1). Price suggests that we have a pedagogical responsibility to teach self-confidence and help students overcome the fear of failure.

What better way to teach confidence than to model to students productive ways to talk about failure, like how teacher response—our own approaches, practices, and habits—might fail. Or how the ecology of response might cause and/or create failure. We can redirect failure away from student writing.

Segal (1996) encourages us to conduct a "structural analysis of failure applying a social-action theory of genre" (p. 176). This allows us to have some concrete language and a shared understanding of how we're analyzing failure. It also demystifies failure, which can complement pedagogical values in alternative classroom assessment practices, like using labor-based grading contracts to decrease the subjectivity of assessing writing (Inoue, 2022). Segal doesn't theorize failure, but she does write about the importance of "good theory." Theory does more than name a concept. It describes the nature of something and provides an explanation of its application. There's opportunity at this moment in time to theorize, conceptualize, question, and unsettle teacher response. I offer *feedback failure theory* to help us do this work.

FEEDBACK FAILURE THEORY

While writing teachers have various approaches to teaching, it remains true that at least one practice unites us all—responding to student writing. If there's one common denominator, even in writing classrooms that use newer classroom assessment models like labor-based grading contracts, it's that teachers read and respond to student writing. Responses can take various forms: marginal comments, end comments, one-on-one conferences, rubrics, audio feedback, feedback in learning management systems (LMS), using screencasting technologies. There's no denying that students have certain attitudes, reactions, and emotional responses to teacher response (Calhoon-Dillahunt & Forrest, 2013; Treglia, 2008). What can we learn from the potential for feedback to *fail our students and even ourselves*?

Since writing is such a vulnerable activity, it makes sense that teacher response affects students, and there are implications for our practices. Writers share their identities and thoughts on a page, and they give them to us to provide feedback. It makes sense that genres of response, such as marginal comments and end comments, might have consequences. In other words, feedback might fail to do what we want it to do, or it might be informed by inequitable policies that shape our response practices. I'm mindful of the peculiarity of failure, too, like how failure doesn't get embodied equally and doesn't take one singular shape. If anything, failure is experiential, unique, and highly individualized, much like student writing.

I offer *feedback failure theory* as a means for teachers and students to explore and investigate how teacher response might fail based on its *production* and *perception*. The goal is to make more visible how teacher response somehow misses the mark, or fails, at least some of the time. Feedback failure theory might help demystify how we respond to student writing and, at the very least, indicate how failure might exist in the systems, structures, and larger ecology of teacher response.

Production

The first part of feedback failure theory examines how feedback is being produced and how the production of feedback can act as failure. The production of feedback is clearly a key component in composition classrooms due to the amount of student writing and revising that is happening over the course of a semester. We might look back at the ecology of response (see Figure 3.1) to understand various elements that might affect feedback production. In doing so, we could ask ourselves questions about the nature of that production. For example, do we consider how our program outcomes might inform what we value and what we say in our response to student writing? Or, to revisit something I mentioned earlier, do we think about how our pedagogies ought to complement our responses? Or maybe how our feedback might be sending contradictory messages to students about those pedagogical values? This is a conversation we could have with students, too. I'm thinking specifically about how a teacher might be committed to antiracism and social justice in first-year writing yet still assess some "standardized" form of English or grammatical errors because of other factors in the university, such as general education learning outcomes. Additionally, the English program or writing program might have outcomes or use other assessment genres, such as rubrics, that value standard academic English and/or call attention to a specific kind of academic languaging. These rubrics, then, are used to assess student writing, which can influence what a teacher comments on.

In the mid- to late 1990s, compositionists explored the nature and tonality of response and encouraged more conversational practices. For example, Peter Elbow (n.d.) shares his response habits, "I write my comments on a separate sheet not only because I'm quicker and neater on my computer, but also because this method makes me comment as a reader about how the writing is affecting me rather than as an editor trying to fix the text" ("About Responding to Student Writing," n.p.). In 1996, Richard Straub argues that "conversational" feedback should employ "calls for revision" and push "the writer to engage in richer pursuits of meaning" (1996b, p. 385). In another article, Straub (1996a) indicates that there's still a problem in understanding the nature of feedback and the purposes for providing feedback. One problem that Straub acknowledges in the production of feedback is the appropriation of student writing. He argues that teachers "should not 'appropriate' student texts by overlooking their purposes for writing and emphasizing our purposes for commenting" (p. 223). Then, Straub concludes that teachers "should be 'facilitative,' providing feedback and support but not dictating the path of revision" (p. 223). Straub's argument and conclusion support a reality—feedback can fail. Though, it doesn't necessarily address the nature of failure through feedback.

Summer Smith (1997) explains how feedback can fail due to its "genre." She examines end comments: "The stability of the genre—the very feature that makes end comments recognizable and, perhaps easier to write—may also reduce the educational effectiveness of the comment" (Smith, 1997, p. 266). Smith writes that teachers establish a "pattern of response" and "history of practice" when forming feedback in part because of institutional power and student expectations. She writes that institutions assert power over teacher feedback to student writing "by determining the focus of the teacher's curriculum, by rewarding or not rewarding the teacher for pedagogical innovations, and, in many cases, by requiring that the teacher return papers with comments within a specified period of time" (Smith, 1997, p. 250). Smith also acknowledges that student expectations play a part in feedback: "The teacher may fear authority challenges from aggressive students who receive poor grades or who oppose the teacher's views on writing" (p. 250). This attention to the production and perception of response is at the heart of feedback failure theory.

The way in which an instructor produces their feedback, in some part, influences whether the student perceives feedback as failure. We can be assured our comments affect our students' attitudes about themselves and their writing. The production of feedback, then, is an essential aspect of understanding how feedback may fail and/or how students might experience failure. Given the larger institutional system under which we work as teachers, we need to think more about how these assessment structures are affecting our production and distribution of feedback.

For example, most universities require that teachers give an end-of-semester letter grade. Traditional grading—giving an "A" or "B" or "C"—on student writing is still the most common assessment method in first-year writing, even though there's been more attention to alternatives over the last decade. If our responses to student writing work under this more traditional hierarchical grading system, then it changes the way we produce feedback. For example, do we see our feedback as a complement to the letter grades we give? Are our responses a justification or a rationale for this summative assessment—the grade? Should they be under this system?

Since letter grades have been problematized in relation to learning and motivation, it might benefit writing teachers who choose to give grades on writing to wait on the production and distribution of the grade itself. For example, under this assessment structure, it seems more beneficial to give feedback to students, and perhaps provide opportunities for revision and reflection, and then assign a letter grade a week later. This would elicit more engagement and response from students—they might read the feedback as opposed to looking for the letter grade. Now, one could argue that feedback is produced through the drafting stages before assigning a letter grade on the final draft. But that brings up a different question: Is there a conflicting message being sent by the production of feedback that, at first, doesn't assign a grade and then, ultimately, produces a grade on student writing? The same conflicting message could be said about feedback on final drafts that include a grade and offer paths for revision, especially if students aren't given the chance to revise or expected to revise.

If teacher response complements the larger classroom assessment ecology and a teacher's pedagogical values, then more than likely, there's going to be less conflict and fewer mixed messages. We might mitigate conflict by seeing how response practices work alongside classroom assessment. In the 1990s, there was an emphasis on portfolios as better representations of writing and pedagogical values, such as writing-as-process, metacognition, and revision. Portfolios as a model for classroom assessment helped complement the belief that measuring multiple written performances is more reliable and valid when assessing student writing. It's possible that classroom assessment could lead to teacher response failing through its production.

Teacher response itself can send contradictory messages, too. Nancy Sommers (1982) communicates that students are "commanded to edit a sentence to avoid an error or to condense a sentence to achieve greater brevity of style, and then told in the margins that the particular paragraph needs to be more specific or developed more" (p. 150). An instructor's annotations could be contradictory by asking a student to fix grammatical errors in one paragraph while asking them to refocus on the content in another: "These different signals given to students, to edit and develop, to condense and elaborate, represent also the failure of teachers' comments to direct genuine revision of the text as a whole" (Sommers, 1982, p. 150–151). This shows how the production of feedback might fail based on what's being said and what students are being asked to do. We might ask ourselves what this means about how students perceive and take up feedback.

For example, is it reasonable to assume that students will be able to negotiate those contradictory messages successfully? It's possible that this failure in feedback also makes students' writing worse. As Sommers (1982) notes, these comments "take the students' attention away from their own original purposes . . . too often revision becomes a balancing act for students in which they make the changes that are requested but do not take the risk of changing anything that was not commented on" (p. 151). Thus, feedback also fails based on whether student agency is removed.

The production of feedback could result in failure based on how a teacher approaches student writing, as well. As Joseph M. Williams (1981) notes, our approach to writing is critical in gauging how feedback will be produced. Williams begs the question of how our expectations for error in student writing act as failure. In many ways, it demonstrates carelessness. We fail students when we don't approach their writing in a spirit of goodwill and eagerness to read and learn. Williams challenges teachers to think more about how we read other texts, such as books, journals, and newspapers, and to approach student writing the same way. Feedback can fail in its production if it's not taken up with intentionality. One way we can potentially avoid failure is to be diligent in how we approach teacher response to student writing and to slow down. Recently, Timothy Oleksiak (2021) coined "slow peer review," which draws on rhetorical feminism. Oleksiak asks teachers to consider how peer review can encourage "students to think more deliberately about inclusivity, accountability, and the consequences of their writing" (p. 370). Likewise, I believe teachers can model this intentionality and compassion through their own response practices.

If we slow down and think more about whether we're approaching student writing with preconceived notions of what "errors" or "failures" we might find, then ideally, this awareness moves us toward more productive feedback that centers students. As others have said, one of the main purposes of feedback is to provide thoughtful commentary that promotes student agency. Thus, feedback facilitates paths that support the student's ability to choose what should or should not be revised in their writing. Teacher response is secondary. Even though teachers spend a significant amount of time producing feedback, we should realize it's not the most important thing. A student's purpose for writing is more important than our comments. To that end, feedback is complementary and should be produced in ways that don't dominate or subtract from student agency. Bruce Horner (1992) writes that teachers should be focused on reinforcing and reaffirming to students that they have power and agency over their own writing. And by inserting our own agendas as teachers through feedback, we remove student agency and discourage them from being invested in our writing classrooms.

This echoes what Straub (1996b) says when he talks about how feedback should facilitate—*not dictate*—paths of revision. The line between productive and nonproductive feedback feels narrow, but most writing teachers agree that a more conversational, probing, facilitative tone that helps support student agency is effective. That doesn't necessarily mean there's not failure through response, which is why I suggest looking at the *perception* of feedback, too.

Perception

The second part of feedback failure theory focuses on how response is perceived by teachers and students and how that could lead to other kinds of failures. In 1972, Thomas C. Gee writes, "In marking papers, English teachers are aware that their comments do affect students. The students' reactions are sometimes quite different from those that the teacher had expected or hoped for" (p. 38). We can understand how feedback affects students by considering how Carr (2013) talks about failure as an "affect-bearing concept" and how failure isolates students. When a student thinks they have failed or feels failure, there's social and emotional implications. This feedback changes how they see themselves, their writing, the classroom, their peers, their teacher. Carr writes, "'failure' (little f) becomes 'Failure' (big f) in our classrooms, the most extensive system of socialization available in the modern world. We are all inculcated into this reductive, do-or-die paradigm. We are *entrenched*" (n.p.).

Failure can exist through teacher perception of student writing and student interpretation and reaction to feedback. Gee (1972) writes, "Students often interpret a marginal notation like *clumsy, poorly written,* or *illogical* as personal indictment or as almost total disparagement of their skills. A student who receives no marks may interpret the dearth of comments as a subtle way of telling him that his paper was so bland, so unworthy as to merit no comment" (p. 38). We have a responsibility as teachers to understand how response might be perceived and how students might feel or react to feedback. A marginal comment like "illogical" could be perceived as a personal indictment, which produces the psychological feeling of failure. Carr (2013) explains how academic failures could produce the feeling of shame: "Shame acknowledges the failure, and in so doing, names the failure *as failure*, causing us to feel isolation while making us painfully aware of our relationality" (n.p.). The feeling of failure and shame as it's related to writing is connected to how we perceive ourselves as writers. There's no doubt that feedback has power to produce affect that embodies failure.

Erica Reynolds (2003) writes about the role of self-efficacy in writing and connects assessment to self-efficacy by encouraging Directed Self Placement (DSP), a writing program placement model that allows students to place themselves in a first-year writing course. Reynolds reveals the correlation between writing assessment/feedback and self-efficacy and addresses the "psychological variables that are related to writing skills and performance" (p. 79). Reynolds acknowledges that writing self-efficacy was "significantly related with written performance" (p. 79). I recommend a simple, reflective in-class activity that generates good conversations about feedback, failure, and affect. On the first day of class, I ask my first-year writing students: How many of you have received feedback that has made you *feel* like a failure? All of them raise their hands. I never have to explain what that type of feedback looks like (e.g., overwhelming comments, red marks, question marks, crossed-out sentences). The students perceive feedback and translate it into their abilities as a writer, or even their abilities as a person and learner. This perception and feeling seems to be universal among students.

The kind of reflective in-class activity I do with students helps us investigate these previous feelings of failure through feedback, or how receiving feedback curates an affective response. There's a range of affective responses that might occur when we receive feedback, right? I use this in-class activity to illuminate other emotions and responses to feedback as well, experiences we might perceive to be more positive. For example, I ask students to reflect and share experiences with teacher response that helped create a sense of pride in their writing. Feedback failure theory isn't just about identifying failure, then. It's about understanding the nature of teacher response and demystifying various productions and perceptions of feedback.

As teachers, some of this happens if we consider our own perceptions of student writing. Since the feeling of failure is highly individualized based on the relationship between a teacher and student, it's beneficial for us to reflect on our own biases. Paul Diederich (1974) writes about this: "There are even particular types of errors to which some teachers react so strongly that they are likely to fail any paper in which they appear, no matter how good it is in any other respects" (p. 11). Diederich adds that bias "appears most obviously when a teacher is grading his own students, knowing who wrote them" (p. 11). In my writing class, I have conversations with students about my own biases when it comes to response. I share with students, for example, that I don't pay much attention to grammar and mechanics, but I do focus on how they analyze a text and develop evidence for a claim. My perception of these rhetorical moves impacts how (and what) I choose to respond to, including how the tone of my feedback might change.

This metacognitive awareness and these conversations with students are helpful. As readers and responders, we're trying to make meaning of a student's text. It's impossible to set aside our biases and preferences for what writing is and does or what it should be or look like. And while *error* has been the subject of teacher response scholarship for a while, I feel as though conversations around error are often positioned in relation to error in student writing and not teacher biases and perceptions of writing. Gee writes about students' responses to teacher comments in 1972, and Straub studies students' reactions in 1997. I appreciate this work, in part, because it centers students' interpretations and perceptions of feedback—and I like how Straub (1997) understands that "the particular context has an effect on how students view teacher response" (p. 113). We need more work on how teachers respond within individual contexts and how students are perceiving and taking up these comments.

Even more so, we need to see how our responses reflect relationships with students and not merely contexts. For example, how do our comments change from Student Y to Student Z on the same writing assignment? This is where feedback failure theory can help because it allows us to see how each student is perceiving and reflecting on response. It provides an opportunity for teachers to better produce feedback with each student in mind and for conversations to happen around failure through feedback production and/or perception. Carr (2013) writes, "We can only become better writers when we acknowledge that writing is a process, that we all make mistakes; denying this reality is futile and reduces a fundamental human experience—expression—to a matter of skills, technicalities, or—worse—a matter of inborn genius" (n.p.). Likewise, I believe we can only become better, more thoughtful and compassionate, responders when we acknowledge that feedback is a process and that we're all capable of making mistakes. And that response is part of a larger ecology that has systems and structures with embedded ideologies and values that can hurt or help teachers and students.

APPLYING FEEDBACK FAILURE THEORY

How we talk with students about feedback can help demystify our response practices and help students better understand the ways response gets produced and perceived. These conversations can be relational and can help build community in classrooms because the feeling of failure through response is something we've all experienced. If we share that we've felt failure through feedback, our students will know they aren't alone. They'll know that teachers and scholars are affected by feedback in negative ways, too. They'll see that feedback is not infallible, including the feedback we give them. If we admit to our students that we are capable of producing failure through our feedback, then our students are, more often than not, going to give us the benefit of the doubt. This models transparency and opens space for honest communication about feedback and failure.

Feedback can be seen as a *negotiation* between teacher and student. I find it necessary to echo Thoune's (2020) attention to identity and vulnerability when talking about failure before I share how to apply feedback failure theory through negotiation:

> Because universities, including writing classrooms, are spaces that replicate and often reinforce systems of privilege and oppression, asking students and instructors to make themselves vulnerable and to reflect on their failure(s) may not always work or be appropriate. (p. 60)

We have to consider our positionalities when we share failure or write about failure or talk about failure with students (and others). Since I'm suggesting how feedback failure can be negotiated, I want to make clear that not everyone has the same access nor the same power to negotiate. I want to acknowledge some identities do not have the privilege to negotiate because of the inequities that pervade systems and structures, both institutionally and culturally. Therefore, I suggest negotiation while recognizing that, for some teachers, negotiation might cause further marginalization, so negotiation isn't even a possibility.

I draw on Bruce Horner's (1992) framework for negotiation because he pays close attention to how feedback has the power to foster or discourage student agency, and he makes more visible the sociality of "error" and its implications. If we start with an understanding that failure is socially constructed and that in student writing, "error" is a "flawed social transaction," then we can see "failure on the part of *both* the writer and reader to negotiate an agreement" (Horner, 1992, p. 174). Acknowledging our responses to student writing—this exchange between us and students—as a social agreement is important for us to see how feedback can be negotiated. In short, it's resisting a "right" and "wrong" binary that teachers are pressured to adopt almost inherently when responding to student writing because of grades and classroom assessment that inform our response practices.

I suggest we see feedback as a *first draft*. Teacher response is an attempt to work towards agreement with students. This indicates that feedback is not final; feedback is a process and is a part of the writing process. Feedback is not a concrete exchange of communication where students better take up comments or else there are consequences (which is fear driven), but instead the first step to a more open dialogue. The tonality of our feedback can shape its perception, of course, but I'm not talking about changing just our tone. I'm suggesting something much more than that. I'm arguing for a reorientation of how we see teacher response through failure and how we can present feedback as negotiable.

One thing this does for sure is challenge traditional response practices that associate failure with student writing. These practices focus on "error" in student writing and mark grammar, syntax, mechanics, spelling, punctuation. I'm recommending the opposite by linking teacher response to failure and asking us to consider how any kind of response might fail. For example, a teacher might make a marginal comment that asks a student to further develop their main claim or suggests using more evidence to support an idea or to revise their thesis statement. These comments might come across as questions in the margins. They might feel negotiable in tonality. Do we know that? Are we sure students feel agency and power through these responses? Even in our best efforts as teachers and responders, we don't know what responses feel negotiable or feel like failure to students.

When we respond, we facilitate revision. And facilitating revision should be an act of compromise between teachers and students. Negotiation is two sides coming together to form some sort of agreement. In regards to feedback, both the instructor and the student have to be willing to compromise. Horner (1992) writes, "Teachers who fail to acknowledge the power of their students likewise reject the opportunity of negotiating with them, and so, however indirectly, reject their own power and agency as well" (p. 176). Like Horner, most of us would probably agree that both the reader and writer "hold a degree of power and authority" (p. 175). Since feedback is based on at least two characteristics, production and perception, then negotiation should be the central balance between teacher and student. Negotiation, like feedback, is an act of communication.

Touching back on Paul Cook's compelling arguments (this volume), the heart of negotiation isn't about winning. That said, it would be naive not to acknowledge how United States cultural values and beliefs might say the opposite (e.g., via capitalism, profit, consumerism). Negotiation is dialogic. The aim is mutual interest. To me, listening is at the core of negotiation and the goal is to learn something through that dialogue. Horner agrees that negotiation "is not a matter of one party persuading a second to adopt the position of the first, nor a process of exchange (barter) between two parties, but a process of joint change and learning in which power operates dialectically" (p. 175). There are a couple of ways teachers can apply feedback failure theory after having conversations with students about what feedback failure theory is and how it can better help us understand response: one-on-one conferences and reflective writing.

ONE-ON-ONE CONFERENCES

Teachers could meet with each student to discuss their feedback for ten to fifteen minutes. I realize not everyone has the same opportunity to do this, though. For example, a teacher with a 4/4 or 5/5 teaching load with 20–25 students in each class would not be able to do this as effectively (or sustainably) given the amount of time, energy, and labor involved in this process. One-on-one conferences represent a dialogue between two people. They make visible that there are two parties; both have something to say. With feedback failure theory, of course, the conversation would be about the production and perception of teacher response. Having this vocabulary for feedback failure theory and embracing a pedagogy that centers teacher response is important because there's a shared vocabulary that can help start the conversation; there's a shared sense of understanding as to what we're talking about and why.

In this situation, I recommend teachers consider their positionality and the physical space itself. Institutions are hierarchical, of course. And based on current systems and structures within institutions, we know teachers have more power than students (e.g., in terms of course outcomes, classroom policies, grading standards). It might be beneficial for teachers to acknowledge this institutional power as a way of surrendering it and communicating how they desire a shared, co-equal conversation about response. Likewise, this also means teachers might reconsider where this conversation happens. As opposed to meeting in the teacher's office, which could be perceived as another sign of institutional power and imbalance between teacher and student, maybe meeting in a more neutral location, like the library or student union, would be better. The goal is to talk about feedback through a more critical lens, whether that be in a teacher's office or public-facing space.

I start these one-on-one conferences by focusing on *perception*. I became disenchanted with these meetings at first because it felt like I was taking up the space with questions and ideas. I was leading the conversation too much. It felt unbalanced. It didn't feel dialogic. I started asking students to reflect on my feedback and write questions and concerns. I asked them to bring those reflections to our one-on-one conferences. That has been a lot more productive. First, I ask students to write down their immediate emotional reactions after receiving my feedback. I think that helps capture the affective nature of response. I also encourage students to identify specific comments in the margins so we can talk more about them, whether there was a positive or negative reaction to it. The goal is to have open communication about feedback and for me to listen and better understand who I'm responding to. I see this as another way to build and cultivate a relationship. I want to have a transparent, honest conversation about my own response practices.

To me, negotiation is about releasing power. After we talk about how they perceived my feedback, how my responses made them feel, I can share how I approached their writing. I can talk about where those comments came from, including what I was thinking as I wrote a specific marginal comment they pointed to. This part of the conversation is all about the production of feedback. I am demystifying the production of my response practices. I am also reflecting and thinking critically about possible errors I made in that process. I try to help students understand what was going on. I try to paint a picture of where I was sitting and writing, what I was doing and whether there were any distractions, what music I was listening to, etc. Maybe I was writing feedback thoughtlessly, making rubber stamp comments that didn't feel like I was commenting to a real individual writer. Maybe they were too generic or too abstract. This is a chance for me to engage in self-reflection to see whether I was being informed and influenced by other elements in the response ecology (see Figure 3.1).

After we engage in conversations about feedback failure theory, we discuss how my feedback has or has not failed. These are productive conversations. A lot of the time, students don't have any issues with my feedback. There's not a negative emotional response or reaction that embodies failure. With that said, these conversations are still incredibly helpful to both of us. Because it's all about creating an open space to share and reflect on response, to deconstruct power and privilege within academic systems and structures, to demystify feedback, and to learn more about each other as writers and humans.

REFLECTIVE WRITING

Teachers don't have to schedule one-on-one conferences to discuss their feedback with students, especially given time constraints. It's also more accessible and accommodating to not ask students to meet face-to-face. Therefore, the second way to apply feedback failure theory is to strategically build into the curriculum reflective writing assignments that ask students to write about teacher response and submit it as part of the writing process. This could be more useful (and less stressful) for students and teachers. After receiving feedback, each student could write a letter to their teacher sharing how their feedback made them feel and what they are taking away. Students could talk about what responses are most beneficial to them. They could share which ones feel productive and which ones don't. They could describe how they are going to take up the feedback to revise and why they are choosing to take up some suggestions and ignore others. Some of us might already be doing something similar in our writing classes, especially ones that center on reflection, revision, and metacognition.

The difference here is that there's a focus on the production and perception of feedback not just how students are going to revise based on comments. Students would spend more time focusing on affect and emotion. They would spend more time sharing their feelings and talking about their perception of specific marginal comments. And again, there would be a true sense of negotiation where the teacher is listening to students' reactions and concerns and responding. Unlike a reflective assignment where students talk about their path for revision and a teacher marks it "complete" or "incomplete," this activity would require teachers to respond. After all, the purpose is to engage in a dialogue. What might be neat here is for the teacher to read the student letter and then record an audio response to the letter (and provide a transcript). There's something more personal and relational about hearing someone's voice. This would also complement multimodal pedagogies. In this situation, the teacher could clarify and share their thoughts about their response practices, including where and how that was happening and what other ecological elements (see Figure 3.1) might be at play.

This doesn't have to be a one-time exchange between student and teacher, either. Teachers and students can gauge whether more conversation and reflection are needed. This could turn into a larger classroom conversation with students that includes an illustration of examples from class where feedback had failed. Through conversations and negotiation, feedback failure theory allows us to investigate and examine the complex ecology of teacher response in our own local contexts. It allows us to build better relationships with students and for us to consider how each one of them might respond differently to a specific comment. We have to get to know them and keep each student in mind as we provide feedback.

CONCLUSION

Failure doesn't have to be isolating. It doesn't have to mimic how systems and structures reassert and reinforce power. It doesn't have to create distance between teachers and students. There's a lot of promise and potential for theorizing failure through teacher response. Our field values feedback more than grades because feedback teaches students about writing, intervenes as students are engaged in the writing process, and often informs what directions a student might take through their writing.

Carr (2017) writes about failure and learning: "Writing—and learning to write—involves a great deal of failure . . . failure is a significant part of the entire scene of learning" (p. 79). My hope is that writing studies stays committed to examining writing assessment practices. I hope we continue to theorize, explore, examine, and research how feedback might fail students, at least some of the time, so that we might identify failure and possibly learn something from it. And, of course, so that we might learn from our students. As a writing teacher, I want to know how my feedback doesn't hit the mark and what and how my responses can be more invitational, more productive, more compassionate.

REFERENCES

Anson, C. (1989) *Writing and response: Theory, practice, and research*. National Council of Teachers of English.

Anson, C. (2000). Response and social construction of error. *Assessing Writing, 7*(1), 5–21. https://doi.org/10.1016/S1075-2935(00)00015-5.

Blum, S. D. (2020). *Ungrading: Why rating students undermines learning (and what to do instead)*. West Virginia University Press.

Bruffee, K. (1980). *A short course in writing: A practical rhetoric for composition courses, writing workshops, and tutor training programs*. Little, Brown.

Calhoon-Dillahunt, C. & Forrest, D. (2013). Conversing in marginal spaces: Developmental writers' responses to teacher comments. *Teaching English in the Two-Year College 40*(3), 230–247.

Carr, A. D. (2013). In support of failure. *Composition Forum, 27*. https://compositionforum.com/issue/27/failure.php.

Carr, A. D. (2017). Failure is not an option. In C. E. Ball & D. M. Loewe (Eds.), *Bad ideas about writing* (pp. 76–81). West Virginia University Libraries.

Carr, A. D. & Micciche, L. R. (2020). *Failure pedagogies: Learning and unlearning what it means to fail*. Peter Lang.

Devitt, A. J. (2004). *Writing genres*. Southern Illinois University Press.

Diederich, P. (1974). *Measuring growth in English*. National Council of Teachers of English.

Elbow, P. (n.d.) *About responding to student writing*. https://wrd.as.uky.edu/sites/default/files/respond.pdf.

Fernandes, M., Brier, E. & McIntyre, M. (2023). We're all still grading: A call for honesty in writing assessment discourse. *Composition Studies, 51*(2), 148–153.

Gee, T. (1972). Students' responses to teacher comments. *Research in the Teaching of English 6*(2), 212–221. https://doi.org/10.58680/rte197220151.

Green, D. F. (2016). Expanding the dialogue on writing assessment at HBCUs: Foundational assessment concepts and legacies of historically Black colleges and universities. *College English, 79*(2), 152–173. https://doi.org/10.58680/ce201628811.

Horner, B. (1992). Rethinking the "sociality" of error: Teaching editing a negotiation. *Rhetoric Review, 11*(1), 172–199.

Inman, J. O. & Powell, R. A. (2018). In the absence of grades: Dissonance and desire in course-contract classrooms. *College Composition and Communication, 70*(1), 30–56.

Inoue, A. B. (2014). Theorizing failure in US writing assessments. *Research in the Teaching of English, 48*(3), 329–351.

Inoue, A. B. (2022). *Labor-based grading contracts: Building equity and inclusion in the compassionate writing classroom* (2nd ed.). The WAC Clearinghouse; University Press of Colorado. https://doi.org/10.37514/PER-B.2022.1824.

Johnson, G. P. (2021). Grades as technology of surveillance: Normalization, control, and big date in the teaching of writing. In E. Beck & L. H. Campos (Eds.), *Privacy matters: Conversations about surveillances within and beyond the classroom* (pp. 53–72). Utah State University Press.

Knoblauch, C. H. & Brannon, L. (1981). Teacher commentary on student writing: The state of the art. *Freshman English News 10*(2), 1–4.

Knoblauch, C. H. & Brannon, L. (1982). On students' rights to their own texts: A model of teacher response. *College Composition and Communication, 33*(2), 157–166.

Oleksiak, T. (2021). Slow peer review in the writing classroom. *Pedagogy: Critical Approaches to Teaching Literature, Language, Composition, and Culture, 21*(2), 369–384. https://doi.org/10.1215/15314200-8811551.

Poe, M., Inoue, A. B. & Elliot, N. (2018). *Writing assessment, social justice, and the advancement of opportunity*. The WAC Clearinghouse; University Press of Colorado. https://doi.org/10.37514/PER-B.2018.0155.

Price, C. (1997). *Changing the rhetoric of failure in writing classrooms: An investigation of teachers' responses to first year writing students* [Doctoral dissertation, New Mexico State University]. ProQuest Dissertations and Theses Database.

Reynolds, E. (2003). The role of self-efficacy. In D. Royer & R. Gilles (Eds.), *Directed self placement: Principles and practices* (pp. 73–103). Hampton Press.

Schneider, J. & Hutt, E. (2023). *Off the mark: How grades, ratings, and rankings undermine learning (but don't have to)*. Harvard University Press.

Segal, J. (1996). Pedagogies of decentering and a discourse of failure. *Rhetoric Review 15*(1), 174–191.

Smith, S. (1997). The genre of the end comment: Conventions in teacher responses to student writing. *College of Composition and Communication, 48*(2), 249–268.

Sommers, N. (1982). Responding to student writing. *College Composition and Communication, 33*(2), 148–156.

Sommers, N. (2013). *Responding to student writers*. Bedford/St. Martins.

Straub, R. (1996a). The concept of control in teacher response: Defining the varieties of "directive" and "facilitative" commentary. *College Composition and Communication, 47*(2), 223–251.

Straub, R. (1996b). Teacher response as conversation: More than casual talk, an exploration. *Rhetoric Review, 14*(2), 374–399. https://doi.org/10.1080/07350199609389071.

Straub, R. (1997). Students' reactions to teacher comments: An exploratory study. *Research in the Teaching of English, 31*(1), 91–119.

Students' rights to their own language (1974). CCCC Position Statement.

Thoune, D. L. (2020). Failure potential: Using failure as feedback. In A. D. Carr & L. R. Micciche (Eds.), *Failure pedagogies: Learning and unlearning what it means to fail* (pp. 53–62). Peter Lang.

Treglia, T. (2008). Feedback on feedback: Exploring student responses to teachers' written commentary. *Journal of Basic Writing 27*(1), 105–137.

West-Puckett, S., Caswell, N. I. & Banks, W. P. (2023). *Failing sideways: Queer possibilities for writing assessment*. Utah State University Press.

Williams, J. (1981). The phenomenology of error. *College Composition and Communication, 32*(2), 152–168.

Wood, S. A. (2020). Engaging in resistant genres as antiracist teacher response. *Journal of Writing Assessment, 13*(2).

Young, V. A. (2010). Should writers use they own English? *Iowa Journal of Cultural Studies, 12*(1), 110–118. https://doi.org/10.17077/2168-569X.1095.

PART 2.
CASE STUDIES AND PROFESSIONAL PROFILES OF FAILURE IN ACTION

Contributors to Part Two bring the concept of failure to practical light with case studies and professional profiles. The first two chapters offer empirical research studies, including case studies of how fail memes can influence students' beliefs about failure, and original research on mindsets in relation to writing development and failure. The next two chapters provide detailed professional and personal profiles, including how feminist rhetorical resilience can offer a lens to scrutinize very personal feelings of failure, and narrative accounts from three women who share their research-framed personal and professional experiences with the effects of failure to achieve high-scoring student evaluations of teaching.

Ruth Mirtz, in **Chapter 4**, "Fail Memes and Writing as Performance: Popular Portrayals of Writing in Internet Culture," offers a taxonomy of types of "writing fail" memes to analyze and suggests ways that our writing students' work is influenced by the notion of failure as represented by these memes. This chapter also suggests ways to study memes with students to deepen their rhetorical understanding of digital information and strengthen their ability to transfer notions about writing to many rhetorical situations. Memes are a particularly expressive way our students learn and express what failure means, both in writing and in wider fields of life. This chapter positions memes as a genre and mode of writing, drawing on research on memes from sources within and beyond composition studies. Thus, Mirtz contends that our students' constant exposure to meme-thinking about writing and failure has to be taken into account if we want them to grow as writers.

In **Chapter 5**, "'I'm a Bad Writer': How Students' Mindsets Influence Their Writing Processes and Performances," Laura K. Miller seeks to illuminate the connections between students' mindsets and their writing processes and performances by presenting empirical findings that highlight growth-minded students' writing practices. Drawing on a larger research project assessing engineering students' literature review essays and exploring how an embedded writing tutor influenced students' mindsets and writing performance, the author uses mindset theory to make sense of their interview and survey data in order to understand how writers' beliefs impact their writing processes and performance. Miller argues that a better understanding of the consequences of students' mindsets could help explain and mitigate challenges writing instructors face, such as students' reluctance to revise, resistance to feedback, and poor response to failure.

In **Chapter 6**, "Recognizing Feminist Resilience Rather Than Seeking Success in Response to Failure," Karen R. Tellez-Trujillo shares some of their experiences with writing struggles that result in failing and resilient responses to adversity in relation to times they failed at writing and labeled themselves a writing failure. They ground these experiences in the concept of feminist rhetorical resilience, the ways that common definitions of resilience and feminist rhetorical resilience differ, and the potential ways that we can use feminist resilience to frame writing prompts for students that can help them balance failing at writing with acknowledging the ways their writing has had an impact on themselves, and the people around them.

And in **Chapter 7**, "Teaching to Fail? Three Female Faculty Narratives about the Racial and Gender Inequalities of SETs," Mary Lourdes Silva, Josephine Walwema, and Suzie Null round out Part Two and prepare readers for Part Three, with their narratives confronting the question: What does it mean to function in an inequitable culture of failure framed by the values and metrics of student evaluations of teaching (SET)? Failure to perform well on SETs can result in some form of administrative action, as well as impact self-esteem, labor conditions, teacher-student relationships, departmental work relationships, and job marketability. After a comprehensive literature review of the problematic nature of SETs—especially for female faculty and female faculty of color—the three authors share their personal accounts with SETs and the psychological, emotional, pedagogical, professional, personal, and health consequences of working in this culture of failure. In the first narrative, Walwema writes about the shame and anxiety experienced while serving multiple leadership roles in faculty development while repeatedly receiving lower evaluations in comparison to her white male subordinates. Next, Silva describes her experience in an almost all-female department, where gendered expectations in the field combined with departmental culture compel her to choose between upholding syllabus policies, a research agenda, and a manageable workload or risk getting lower SET scores. And Null shares her experiences of shame and its heavy toll throughout her academic career, where low SETs even compelled her to withdraw from a job search. These narratives will begin a conversation in our field about the psychological, professional, and pedagogical consequences of navigating a field that leaves intelligent, skilled, experienced female experts constantly negotiating the conundrums of failing in one or more areas of their professional lives.

CHAPTER 4.
FAIL MEMES AND WRITING AS PERFORMANCE: POPULAR PORTRAYALS OF WRITING IN INTERNET CULTURE

Ruth Mirtz
Kansas State University

When Kate Ronald (1990) wrote about dichotomies that threaten our sense of self, such as personal vs. public realms, she pointed out that these dichotomies force writers and writing instructors to view writing as objectively manageable. In the context of writing processes, writing instruction often over-manages the writing process with defined processes of prewriting, drafting, revising, and proofreading in the attempt to control the messy work of writing. Failure/success has also become a limiting dichotomy in academia, borrowing from the business world's work ethic, which implies that hard work means success and the only alternative to success is failure. Scott Sandage (2005) pointed out, in his history of failure in the US, that to be a failure or bankrupt in business morphed in the late 1800s to include any average, plodding, uninspired life. Saddest of all, in our American concept of failure, Sandage said, the lack of a "story" to tell about ourselves is also a sign of failure (p. 256). The business model that academia leans toward requires statistical proof that students succeed rather than that they learn, which is, in turn, internalized by our students to mean a successful paper is a one-draft essay and a grade. This attitude also carries over into how students handle writing processes: When a paper is complete, it is a success; a written text in draft form is a failure.

As a means of identifying and analyzing the true power of this fail/success dichotomy, looking at memes that my undergraduate writing students create about their writing processes is illuminating. This chapter studies "writing fail" memes, offers descriptive types of memes with which to analyze our students' theories of writing, and suggests ways that our writing students' work is influenced by the notion of failure as represented by these memes. This chapter also suggests ways to study memes with students to deepen their rhetorical understanding of composing-as-failure and strengthen their ability to transfer notions about writing to many rhetorical situations.

DOI: https://doi.org/10.37514/PER-B.2024.2494.2.04

INSTITUTIONALIZED FAILURE AND COLLEGE WRITING STUDENTS

As the Director of the Student Success Center on my branch campus (and former writing instructor), I have a complex relationship with the fail/success dichotomy when applied to undergraduate students. The Student Success Center operates as a resource for all students but also expects students who are on academic warning or who were conditionally admitted to participate in weekly meetings to share, reflect, and practice good study habits, theoretically intervening in their failed performance to turn them toward success. The dichotomy of fail/succeed is even embedded in the title; we're not the Academic Manage-Your-Expectations Center or even, my preference, the Academic Resilience Center. The institution's definition of failure by one-semester GPA or high school GPA (in the case of conditionally admitted students) is so fraught with its own failed sense of academic accomplishment that it's no wonder that about 25 percent of these students resist or refuse to participate. How can a student be failing and require "remediation" or "intervention" with no-credit work before they've attended a single college class? On the one hand, I hope all my students are successful (and I'm secretly happy with those who resist the stigma of failure by not participating). On the other hand, I don't want these students interpreting a lack of institutional success as a learning failure. In most versions of contemporary writing instruction, descriptions of writing processes specifically address drafting as a mess and a muddle, and we refrain from calling early drafts "failed" because of the connotations of failed exams and failed classes, which are absolutes in the fail/success dichotomy. And yet, for those students struggling with writing, any feedback on rough drafts is often the last straw after overcoming multitudes of obstacles to get that first draft submitted. Lengthy revisions and feedback intended to help students re-envision what they are composing is too frustrating for them to ever be seen as a successful process. For non-writers (students who prefer any activity over writing, even when quite skilled at writing), one-draft writing is the only "successful" writing, despite their experiences to the contrary in their engineering and computer classes. Students at my technical school are mostly STEM majors in lab-central and project-oriented classes, where the notion of failure is more readily defined as iterative steps toward success when learning Python to code a new video game, for instance, than in writing classes.

Embracing failure as a sign of growth is identified as a threshold concept for writers, without which students are less likely to move forward toward more rhetorically-aware writing (Brooke & Carr, 2015). However, the notion that the creation of failure is a result of constant high-stakes testing has been extensively described as a systemic problem that affects how students and instructors view writing; testing seems to drown out any other voice on the topic of failed writing for our students. As Inoue (2014) pointed out, testing creates failure where none existed before, which leads to student performance (not writing) as failure or success. Even in our process-oriented classes with no exams, as such, every paper becomes just another place where students fail by not following their instructor's sense of a successful paper. West-Puckett and her coauthors (2023) point out that "In writing studies, when students fail, they have not demonstrated what has already been constructed by someone else as the ideal or appropriate text for a particular situation; normally, this someone else has both the power and the privilege not only to name that distinction but also to make it have meaning" (p. 47). I've been guilty of giving a lower grade to a rhetorically successful paper because it didn't follow the instructions.

Recent research on transfer in knowledge-making shows the difficulty students have in transferring or integrating writing skills into new sites and purposes for writing. Students tend to see writing assignments as discrete tasks that can be finished and then forgotten (Adler-Kassner et al., 2017, p. 19). These studies point directly to the failure of standard writing instruction practices such as writing workshops and peer reviews to help students apply writing skills from one similar setting to another (Smith et al., 2017; Brent, 2012). Our writing process teaching simply does not transfer past single assignments; as Thoune (2020) noted, students are required to "fail" a draft, in their eyes, to get feedback (p. 55).

On a wider scale, the 16-week, final exam, Carnegie credit hour paradigm of higher education, based on a completely different funding model than what my students have available to them, sets up so many students for failure that "retention" becomes the institutional version of "success." Programmatic changes that are designed to mitigate these barriers, such as delayed grading, labor-based or contract grading, portfolio assessment, and others, are hallmarks of critical pedagogy but not universally found in first-year college composition classes. My university constantly harps on early grading, requires 6-week progress reports rather than midterms, with the intention of getting feedback to students about their lack of progress, but in turn creating anxiety and early withdrawals. Hjortshoj (2001) pointed out that institutions assume writing skills are a freshman-level issue, solved once and for all with an introductory-level course, which does not allow for extensive drafting and messy, confusing learning processes. The students who can't manage this one-and-done kind of learning by Week 6 are encouraged to withdraw rather than change the environment, which creates this institutionalized failure to learn. In this testing-focused, failure-first environment, students' memes about their writing expose their intertwined notions of writing and failure.

Figure 4.1. Student meme from English 200; "Hide the Pain Harold" template.

ARGUMENT 1: MEMES ARE ARTIFACTS OF CREATIVE FAILURE, THROUGH CONSTANT REMIXES, BUT ALSO INDICATIONS OF THE STATUS OF FAILURE IN POPULAR CULTURE

Scholars have been arguing over the definition of meme since Dawkin's 1976 book, using the term to mean complex, spreadable, memorable cultural ideas. For our purposes, memes are simple visuals, often with text, that undergo constant remixing as they are repurposed for different messages spreading over social media. Generally, at least one element of the original meaning remains with the remix in order to participate in the string of revisions, but often, that original meaning is utterly transformed by the time a meme goes "viral" and reaches a substantial audience.

The term meme also covers a wide variety of mimetic and viral material spread over the internet. But for my purposes here, I will focus on what Shifman (2013) calls "stock character macros" (p. 112): still photos of animals or humans with particular associations toward community values and behaviors, such as "advice dog," "success kid," and "Hide the Pain Harold" (see Figure 4.1). This genre of meme is favored by students in my writing classes when they choose meme templates; plus, as Shifman points out, they are part and parcel of expressing success and failure as a way of showing how one belongs to a group (p. 113). For instance, the image macro meme "Confession Bear" shows a bear with a rather human-like sad expression and text that confesses a usually taboo activity, such as "I actually like Nickelback." Another one that connects to the theme of failure is "success kid," which shows a small child with a fierce expression and a fist. The meme started out with the message "I hate sandcastles" but morphed as it was remixed to be an image of unexpected success with text such as "Late to work—boss was even later."

One of the first popular meme collections was "Fail Blog," which chronicles "fail" memes. Although it is now part of the Cheezburger website, the glee with which internet readers liked and reposted photos, descriptions, and visuals of embarrassing falls, silly slips, and faux pas show how much we love *schadenfreude* and how much we seek to show how we belong to a world of ineptitude, which is also a testament to the pervasive but depressing vision of success that we are surrounded by. There are "epic fails," a section on "autocowrecks," a place for "Fail Nation," and a "School of Fail" specifically for school-related assignment failures with many variations on "the dog ate my homework" excuses. We apparently need to prove to the world that most of us are not shining examples of American work ethic and athletic grace. As Paul Cook (this volume) points out, memes participate in the "Internet Ugly" aesthetic where failure is a stock joke and complaint about modern life.

Thus, what makes stock character macro memes expressive and interesting also makes them limiting and superficial: Simple, visual, part of stereotypical experiences (so that wide audiences understand them). The fact that memes are funny and self-deprecating, therefore prone to be about failure, makes them good for bringing up the challenges and myths about writing and research, but ultimately show the lasting power and draw of those stereotypes about writers and writing. These memes don't "hold" positive messages well; the predominant activity of memes is to poke fun at someone. Many memes that my students choose are those with exaggerated, over-the-top emotions, easy prey for meme-makers to mock. For instance, one student used the "American Chopper Argument" meme with several stills taken from the scene where the father and son shout at each other as the father fires the son and they throw furniture, with both characters completely out of control, but likely a staged scene for the show; one of my students turned this meme into the argument between her need to pass the writing course and her desire to binge Netflix all night, an argument also staged for class participation since she was clearly doing well in the course.

A scan of the memes about writing on Fail Blog shows that most contributors believe writing is hard work and the special skills needed as writers are for padding a report and waiting for the miracle of an original idea. For instance, one fail meme shows Captain America ripping up a log with his bare hands, with the inscription indicating that the writer turns the word "don't" (aka the log) into "do not" (aka the ripped log now in two pieces) to add more words to the essay. This is a funny exaggeration as if non-contracted words will add any significant number of words to an essay, and yet this is not an exaggeration at all for struggling writers who can't, that is, can not, think of anything more to write. Lots of other memes are of cats procrastinating as they sit on a pad of paper or on a computer keyboard. A recent listicle of memes about writing by Hayes (2021) in Buzzfeed shows that the popular vision of even professional writers emphasizes procrastination, holes and gaps in stories, late-night revelations, and basic descriptive writing skills as material for jokes based on failed writing skills. The work of memes in most contexts is to find empathetic audiences that can "get" the joke and to show that one is part of the writing community that sees writing as a distraction and a chore. Many memes targeting the work of creative writing show "not-writing" as a failure as well, indicating a stereotype of writing as "putting words on a page" and leaving out every other stage or activity involved in writing: researching, reading, reciting, interviewing, re-envisioning, sketching, and so on (see Figure 4.2 as an example). Many of these fail memes are, therefore, not directly about failure but about the *management* of failure, about how we deal with failure (and impending failure) by making jokes and pointing out ironies in education. They help us manage the utter meaninglessness of some failures, as the opposite of making every failure into a "learning opportunity."

Shifman (2013), along with others, argues that memes are important objects of study because they are "cultural information . . . which scale into shared social phenomena" (p. 18). Writing fail memes share this contact in scale with the failure/success dichotomy and its close relative, the lose/win dichotomy. Because of this integration with social values, Jenkins (2014) suggests that rhetorical study of memes requires a modal approach rather than a textual or visual approach to account for the rapid delivery and constant remix of memes. His modal study of fail/win memes argues that they are expressions of anxiety in a digital world where humans are expected to succeed or fail the same way that computers do. The reductionist view of writing exhibited in most memes, when combined with the stereotypical view of failure in culture, creates a popular version of writing as failure in almost every aspect and experience. Internet memes about productive, meaningful writing that makes a difference in the world are nearly non-existent.

ARGUMENT 2: WRITER-GENERATED MEMES ARE WAYS TO FOCUS ON THE PROBLEMATIC RELATIONSHIP OF SUCCESS AND FAILURE IN WRITING

What happens when you ask college writing students to make memes about their writing processes? I started using memetic and viral materials in college writing classes when Padlet added a feature that allowed users to quickly and easily post a GIF on a virtual wall. I asked the students to do a "temperature check" at various times during the semester to share simply "how things are going" in their lives without the need to make comments or explanations. The GIFs they chose generated enough discussion that I moved to asking students to create memes about their writing processes (not about failure), first as an experiment and later as a regular activity to create an alternate mode of self-expression, allow students to make visuals instead of writing, and start discussions about writing processes. I gave them the option of any family-friendly, appropriate meme, using any program they wanted, but I walked them through the Meme Generator on the imgflip.com site as a simple, quick way to choose a well-known meme from templates. The Meme Generator allows them to add text in certain places but not manipulate the image template. Their memes were created during class and had minuscule points assigned, mainly a participation activity.

- Most students created a procrastination fail: a failure to focus. The memes were self-mocking—they know better but don't do better. The two points of greatest struggle for college writers, according to their memes, are getting started and getting the final draft submitted.
- Some students created a meme to describe the difficulty of balancing homework with their other preferred activities: a failure to juggle. Inherent in their memes is the idea that if they could keep all the parts of their lives in motion, they could succeed.
- Some students created a meme that describes a writing or research struggle: a failure to complete, generally located in the performance of the assignment: the number of words required, the number of sources required, the deadlines, etc.
- No students reinterpreted the template in a remix of images or concepts about writing (as with the Chuck Norris version of "Bicycle Fail" shown in Figure 4.3).

In Figure 4.2, the skeleton meme shows the most common type, illustrating the empty body/mind connection when searching for a topic or a way to phrase an idea. The second one is also common, showing the procrastinating of most writers who know they need to start writing but get pulled away by distractions and alternative activities. The third one illustrates a fairly complex idea and is much rarer among the memes that my students create. The astronaut meme is illustrating a trope in action movies where the protagonist has a revelation that he was lied to from the beginning of the story, and the villain reveals his treachery. The student turned this into a revelation about how his good intention to revise a draft was really only a pipe dream, and his first draft was, to be honest with himself, always going to be his final draft.

In Figure 4.3, a webcomic illustrating a metaphoric version of self-sabotage by Corentin Penloup was appropriated by other meme-makers. The first image is the original webcomic by Corentin Penloup. The second meme shows the use of the comic with added text, which reinterprets the original. The third one shows a more typical self-mocking, everyday version expressing the way our good intentions get sidetracked by others' agendas. The fourth one is Penloup's favorite, which shows a re-imagining of the original where Chuck Norris, the ultimate strongman good guy, simply keeps biking despite the stick and overcoming what for him is a small obstacle.

Figure 4.2. Three examples of student-created memes about writing processes.

Figure 4.3. Bike Fail meme [Know Your Meme website].

Fail Memes and Writing as Performance

Figure 4.4. Student-created memes using the "Bike Fail" template.

In Figure 4.4, student-created memes took on the same visual. The first one follows the original web comic closely, showing the self-destructive writing habit of citing the source before reading it. The second one shows a slight reinterpretation of the visual as just a failed bicycle ride as a metaphor for a failure of the assignment despite finding the first seven sources. The third one shows the same sense of writing as performance failure, equating the finding of a number of sources as the measure of writing success.

Memes are a particularly expressive way our students can convey what failure means, both in writing and in wider fields of life. Most of my students are thoroughly familiar with these memes through constant exposure to online content platforms. Many "writing fail" memes are humorous and relatable, expressing a shared experience with the difficulty of writing. Any meme with a panicked or confused expression is useful for students to express their problems with procrastination and distractions. Other memes quickly cycle through a variety of attitudes, such as rueful disdain toward writing, scathing satire of "schooled" essays, and competition among epic procrastinators. The notion of writing failure embodied in these memes is closely connected to broader memes about writing, which often portray writing and writers as unable to express themselves in language and highly distractible. Despite their ephemeral qualities, writing fail memes reveal the popular internet culture's attitude toward writing, including unmanageable emotional responses to writing complexity and a very narrow view of writing. Creating memes in class, then, is important for the "social bonding effect" of sharing common feelings (Zenner & Geeraerts, 2018, p. 190) and for joining the club of students who dislike performing writing with deadlines.

Students' memes point out the failure of pedagogy: that nothing I said about writing processes or messy drafts transferred or seemed applicable in the real world that the students' memes pointed to. "Writing fail" memes clearly

99

contribute to social bonding over the common anxiety-producing problems of emotional management during difficult stages of writing. Peeling back another layer of failure in the students' memes, we can see how students used the memes to embody themselves in their resistance to the version of writing their instructor gave them. They found bodies not their own (astronauts with guns, skeletons, bicyclists) to say they know they are self-sabotaging their papers (thus their liking for the Baton Roue meme); they know writing is NOT exploratory, provisional, or interesting, but just another hoop to jump.

CONCLUSION: STUDENT MEMES ARE EVIDENCE THAT WE NEED TO DO SOMETHING DIFFERENTLY

Are memes worth studying, worth classroom time, or just another attempt to use pop culture in cringe-worthy ways? Can they be transgressive as well as socially bonding? By asking students to create memes and participate in a part of culture heavily weighted toward a fail/succeed dichotomy, I am, in effect, asking a leading question, leading them to fall back on popular notions of writing processes and, thus, writing failure. These memes also perpetuate myths about writing blocks and writing processes, portraying writing as a performance rather than an inventive, meaning-making process. This version of writing is exactly what causes the kinds of failed writing described by Mike Rose (1980) in his case studies of students who operated with rigid rules and absolute control of writing processes. The one-shot approach behind some of the "writing fail" memes (a writer has one chance to succeed and, if not, the work is a fail) reinforces students' tendency to take any small criticism of their drafts as an utter failure of the draft.

And as Yancey, Robertson, and Taczak (2014) point out, prior knowledge profoundly affects students' ability to theorize, generalize, and apply ideas about writing across writing tasks. Thus, our students' out-of-class exposure to meme-thinking about writing and failure has to be taken into account if we want them to grow as writers by seeing failure as iterative growth in meaning-making. Helping students find and analyze the sources of their writing approaches, such as these fail/win memes, makes them stronger writers and rhetors. While making memes in first-year writing classes began as a lighthearted way to bring joy into a prosaic class, a deeper look shows the ability of meme-making to be an "assessment killjoy," as West-Puckett and her coauthors (2023) call the ability to move writing sideways, allowing writers to "take up more space" than the assessment, by not being the assessment (p. 84). Meme-making gives students a chance to speak out, to be unhappy, to show themselves as bodies in the world,

Fail Memes and Writing as Performance

and that they are not just the uploaded files that will be graded. Meme-making with our students can be, as West-Pucket, Caswell, and Banks (2023) suggest, a "sideways" assessment that "points us toward the shadowy, messy, complicated, contradictory, fluid, and foundering practices of writing and the teaching of writing" (p. 106).

Memes can be used to resist the cultural standards surrounding failure. For example, the "What People Think I Do/What I Really Do" meme elicits the gaps among audiences and interpretations based on stereotypes and popular images of a particular profession or activity. Figure 4.5 is an example, created by J. W. Eberle (2012), of how this meme works with the role of writer. Our mothers will forever think we are cute, our friends assume we live some kind of hippie Utopian fantasy of working in a meadow, society assumes we are alcoholics, and the last two images show the contrast between how we wish our writing progressed with how it more often fails to progress.

In a writing class, using this meme along with a collection of images of writers and writing, accompanied by a student-led search of stock images for writers and writing, could help students start to articulate the conflict between how they are asked to write in class with how they manage the failure of writing, through more visually-loaded meme-making. Another classroom use of meme-making is creating "anti-memes," which spin the mocking, ironic use of memes into the ultra-obvious aspects of life. The skeleton (in Figure 4.2) would be relabeled the technically accurate "Anatomically Inaccurate Skeleton Chilling on a Park Bench," and the images in the "Writers" meme (Figure 4.5) would be filled with actual selfies of the students as they write.

Figure 4.5. What People Think I Do/What I Really Do "Writers" meme. Reprinted with the permission of the author.

Teaching writing as an iterative, messy process may not be enough. We also need to show students the way through the fail/success dichotomy by acknowledging the social media world they live in and around and discussing the limitations of choosing "fail" as the predominant reaction to writing. Simply replacing the dichotomy of fail/success with another dichotomy of recursive/linear ignores the material world our students live in. We need to be explicit in our talk about room for failure in writing processes and the difference between getting work done and intellectual failure. Yancey (2024) calls for us to engage students in articulating their own theories of writing and to continue developing those theories through intentional reflection and practice (p. 232). But ultimately, we have to make room for less fossilized versions of composing and failing. Kate Ronald (1990) argued that rather than swinging from one extreme to another with such dichotomies or cementing a position on one side or the other, we as rhetoric/composition scholars and practitioners need to act in the tension between the two and rather than seeing writing as either a subjective or objective writing practice, that we seek "connected" knowledge. This third position holds the other two in tension rather than against each other. Studying memes in writing instruction is one of those bridges to connected learning, or as Allison Carr (2013) describes her journey through failure to write, to an "enlarged" place for connecting mind and body. Not only do we as writing instructors need to present an iterative, recursive, robustly meaning-making activity, but we need to actively present the stereotypical version of writing as a physical and psychologically difficult (and sometimes boring) job as something to be considered.

REFERENCES

Adler-Kassner, L., Clark, I., Robertson, L., Taczak, K. & Yancey, K. B. (2017). Assembling knowledge: The role of threshold concepts in facilitating transfer. In C. M. Anson & Jessie L. Moore (Eds.), *Critical transitions: Writing and the question of transfer* (pp. 17–47). The WAC Clearinghouse; University Press of Colorado. https://doi.org/10.37514/PER-B.2016.0797.

Baton Roue Meme. (n.d.). Know your meme. https://knowyourmeme.com/memes/baton-roue.

Brent, D. (2012). Crossing boundaries: Co-op students relearning to write. *College Composition and Communication, 63*(4), 558–592. https://www.jstor.org/stable/23264229.

Brooke, C. & Carr, A. D. (2015). Failure can be an important part of writing development. In L. Adler-Kassner and E. Wardle (Eds.), *Naming what we know: Threshold concepts of writing studies* (pp. 62–64). Utah State University Press.

Carr, A. D. (2013, Spring). In support of failure. *Composition Forum, 27.* https://compositionforum.com/issue/27/failure.php.

Dawkins, R. (1976). *The selfish gene*. Oxford University Press.

Eberle, J. W. (2012). *Jumping on the meme bandwagon*. J. W. Eberle [blog]. https://jweberle.com/2012/02/13/jumping-on-the-meme-bandwagon/.

Hayes, A. (2021). 26 writer jokes that'll make you laugh. *Buzzfeed*. https://www.buzzfeed.com/alliehayes/writer-jokes-for-writers-who-write-sometimes.

Hjortshoj, K. (2001). *Understanding writing blocks*. Oxford University Press.

Inoue. A. B. (2014). Theorizing failure in US writing assessments. *Research in the Teaching of English*, 48(3), 330–352. https://www-jstor-org.er.lib.k-state.edu/stable/24398682.

Jenkins, E. S. (2014). The modes of visual rhetoric: Circulating memes as expressions. *Quarterly Journal of Speech*, 200(4), 442–466. http://dx.doi.org/10.1080/00335630.2014.989258.

Ronald, K. (1990). Personal and public authority in discourse: Beyond subjective/objective dichotomies. In K. Ronald and H. Roskelly (Eds.), *Farther along: Transforming dichotomies in rhetoric and composition* (pp. 25–40). Boynton/Cook Heinemann.

Rose, M. (1980). Rigid rules, inflexible plans, and the stifling of language: A cognitivist analysis of writers' block. *College Composition and Communication, 31*(4), 389–401.

Sandage, S. (2005). *Born losers: A history of failure in America*. Harvard University Press.

Shifman, L. (2013). *Memes in digital culture*. MIT Press.

Smith, K., Girdharry, K. & Gallagher, C. W. (2021). Writing transfer, integration and the need for the long view. *College Composition and Communication 73*(1), 4–26.

Thoune, D. L. (2020). Failure potential: Using failure as feedback. In A. D. Carr and L. R. Micciche (Eds.), *Failure pedagogies: Learning and unlearning what it means to fail* (pp. 53–62), Peter Lang.

West-Puckett, S., Caswell, N. I. & Banks, W. P. (2023). *Failing sideways: Queer possibilities for writing assessment*. Utah State University Press.

Yancey, K. B. (2024). Afterword: Transfer happens; transfer doesn't happen: Maps, tensions, questions, and ways forward. In K. P. Alexander, M. Davis, L. W. Mina & R. Shepherd (Eds.), *Multimodal composing and writing transfer* (pp. 225–233). Utah State University Press.

Yancey, K. B, Robertson, L. & Taczak, K. (2014). *Writing across contexts: Transfer, composition, and sites of writing*. Utah State University Press.

Zenner, E. & Geeraerts, D. (2018). One does not simply process memes: Image macros as multimodal constructions. In E. Winter-Froemel & V. Thaler (Eds.), *In cultures and traditions of wordplay and wordplay research* (pp. 167–193). DeGruyter.

CHAPTER 5.

"I'M A BAD WRITER": HOW STUDENTS' MINDSETS INFLUENCE THEIR WRITING PROCESSES AND PERFORMANCES

Laura K. Miller

James Madison University

Writing teachers and tutors often hear students characterize themselves as "bad writers," but how does this self-belief and feeling of failure affect them? Decades ago, Mike Palmquist and Richard Young (1992) hypothesized that viewing writing as a natural gift could be harmful for students because this "notion of giftedness" can lead to writing apprehension and resistance to instruction (p. 162). However, their study was inconclusive; we still do not fully understand how students' beliefs about writing affect them. Psychological research on students' mindsets, characterized by their beliefs about the expandable nature of ability, can help us unpack students' belief systems and behaviors (Dweck, 2006). Better understanding the consequences of students' mindsets could help explain and mitigate challenges writing instructors face, such as students' reluctance to revise, resistance to feedback, and poor response to failure.

The goals of this chapter are to illuminate the connection between students' mindsets and their writing processes and the connection between their writing processes and performances by presenting empirical findings that highlight growth-minded students' writing practices. The study I describe is part of a larger project with additional research questions and data that exceed the scope of this chapter. For the larger project, I assessed engineering students' literature review essays and explored how an embedded writing tutor influenced students' mindsets and writing performance. I found that tutored students became significantly more growth-minded, and they revised their final essays more significantly than control group students did (Miller, 2020). In this chapter, I use mindset theory to interpret my interview and survey data, to understand how writers' beliefs can impact their writing processes and performances.

DOI: https://doi.org/10.37514/PER-B.2024.2494.2.05

MINDSET THEORY

According to Stanford Psychologist Carol Dweck (2006), people's implicit beliefs about their intelligence and abilities characterize their "mindset." Through decades of research, Dweck has discovered that people tend to have either a "fixed" mindset—the belief that intelligence and ability are mostly unchangeable—or a "growth" mindset, the belief that people can improve themselves through effort. Studies have shown that growth-minded students typically outperform fixed-minded students: They tend to earn higher grades (Aronson et al., 2002), improve their standardized test scores (Good et al., 2003), work harder with greater motivation (Blackwell et al., 2007), and enjoy school more (Aronson et al., 2002). Fixed-minded students tend to avoid challenges because they are afraid of failing, which they perceive as a reflection of their innate qualities (Dweck, 2006). Thus, they aim to display their intelligence and are more concerned with performance than learning. Fixed-minded students also tend to avoid effort because they see it as a sign of weakness, assuming only weak students must work hard (Dweck, 2006). Although researchers have studied the consequences of students' implicit beliefs in a variety of domains, very few studies examine mindset in the context of writing (e.g., Limpo & Alves, 2014; 2017; Powell, 2018).

According to psychological research, students' mindsets directly affect their attitudes, learning strategies, performance, and success (Good et al., 2003). Importantly, psychologists argue that mindsets influence people most when they encounter obstacles and challenging subject matter (Blackwell et al., 2007). Several groundbreaking studies have sought to change students' mindsets and then assess the effects of that intervention (e.g., Aronson et al., 2002; Good et al., 2003). Such intervention studies typically encourage students to adopt a growth mindset by teaching them about brain plasticity; they find that most students who learn about mindset theory have later increased academic performance (Aronson et al., 2002), improved persistence (Blackwell et al., 2007), better health and decreased stress (Yeager et al., 2014), and less hostility toward others (Yeager et al., 2013). These studies suggest that mindsets are malleable, and even relatively small interventions can significantly impact students' beliefs and behaviors (Blackwell et al., 2007).

Although scholars argue that a growth mindset can improve students' performance, they acknowledge that this mindset is not a panacea for all obstacles (Blackwell et al., 2007; Mercer & Ryan, 2010). It is important to note, too, that people do not display the same mindset all the time. Instead, psychologists generally view mindsets as operating on a continuum, and they "think of learners as having a tendency towards a particular mindset to varying degrees" (Mercer & Ryan, 2010, p. 438). Since mindsets are situationally bound, this study investigates students' mindsets in the context of writing with a specific emphasis on how students' beliefs about their writing ability, not intelligence in general or aptitude in other areas, affect them.

METHODOLOGY

The context for this mixed methods study, consisting of surveys, interviews, and grades, was a Mid-Atlantic comprehensive state university with an enrollment of over 20,000 students. The study's methodological approach was designed to answer the following research question: How do students' mindsets affect their writing processes and writing performance? The participants included students enrolled in three sections of a junior-level engineering class who volunteered to participate. One section had an embedded writing tutor assigned to the class, but students were not aware of this course component when they registered.

At the beginning of the semester, study participants completed an online self-administered survey during class. The survey instrument was a modified version of three previously validated surveys (Dweck, 2000; Limpo & Alves, 2014; Palmquist & Young, 1992). It contained eight Likert-scale statements that assessed students' beliefs concerning the malleability of writing skills (e.g., "Good writers are born, not made"; "No matter who you are, you can significantly change your writing ability"; "Good teachers can help me become a better writer"). Students rated these statements on a 6-point scale from "strongly disagree" to "strongly agree." I calculated students' mindset scores by assigning a numerical value to each statement (1=strongly agree to 6=strongly disagree, reverse scored for growth-minded statements), and then I calculated the mean. I did not identify cut-off points for growth and fixed mindset scores. Instead, mindset scores fell along a spectrum, with higher scores indicating more of a growth mindset and lower scores reflecting more fixed-mindedness.

At the end of the survey, I invited students to participate in a short interview. Five students volunteered to be interviewed individually about their mindsets and writing experiences in a semi-structured interview setting. I also interviewed the course-embedded writing tutor. I coded interview transcripts inductively to identify emerging codes and categories. I initially coded on paper, using underlining and color-coding techniques to highlight salient quotations and patterns. Then, I used NVivo software to organize and tag the data. To identify and organize major themes, I created a codebook with emerging codes, categories, and salient quotations. Finally, I used structural coding to connect the codes to my research questions and to relevant literature in psychology. Structural coding initially yielded 28 codes, and I condensed these into seven major categories: Difficulties, failure, improvement, motivation, teachers, performance, and writing process.

To interpret interview participants' experiences and behaviors, I operationalized mindset theory to illuminate how mindsets may manifest in a writing context. Operationalizing mindset theory revealed coding categories that were relevant to mindset literature. Since researchers have found that students' mindsets directly influence their attitudes, learning strategies, performance, and success (Blackwell et al., 2007), I hypothesized that students' mindsets influence their (1) revision practices, (2) responses to feedback, and (3) reactions to challenge and failure. The following three hypotheses guided the data analysis:

1. Growth-minded writers see revision as a natural component of learning and are, therefore, willing to compose multiple drafts. Fixed-minded writers tend to avoid drafting and revision to save face, especially if they see effort as fruitless or believe that only weak writers need to revise.
2. Growth-minded writers see feedback as an opportunity to improve and are motivated to revise their drafts after receiving constructive criticism. Fixed-minded students resist receiving negative feedback, even if constructive criticism could help them improve their drafts.
3. Growth-minded writers welcome challenging writing assignments that require substantial effort because they see difficult writing tasks as opportunities to improve their skills. Fixed-minded writers do not welcome challenge or risk-taking but instead tend to give up easily to avoid failure.

This operational scheme was used to code and analyze the interview data.

To triangulate the data, I also collected students' grades from their literature review assignment that required multiple drafts. I analyzed the data using bivariate correlation tests to see whether students' mindset scores correlated with their final essay grades. When conducting these statistical analyses, I consulted a statistician to help me select the most appropriate tests and interpret the results accurately. For the correlation test, we opted to run Spearman's correlation to minimize the effect of outliers because the data had a small departure from normality; the growth end of the curve was slightly higher than normal.

RESULTS

Survey

Of 66 total students in the three engineering sections, 57 completed the survey, resulting in an 86.4 percent response rate. On average, 15 percent of students displayed a fixed mindset in response to the survey statements, and 85 percent displayed a growth mindset. Notably, the highest percentage of students expressed a growth mindset (98.2%) in response to the statement, "Good teachers can help me become a better writer." Only one of the 57 participating students even disagreed slightly with this statement. The highest percentage of fixed-mindedness was displayed in response to the statements "Good writers are born, not made" (28.1%) and "I believe I was born with the ability to write well" (36.8%). Both statements assessed students' beliefs regarding the innateness of writing ability, whereas the remaining statements assessed students' beliefs regarding effort and dedication. Table 1 highlights these findings. The final column reports the overall percentage of students who agreed and disagreed with growth- and fixed-minded statements, respectively.

Table 5.1. Survey Responses

Statements	Strongly Disagreed	Disagreed	Disagreed Slightly	Agreed Slightly	Agreed	Strongly Agreed	Growth vs. Fixed Mindset
No matter who you are, you can significantly change your writing ability.	0%	1.8%	7%	31.6%	45.6%	14%	8.8% Fixed 91.2% Growth
Hard work, desire, dedication, and enough time are all I need to become a good writer.	0%	1.8%	10.5%	28%	42.1%	17.5%	12.3% Fixed 87.7% Growth
Good teachers can help me become a better writer.	0%	0%	1.8%	24.6%	54.4%	19.3%	1.8% Fixed 98.2% Growth
You have a certain amount of writing ability, and you can't really do much to change it.	17.5%	50.9%	21.1%	10.5%	0%	0%	10.5% Fixed 89.5% Growth
Good writers are born, not made.	8.8%	50.9%	12.3%	22.8%	5.3%	0%	28.1% Fixed 71.9% Growth

Statements	Strongly Disagreed	Disagreed	Disagreed Slightly	Agreed Slightly	Agreed	Strongly Agreed	Growth vs. Fixed Mindset
I believe I was born with the ability to write well.	12.3%	28.1%	22.8%	28.1%	8.8%	0%	36.8% Fixed 63.2% Growth
My essays will always have the same quality, no matter how much I try to change them.	15.8%	54.4%	14%	12.3%	3.5%	0%	15.8% Fixed 84.2% Growth
No matter how hard I try, I will never be a great writer.	33.3%	35.1%	22.8%	8.8%	0%	0%	8.8% Fixed 91.2% Growth

In addition to containing Likert-scale items, the survey posed the following question: "When it comes to writing success, which is more important: effort or talent?" Over 87 percent of students reported that effort is more important. Only seven students indicated that talent is more important, and they provided the following reasons why talent matters more than effort:

- "It is the accumulation of skills you have acquired over time."
- "Because it takes creativity to write well and that is talent."
- "It comes easier to those writers."
- "Because at this point in our career our writing abilities are engrained in [our] minds so in order to alter them it will take a lot of effort."
- "I feel that people acquire the ability to convene words better than others."
- "Some people are left brain creative thinkers. Writing is easier for them."

Most of these comments suggest a belief in "giftedness," as Palmquist and Young (1992) hypothesized. However, at least two comments also reflect an appreciation for effort, which underscores the complexity of the effort/talent binary, a phenomenon I will examine in the discussion section.

Grades

The bivariate correlation test showed that students' mindset scores and their final grades correlated moderately, Spearman's $r = 0.481$, $p = .008$. This finding suggests that a relationship exists between students' mindsets and their writing performance: Growth-minded students tended to earn higher essay grades, and fixed-minded students tended to earn lower grades.

INTERVIEWS

The interviews provide insight into students' (pseudonyms given) writing mindsets and their effects on students' motivations, attitudes toward performance, and beliefs about writing and learning. Table 2 provides an overview of each interview participant's mindset score with quotations that reflect the interview categories. As shown, all interview participants' mindset scores displayed growth mindsets. Thus, lingering on the interview data offers examples of growth-minded students' writing processes and experiences with writing. In the next two subsections, I highlight interview comments that illustrate connections to mindset theory; I will analyze and interpret these findings in the discussion section.

Table 5.2. Combined Data for Interview Participants

Name	Mindset Score (0–6)	Quotations That Reflect Interview Categories
Jenna	5.125	"I hear a lot of people say 'I can't spell because I'm an engineer' or they just say 'I'm a math person, I'm not a writer.'" (Challenges)
		"If I'm just really getting stuck on something, I'll just kind of take a look back, read over everything, make sure it sounds nice. And then go back to where I was stuck, maybe, and that'll help me a little bit." (Writing process)
Elijah	5.125	"Constructive feedback is the driving thing that makes me do things better, to learn things more." (Teachers/Motivation)
		"I take from an English class and I use that and apply it in an engineering class." (Improvement)
Paula	5.25	"If I am doing it a lot in the semester, I'm getting better." (Improvement)
		"I'm not sure if I did it right." (Performance)
Jordan	4.625	"What did we do on this one that we didn't do on this one; how can we improve?" (Improvement)
		"I like to have built in times of reflection, as that can be a really powerful way to improve one's performance." (Improvement)
Maria	5.25	"That was like a negative experience. Because I did not know exactly what, how it was supposed to be done." (Failure)
		"So I would write different things. Read it over. Take my time to write. Understand. It's just like writing; you just keep writing, writing, writing. You make a mistake. Write. You make sense out of it" (Writing process).

Growth-Minded Writers' Traits

Applying mindset theory to the interview data reveals three themes: Growth-minded writers are characterized by (1) an appreciation for effort, (2) an openness to learning and application, and (3) a positive response to challenge and failure. For instance, appreciation for effort is displayed in statements like "Unless you go out of your way to develop writing skills, you're probably not going to" and "[You must be] intentional about trying to grow your skills or make a change if you feel like you need to become a better writer." These comments suggest my subjects understand that writing improvement requires investment and effort. Students' openness to learning was also salient in the data. For instance, Elijah described how he applies his learning from one context to the next: "I take from an English class and I use that and apply that in an engineering class and see how my professor kind of reacts to that." Even professors' "conflicting" messages regarding writing conventions helped Elijah apply what he learned in one class to another class because he developed different skills. Jordan also emphasized reflection and an "iterative" writing process. In fact, Jordan used variations of the terms "reflection" and "iteration" 12 times in the interview and referenced mindset theory without any prompting. Finally, several students indicated that challenging assignments fostered their most substantial writing improvement. Even when a writing task is challenging, these students find the process to "be very rewarding to at the end have a project, a paper at the end, a product that is incredibly well sourced." For these growth-minded students, failure is an opportunity to reflect on an assignment and improve. For instance, Jordan explained how he reflects on poor performance by recalling past success: "What did we do on this one that we didn't do on this one; how can we improve?"

Despite approaching writing from a growth perspective, these students also made comments that were inconsistent with growth-minded tendencies. This finding is important because mindset literature does not typically describe students who simultaneously display characteristics of both growth- and fixed-mindedness. Specifically, my interview subjects did not actively seek feedback from others, and they tended to be preoccupied with performance—both behaviors that are more common in fixed-minded students. For instance, although Jenna reported that her professors' specific guidance and feedback helped her in the past, she indicated that she does not usually request it. Both she and Maria were confident reviewing their own work, and they only sought feedback when it was required. Elijah also endorsed faculty feedback, but he did not willingly seek peer review. Additionally, all interview participants discussed their grades, and some exhibited a preoccupation with performance. For instance, Jenna said, "In college, I would get a lot better grades on essays than I did in high school, and I took that as, like, oh, my writing improved." In this comment, Jenna seems to equate writing improvement with higher grades. Paula also reported using grades to gauge her abilities, saying that she was unsure how well she performed on her literature review because she had not received her grade yet. Her linking of grades to quality suggests she relies on grades to assess herself. Jordan also displayed a concern for grades when he indicated that his grades correlate directly to his interest level. Maria suggested that low grades might incentivize her to change her writing process, but she believes her process is currently working because her grades are satisfactory.

Fixed-Minded Writer's Traits

Although no fixed-minded writers volunteered to be interviewed, data from my interview with the course-embedded tutor provide a glimpse into fixed-minded students' beliefs and behaviors. In the interview, the tutor, Sara, talked at length about her interactions with one student, Alex, who was remarkably resistant to her feedback. According to Sara, Alex appeared distracted and impatient throughout the session, and he quickly dismissed suggestions when she offered them. He even characterized his literature review as "terrible," saying, "There's nothing you can do. This is all a waste of time." According to Sara, every time she offered advice or explained a genre convention, she was immediately "shut down." The tutor interpreted Alex's demeanor as "very closed minded," which was consistent with his survey data: He scored a 3.5 on the survey instrument, indicating a fixed mindset. He was also one of the few students who reported on the survey that his writing process and performance did not change over the course of the semester. He also said that talent influences writing success more than effort does. This snapshot of a fixed-minded writer's beliefs and behaviors provides useful comparison data for discussion.

DISCUSSION

For students like Alex, who believe writing success is dependent on natural talent, drafting and revision may seem like futile processes. Such beliefs can have negative effects, as demonstrated in the tutor's experience with Alex: He rejected all attempts to help him, and he seemed to resist the very practices that could help him, such as feedback and revision. Avoiding these practices likely impairs the 15 percent of students like Alex who have fixed-minded approaches to writing—as demonstrated by the correlations seen in the data between students' essay grades and their mindset scores. Although this window into one fixed-minded writer's beliefs and behaviors can only suggest the importance of mindset, the interviews with growth-minded writers offer compelling illustrations of how students' mindsets affect their writing processes and performance. In the next section, I will draw from mindset theory to interpret these results.

How Do Students' Mindsets Affect Their Writing Processes?

Growth-minded writers are willing to revise, but they still need motivation. Mindset theory would suggest that growth-minded writers are willing to revise their drafts because they embrace effort and challenge (Dweck, 2006). The interview findings confirm this hypothesis. For example, Jordan's description of his writing process underscored a willingness to revise and to embrace the "iterative process," as he called it. When given an assignment, he typically starts by gathering information from sources and synthesizing them into a document that is "just a mess." Once he collects the major parts of his paper, he begins writing, "and as that grows, the mess that's underneath kind of shrinks and becomes more organized." Jordan's belief that "the natural disorganized nature" of his writing process will turn into a cohesive final product reflects a belief in growth and improvement. In this way, his process seems directly correlated to his mindset. Jenna provided evidence of a growth-minded approach, too, when she described her drafting process: "If I'm just really getting stuck on something, I'll just take a look back, read over everything, make sure it sounds nice. And then, go back to where I was stuck, maybe, and that'll help me a bit." She suggests not being discouraged by writer's block but instead believing that she will overcome the obstacle. Comments from other interviewees reflected growth-minded approaches toward drafting and revision as well: "The second time it came out a little better"; "Usually I finish papers in one or two or three sittings"; "The whole process . . . was like a learning curve."

Although I had expected growth-minded writers to be unruffled by challenge, I found that growth-minded writers sometimes resist effort when they believe the assignment or subject is insignificant. Since resistance toward effort is more characteristic of fixed-minded students (Dweck, 2006), hearing growth-minded students report times when they resisted investing in tasks was surprising. Elijah expressed this view when he described a math class that was both difficult and, according to him, unimportant. He said, "The chance that I'm going to use one of the four calculus classes that I took is slim to none." This belief in the subject matter's irrelevance caused Elijah to take calculus "at a community college where it was easier." Rather than exerting the necessary effort, he "took the path around it." Yeager and Dweck (2012) assert that growth-minded students are motivated to put effort into anything that affords learning and development because growth-minded students see "everything (challenges, effort, setbacks) as being helpful to learn and grow" (p. 304). However, Elijah's story shows that relevance matters, too, and it may affect effort.

Elijah's comment underscores the central role that both motivation and a growth mindset play for writers. While my interview subjects were motivated for different reasons, subject matter interest and a belief in their work's relevance emerged as patterns in the data. These findings complement Michele Eodice, Anne Ellen Geller, and Neal Lerner's (2016) conclusions from *The Meaningful Writing Project*. They found that meaningful writing projects give students "the satisfaction of knowing the work they produced could be applicable, relevant, and real world" (p. 5). Such projects give students the freedom to write about their passions, and my interview subjects confirmed these findings. Students identified periods of growth as times when they were "writing more about things that interested [them]," when they felt "passionate," and when the "prompts in class would be more interesting." Jordan explained why interest and passion are so important:

> Not having a real interest or passion for the work that was being done really kind of removed a lot of the motivation that I have to kind of allot that extra time to go through a solid process to actually create something that I can walk away from feeling really proud of.

Here, Jordan connects three important elements: interest, effort, and pride. The linear sequence Jordan implies suggests that interest creates motivation, which leads to increased effort and pride and, ultimately, success. This finding aligns with expectancy-value theory, namely the notion that "If students don't value what they are learning or don't see how what they are learning will be useful to them in the future, they will not engage in mindful abstraction" (Driscoll & Wells, 2012, para. 1). Just as Driscoll and Wells connect motivation to learning transfer, it seems growth-minded writers also invest more effort when they see value in their work.

Growth-minded writers welcome constructive (and sometimes prescriptive) criticism. As I hypothesized, interview subjects confirmed that they see feedback as an opportunity to improve. Elijah expressed this view fervently, identifying moments when he improved the most as the times when he was "criticized most harshly." He acknowledged that not everyone would respond to criticism positively, saying, "There's some people who would just sit there and cry." This distinction between himself and others suggests that a positive response to criticism is characteristic of growth-minded students. Several students emphasized the role that concrete feedback and instruction have had on their writing development. They talked about "nitty gritty feedback," "reworded . . . sentences," and times when professors explained exactly how an assignment "was supposed to be done." Students' desires for concrete guidance surprised me because I had assumed growth-minded writers would be more concerned with learning than following prescriptive directions, as mindset literature would suggest. Students' preference for specific feedback also seems at odds with our field's prevailing writing pedagogies that resist prescriptive approaches and stress higher-order over lower-order concerns when it comes to responding to student writing (Brooks, 2001; Sommers, 1982).

How Do Students' Mindsets Affect Their Writing Performance?

Growth-minded writers welcome challenge and are unshaken by failure. Challenging writing situations did not deter these growth-minded students. In fact, several of them linked challenge to improvement. For instance, Jordan said, "It was a really challenging time, but I really grew as a writer during that time." Elijah expressed a similar sentiment: "I feel like negative feedback or constructive feedback is the driving thing that makes me do things better, to learn things more." For these growth-minded writers, failure is an opportunity to learn and improve. Elijah explained the connection between failure, effort, and success: "If I get a D on a paper, an F on a paper, I'm going to go back and spend a bit more time on that, and I'll probably get better at it because I spent a little more time on it." Here, Elijah's growth mindset correlates directly to his response to failure; he responds by emphasizing the value of effort rather than interpreting the failure as indicative of innate deficiencies. Importantly, none of my subjects said their sense of themselves or their abilities was shaken by failure, a characteristic of fixed-minded students that suggests growth-minded writers are more likely to bounce back from failure.

It is important to note that diverse writing experiences helped my interview subjects. Several participants mentioned that "writing for different classes" helped them improve, and Elijah described it best:

> When you write about different things, too, you write in different styles and take different approaches. When I'm in a religion class, I'm taking a different approach to talk about a religion than I am when I'm in a lab class and I'm talking about how a chemical is made.

Learning different genres, conventions, and styles has helped these students develop their writing repertoire. Hearing professors' different viewpoints has helped, too, because they give students insight into different audiences' responses to their work. It is important to note that this emphasis on variety came from growth-minded students. Fixed-minded students may not respond so positively to conflicting messages about writing because adapting to different writing situations requires flexibility and openness. If it is true that fixed-minded writers do not thrive in diverse writing situations, then their ability to develop rhetorical dexterity could be at stake. Such a potential finding is important, given my interviewees' emphasis on the positive influence that diverse writing experiences have had on their development as writers.

Growth-minded writers are sometimes performance-oriented. Although Dweck (2006) has found that growth-minded students tend to be more learning-oriented, my interview subjects' growth mindsets did not shield them from grade preoccupation. All participants mentioned grades in their interviews—the term appears 29 times in the transcripts—suggesting some preoccupation with performance. This trend, of course, could relate to the local student culture; anecdotally, many of my colleagues would agree that students at this university are especially concerned with grades. While interview subjects expressed interest in learning about genres, conventions, and writing processes, their comments showed that grades were a strong motivating factor. As Elijah said, "Grades kind of push you to do better." He also used rubrics as a guide for revision, saying, "If a rubric said I did a perfect score on one section, I wouldn't go back and touch it; I'd leave it." Most often, students referred to grades as evidence of their success rather than as primary sources of motivation. This distinction is important because Dweck classifies students as performance-oriented when they are more motivated to prove their abilities than they are to learn. Performance-oriented students are fixated on competence, whereas learning-oriented students are focused on skills acquisition (Dweck et al., 1995). The fact that my participants talked much more about research skills and genre proficiency—focusing on skills acquisition—than they did about grades indicates a potential problem with the binary posed by Dweck et al. in that my participants showed they were still invested in learning, despite their desire to earn high grades.

Mindsets are complicated. Although psychologists are careful to describe mindset as a continuum, Yeager and Dweck (2012) assert that mindsets "create different psychological worlds for students" (p. 304). These opposing worlds can sometimes sound all-encompassing in the literature when they are described as either "a world of threats and defenses" or "a world of opportunities to improve" (Yeager & Dweck, 2012, p. 304). My findings suggest that writers can experience aspects of both worlds at the same time, when they care about both grades and learning or when they are both resilient and risk-averse, for instance. These findings challenge the notion of separate "worlds" and suggest that students' mindsets are not always congruent, even within the same domain. Yeager and Dweck acknowledge that students can have different mindsets regarding different subjects, but they do not consider students who simultaneously display features of both mindsets. It may be that writers accumulate growth- or fixed-minded traits over time and eventually become more fully situated in one world or another. However, the students in my study demonstrate that mindsets may have a fluidity not described in Dweck's research, and thus, my research challenges the growth/fixed binary that characterizes much of the current literature.

The study's findings concerning growth-minded students' approaches to feedback reinforce the complicated nature of mindsets. While on the one hand, the interview data suggest growth-minded writers seek opportunities for improvement, their comments also indicate a reluctance to seek feedback. Although most interview subjects spoke positively about times they received feedback, four of five students explicitly reported hesitancy to ask for help. Instead, they seemed either already confident in their work or capable of revising on their own. For instance, Jenna said, "I'm good with what I wrote," so "I don't really need much feedback." Elijah expressed similar confidence: "I'll write it and then I'll go back and look over it, but I'm not going to, like, hand it to somebody else and ask them to revise it extensively." His reluctance to seek help suggests he wants to maintain agency because he feels capable of working independently. Maria also sounded self-reliant when she said feedback is unnecessary because she has "grown as a writer" and can "read through the eyes of who's going to be grading." For Maria, feedback is only necessary if the assignment is "really, really big" or, as Paula said, "a big assignment like a final or something." These comments suggest a preoccupation with performance over learning, and they reinforce the notion that even growth-minded writers might not always be concerned about growth. This finding reinforces the importance of scrutinizing the dichotomies that sometimes take hold in the field.

While I had expected growth-minded writers to express confidence and self-reliance, I was surprised to hear they would not seek more avenues for improvement. Jordan, however, did say he regularly invites his roommate, a writing center tutor, to offer feedback. This interview subject, who was so committed to reflection and an "iterative" writing process, seemed to defy the norm. He stood out as emblematic of the growth-minded writer. He had faced and benefited from challenges; he had failed but saw it as an opportunity to reflect and improve, and he declared, "If I continually practice my writing ability because I have the motivation and rationale to do so, then [I] can certainly become a stronger writer." Contrasting him to the other growth-minded students reinforces the idea of a mindset continuum: There are common traits to look for in growth- and fixed-minded writers, but students may not present all of them.

Although these findings illustrate how a growth mindset influences students' writing processes, questions remain concerning the potency and effects of these individual traits. It is unclear which traits are most influential to writing improvement. For instance, is it more important for writers to be reflective (on their own) than it is to seek feedback (from others)? Is a preoccupation with performance less important than overcoming failure? Which of the growth-minded traits make the most impact on writers, and how do writers like Jordan acquire the whole growth-mindset package?

My study makes it clear that the growth mindset is not a cure-all, as other researchers have noted (Mercer & Ryan, 2010). In the interviews, growth-minded students expressed difficulties with writing assignments, moments of failure, and uncertainty about their abilities. Many of the interviewees underscored the value of clear and concrete instruction, along with exposure to a variety of genres. Simply having a growth mindset was not enough for them to succeed. I am reminded especially of Paula, who repeatedly expressed uncertainty regarding her ability. Her interview displayed many comments like, "I'm not sure if I did it right," "I don't really know how to change it," "I don't know if I would be able to catch that on my own," "I don't know if what I'm saying is better necessarily," and "I don't really know what my skills are doing." She had a high growth mindset but low self-efficacy.

These findings raise the question of whether a growth mindset for students like Paula could make them more aware of their need for improvement. That is, if they see themselves as capable of improving, they might be more aware of their shortcomings, as Paula seemed to be. Researchers have discovered a similar phenomenon occurred in patients who increased their emotional awareness through mindfulness training (Boden et al., 2015). Boden and his colleagues found that patients reported increased anxiety and depression after engaging in mindfulness training, most likely because they had become more aware of these thoughts and feelings. Similarly, Paula's growth mindset might simply make her more aware of growing pains.

Mindsets may affect transfer. Although this study did not intentionally investigate transfer, several interview participants referred to times when they accessed previous knowledge, implying that growth-minded students are attuned to transfer. For instance, Elijah said he will "take from an English class and use that and apply that in an engineering class and see how my professor kind of reacts to that." According to Elijah, applying his learning from one context to another has helped him improve, especially because he can navigate the conflicting messages he receives about writing. Maria also indicated she could apply her genre knowledge to another writing task:

> It was like a learning curve kind of thing. But at the end I was like, so in the future I could actually do it this way . . . So my next literature review after that was really good. It was not a critical review. It was just a literature review. But that was really good because I think I understood what they were

asking for. And I understood how to do it. I didn't just know what to do.

Here, Maria expresses an ability to apply her knowledge of one genre to another similar genre, an example of near transfer. It is also important to note her emphasis on learning "how" to write in a specific genre versus simply knowing about a genre. Knowing "how" to do something is important to Maria, and this emphasis on the process seems to influence her ability to transfer her learning because she can adapt the process for other writing occasions. Jenna also attributed her success writing a literature review to her previous experience with the genre. She said she was confident because she had written one before and, therefore, "had a bit of a sense [of] what was going on." Jenna's unprompted discussion of transferring her learning from a previous class shows she is aware that previous knowledge should be accessed in new situations. Interpreting these comments from a mindset lens suggests that students who believe they can improve are more likely to recognize opportunities to apply their learning simply because they see their abilities and intelligence as malleable.

Since these findings suggest growth-minded students are highly aware of transfer, compositionists studying the connections between dispositions and transfer should examine the impact of mindsets on transfer, too. Roger Powell and Dana Driscoll (2020) have begun making these connections, for instance, observing how one case study participant's fixed mindset "inhibited her ability to transfer previous learning" (p. 53), particularly during challenging moments and when receiving critical feedback (p. 60). In contrast, their second case study participant, a growth-minded student, "could engage in learning transfer by receiving any type of response—critical comments that were harsh or blunt or praise-oriented comments that were supportive and nurturing" (Powell & Driscoll, 2020, p. 61). While Powell and Driscoll found that mindsets impact students' ability to apply teacher response to their writerly development, my findings suggest growth mindsets help writers simply be more open to applying their learning. It makes sense that growth-minded students would make connections between past and future learning because they see themselves as capable of change, growth, and improvement. Therefore, the belief that one can improve seems fundamental to learning transfer.

LIMITATIONS AND OPPORTUNITIES FOR FUTURE RESEARCH

Despite breaking ground in mindset research, the generalizability of this study is limited due to the small sample sizes. In particular, the interview sample was limited to only growth-minded students. Since none of the subjects on the fixed end of the mindset spectrum volunteered to be interviewed, it is difficult to draw conclusions about the interview data without making comparisons to more fixed-minded writers. Despite limited sample sizes, the methodology is replicable and can be used in future studies of larger and different groups.

The survey was also general in nature and did not define "writing" for participants. Students may have considered only their beliefs concerning creative writing or technical writing, for example. Their different conceptions of writing genres may have influenced their answers, raising the question of the roles that genre and disciplinarity play in influencing students' writing mindsets. An underlying assumption of the study was that engineering students' views toward writing are worth exploring because their disciplinary choice may imply a distaste for the humanities. Thus, attention to disciplinarity influenced the study's main questions. Future researchers might adapt the survey to define specific writing terms, depending on the researchers' interests in students' beliefs concerning specific genres.

While this study demonstrates that students' mindsets correlate moderately with their writing performance, whether there is also a causal relationship has not been established. Since this study sought to break ground in this research area, the many variables that affect students' mindsets exceed the scope. For instance, what pedagogical practices are most influential in changing students' writing mindsets? How much and what kind of influence do writing teachers have? To what degree can writers change their mindsets? In addition, future research should investigate how fixed mindsets affect writers.

Future researchers should also explore how students' demographics and backgrounds influence their writing mindsets. Dweck (2010) found that students from minoritized groups benefit the most from mindset interventions because recognizing the value of effort can alleviate stereotype threat. However, we need to understand how mindsets intersect with environmental barriers and systems of oppression. To what extent are mindset interventions effective for groups facing prejudice and other harms that extend beyond the individual's control? What are the ethical implications of studying mindset in these contexts? Is it insensitive, insulting, or even harmful to promote growth mindsets in the face of systemic racism without recognizing that context and working for justice?

In addition to examining writers' mindsets in greater depth, future research could explore the impact of mindsets on revision practices. Researchers could compare students' first and final drafts to identify patterns in changes and then correlate these patterns to mindset differences. Comparing drafts might show that growth- and fixed-minded students tend to revise differently.

Understanding the nuances of different revision tendencies could help teachers detect evidence of mindset interferences in students' writing practices. Although such research should avoid essentializing revision practices according to mindsets, the findings could help teachers provide even more meaningful feedback.

CONCLUSIONS

By building on seminal studies in psychology, this research offers further evidence to demonstrate that mindsets matter: They are moderately correlated to grades, and they influence students' writing processes. These results demonstrate the value of compositionists learning about mindset theory, facilitating conversations with students about their mindsets, and discussing ways that mindsets might influence their students' responses to feedback, willingness to revise, and attitudes toward failure and challenge. The research might also prompt us to identify best practices for intervening when students' mindsets seem to be hindering them.

Since we are increasingly aware of the role internal factors play in learning (Driscoll & Wells, 2012), writing experts are well-positioned to contribute to unfolding interdisciplinary discussions about the connections between mindsets and writing. This study has identified a possible relationship between growth mindsets and successful transfer, and future research can build on this finding to contribute to evolving understandings about the best conditions for transfer. Important gaps remain in mindset theory, particularly regarding the efficacy of pedagogical interventions, especially within inequitable learning environments. Although this study and others have shown that mindsets affect student success, it is incumbent upon all of us to also dismantle the systems that don't allow the individual, whether growth- or fixed-minded, to thrive.

REFERENCES

Aronson, J., Fried, C. B. & Good, C. (2002). Reducing the effect of stereotype threat on African American college students by shaping theories of intelligence. *Journal of Experimental Social Psychology, 38*, 113–125. https://doi.org/10.1006/jesp.2001.1491.

Blackwell, L. S., Trzesniewski, K. H. & Dweck, C. S. (2007). Implicit theories of intelligence predict achievement across and adolescent transition: A longitudinal study and an intervention. *Child Development, 78*(1), 246–263. https://doi.org/10.1111/j.1467-8624.2007.00995.x.

Boden, M. T., Irons, J. G., Felder, M. T., Bujarski, S. & Bonn-Miller, M. O. (2015). An investigation of relations among quality of life and individual facets of emotional awareness and mindfulness. *Mindfulness, 6*, 700–707. https://doi.org/10.1007/s12671-014-0308-0.

Brooks, J. (2001). Minimalist tutoring: Making the student do all the work. In R. W. Barnett & J. S. Blumner (Eds.), *The Allyn and Bacon guide to writing center theory and practice* (pp. 219–224). Allyn and Bacon.

Driscoll, D. L. & Wells, J. (2012). Beyond knowledge and skills: Writing transfer and the role of student dispositions. *Composition Forum, 26*. http://compositionforum.com/issue/26/beyond-knowledge-skills.php.

Dweck, C. S. (2006). *Mindset: The new psychology of success*. Ballantine Books.

Dweck, C. S. (2010, January). Mind-sets and equitable education. *Principal Leadership, 10*, 26–29.

Dweck, C. S., Chiu, C. & Hong, Y. (1995). Implicit theories and their role in judgments and reactions: A world from two perspectives. *Psychological Inquiry, 6*(4), 267–285. https://doi.org/10.1207/s15327965pli0604_1.

Eodice, M., Geller, A. E. & Lerner, N. (2016). *The meaningful writing project: Learning, teaching, and writing in higher education*. Utah University Press.

Good, C., Aronson, J. & Inzlicht, M. (2003). Improving adolescents' standardized test performance: An intervention to reduce the effects of stereotype threat. *Applied Developmental Psychology, 24*(6), 645–662. https://doi.org/10.1016/j.appdev.2003.09.002.

Limpo, T. & Alves, R. A. (2014). Implicit theories of writing and their impact on students' response to a SRSD intervention. *British Journal of Educational Psychology, 84*, 571–590. https://doi.org/10.1111/bjep.12042.

Limpo, T. & Alves, R. A. (2017). Relating beliefs in writing skill malleability to writing performance: The mediating role of achievement goals and self-efficacy. *Journal of Writing Research, 9*(2), 97. https://doi.org/10.17239/jowr-2017.09.02.01.

Mercer, S. & Ryan, S. (2010). A mindset for EFL: Learners' beliefs about the role of natural talent. *ELT Journal, 64*(4), 436–444. https://doi.org/10.1093/elt/ccp083.

Miller, L. (2020). Can we change their minds? Investigating an embedded tutor's influence on students' mindsets and writing. *Writing Center Journal, 38*(1), 103–128. https://doi.org/10.7771/2832-9414.1922.

Palmquist, M. & Young, R. (1992). The notion of giftedness and student expectations about writing. *Written Communication, 9*(1), 137–168. https://doi.org/10.1177/0741088392009001004.

Powell, R. (2018). *The impact of teacher and student mindsets on responding to student writing in first-year composition* [Doctoral dissertation, Indiana University of Pennsylvania]. ProQuest Dissertations & Theses Global.

Powell, R. L. & Driscoll, D. L. (2020). How mindsets shape response and learning transfer: A case of two graduate writers. *Journal of Response to Writing, 6*(2), 42–68.

Sommers, N. (1982). Responding to student writing. *College Composition and Communication, 33*(2), 148–156.

Yeager, D. S. & Dweck, C. S. (2012). Mindsets that promote resilience: When students believe that personal characteristics can be developed. *Educational Psychologist, 47*(4), 302–314. https://doi.org/10.1080/00461520.2012.722805.

Yeager, D. S., Johnson, R., Spitzer, B. J., Trzesniewski, K. H., Powers, J. & Dweck, C. S. (2014). The far-reaching effects of believing people can change: Implicit theories of personality shape stress, health, and achievement during adolescence. *Journal of Personality and Social Psychology, 106*(6), 867–884. https://doi.org/10.1037/a0036335.

Yeager, D. S., Miu, A. S., Powers, J. & Dweck, C. S. (2013). Implicit theories of personality and attributions of hostile intent: A meta-analysis, an experiment, and a longitudinal intervention. *Child Development, 84*(5), 1–17. https://doi.org/10.1111/cdev.12062.

CHAPTER 6.

RECOGNIZING FEMINIST RESILIENCE RATHER THAN SEEKING SUCCESS IN RESPONSE TO FAILURE

Karen R. Tellez-Trujillo
Cal Poly, Pomona

> It's okay to fail. Our goal should be to fail miserably and to fail often—as long as we keep learning from those failures and keep moving toward the goal we have set. Failure is a bruise, not a tattoo.
> — Michelle LaFrance, "Discourse Community Fail!"

My writing body is a balance. My torso is a pillar, my head a beam, and on each hand of an outstretched arm, I hold a pan that informs a scale that sits in my unsettled stomach. When the pan on the right becomes stacked with white paper filled with edits and recommendations, I halfheartedly pull pages from the top of the pile for revision, telling myself that I will feel better when the weight lifts. My inner voice says, "There are so many comments on this page," and the pan on the right slams to the table of my mind. The weight of writing failure is heavy and makes a raucous. I immediately seek ways to weigh down the pan on my left by gathering successes and opportunities to win. Desperate to tip the scale back into my emotional favor, I imagine scheduling blocks of time in my day where I can work harder on drafts, ways to give more of myself to service on campus or in my field, or I remember a grant application I can complete to see a project through. "Whew! That was close," I say to myself, imagining the pans floating, level, at last. I know that using my body in this way is not sustainable, but rather than finding ways to build resilience to the weight of failure, I have consistently sought success to ensure that the scale doesn't tip.

Managing the feelings of failure that come with writing is something I deal with often. As a junior faculty member who is in the process of fulfilling publication requirements for future retention, tenure, and promotion, I am once again back in the seat of the student writer. I imagine that receiving revision comments for some is truly generative or invigorating even. Paul Feigenbaum (2021)

DOI: https://doi.org/10.37514/PER-B.2024.2494.2.06

writes, in "Welcome to 'Failure Club'": "In fact, for students across English studies, the learning rewards of failure potentially include: finding unexpected and poignant connections between disparate ideas or domains of knowledge, cultivating a more nuanced understanding of complex concepts, and composing compelling and vibrant (if unruly) texts in various genres and modes" (p. 403). This is what I imagine when I think about my students reflecting on drafts, re-envisioning what their next draft might be.

The feelings I associate with receiving feedback on my writing are what Allison Carr (2013) describes as "a *deeply felt*, transformative process that incorporates feelings of anxiety, desperation, confusion, and shame" (p. 2). I am the educator Darci Thoune (2020) describes who balances protecting students from failure while encouraging them to fail gently but also wrestles with my own past and present failures (p. 53). These details are important to my trajectory as a writing teacher because my feelings of failing and being a failure are tied to writing more often than to any other activity with which I engage and have shaped my identity and the way I relate to writing.

I am a forty-something Chicana who returned to and graduated from my hometown Southwest Border university as a non-traditional student. I was not mainstreamed from high school to college with the writing skills many of my peers possessed. My ambivalent relationship with writing is complicated, more so due to taking a fifteen-year break between early college and my return in my thirties. When it comes to writing, I relate best to Charlie Brown in "A Boy Named Charlie Brown" (Schultz, 1969), in a yellow and black sweater, my mouth in a squiggly line with all but the Peanuts gang singing "Failure Face" to me as I peck away at my keyboard. I can say I still haven't adapted to this negative association with writing, nor to situations I find myself in related to writing struggle but am always willing to try something new to see my way out of it.

Taking new approaches to writing failure is not a new idea. For example, Paul Feigenbaum (2021) asserts that "helping students reconceptualize motivation and failure is an ethically, affectively, and progressively critical component of writing pedagogy" (p. 405). As a part of writing pedagogy, one can deduce that for every writer, there are failure stories, and for every teacher, a cliché, or an approach to helping ourselves and our students access the possibilities that come from feedback rather than the stifling products of failure that threaten to keep us from writing.

Feelings of failure tied to writing are not unique. Each of us seems to have a story we can share about the sick feelings we get as a result of a writing failure that might be as brief as a text interaction that led to a misunderstanding or longer, but not necessarily less devastating. There are so many failure experiences and such a need to find ways to move forward that in 2020, Allison Carr and Laura Micciche edited the first entire volume of essays addressing failure in *Failure Pedagogies: Learning and Unlearning What it Means to Fail*, offering narratives, suggestions for ways we can support our students, and varying definitions of success and what it means to fail.

As a commonplace, failure means something different to everyone, and each relationship with failure has developed in a unique way. This is one of the reasons I believe it's so valuable to have numerous approaches to handling writing failure because there is not one answer. I began using failure as a way of motivating myself to do better as a child. I didn't fail on purpose but used the shame, embarrassment, sadness, and sometimes anger to fuel action. Although I hadn't paid close attention to this tactic until recently, I have spent a lifetime believing that negative self-talk would produce positive results, and this is probably because there were times when I saw a correlation that wasn't there. I think of Allison Carr's (2013) advisor telling her, "I think you like to fail," and wonder if I have used failure as a way of benefiting from what I thought were positive results from self-scolding (p. 14). I may have never addressed this behavioral pattern had I not realized that over the years, my physical responses to failing, such as anxiety and insomnia, are far more powerful and damaging than any motivation failure has ever produced.

Throughout these processes of learning about myself that are long overdue, I discovered that I am not resilient to failure in the ways I believed I was, at least not according to traditional definitions of resilience. Rather than being a master of bouncing back from adversity, I have only sought winning in ways not related to writing as a balm to the emotional and physical effects I'd feel after failing. I've learned more about the false truths I'd owned for so long, as well as about resilience and the possibilities of responding to failure with resources that come from places that don't require that I work harder. This chapter is an opportunity for me to share some of my experiences with writing struggles that result in failing and resilient responses to adversity in relation to times I've failed at writing and labeled myself a writing failure. I will also share the concept of feminist rhetorical resilience (Flynn et al., 2012), the ways that common definitions of resilience and feminist rhetorical resilience differ, and the potential ways that we can use feminist resilience to frame writing prompts for students that can help them balance failing at writing with acknowledgment of the ways their writing has had an impact on themselves and the people around them.

SOME WORDS ON RESILIENCE AND FEMINIST RHETORICAL RESILIENCE

Resilience is one of the most commonly used words to describe students since the beginning of the 2020 COVID pandemic. The American Psychological

Association (APA) even created a page on their website titled "Building Student Resilience" (2023) containing a letter for families and guardians as a reassurance and grade-appropriate modules with lessons addressing "Actions," "The Body," and "The Mind" that encouraged the building of resilience to pandemic life. While I can identify the well-meaning motivations behind using these lessons, I argue that efforts to build resilience overnight, or ascribing resilience as a character trait, is a way of ignoring the need to pay attention to the well-being of a population or person, assured that they are tough and bounce back easily. I believe this takes place especially when we tell ourselves that we have provided the tools necessary to build resilience. But resilience isn't solitary, nor maintained without community. As a term that is used widely, from economics and political science to urban planning and globalization, resilience in each context shares similar definitions that center on adapting to the experience of adversity, including the ability of the individual to return to the state they were in prior to experiencing a crisis or struggle. These definitions give the impression that a person is not changed or taken down by adversity, and if they are, it is because they didn't have special resilient traits to see them through. There is also the impression that one can mold themselves back to who they were in the before times, before things got rough, if only they have what it takes.

Conversely to popular definitions and beliefs on resilience, no matter the magnitude of the adversity a person faces, they do not ever return to who they were before, and no one emerges from adversity unscathed, if they emerge at all. Adversity is ongoing and reveals itself in a variety of magnitudes, so much so that adversity is often accepted as the way life is. Further, expecting someone to adapt to the adversities they face suggests that one doesn't emerge from their crises but learns to feel comfortable in them, lacking the agency to seek a way out or to change. Feminist rhetorical resilience says otherwise. Elizabeth Flynn, Patricia Sotirin, and Ann Brady (2012) introduced feminist rhetorical resilience as a metaphor used in feminist rhetoric that "places greater emphasis on agency, change, and hope in the daily lives of individuals or groups of individuals," and ". . . suggests attention to choices made in the face of difficult and even impossible challenges" (p. 2). Further, these theorist's define feminist rhetorical resilience as enactments that are "communal, relational, and social" (Flynn et al., 2012, p. 5) while attending to concepts such as "agency, mêtis, and relationality" (Flynn et al., 2012, p. 7). These descriptors differ greatly from commonplace approaches to resilience as feminist resilience focuses on the resources available to an individual, particularly those who do not have power, but rather on the individual to see themselves through, to the end of a crisis. While it is not my main argument in this chapter, I assert that one never emerges from major life crises but feels their presence off and on throughout their lives.

Attracted to Flynn, Sotirin, and Brady's (2012) concept of feminist rhetorical resilience, I completed a dissertation titled "Enactments of Feminist Resilience in the Composition Classroom: Re-Scripting Post-Adversity Encounters Through Writing" (2020) involving a study on the feminist resilient responses of students in three first-year composition classes at a Southwest Border university where I was participant-observer. The objective of this study was to examine the occurrences of feminist resilience enacted by students as they recall their responses to adversities faced inside and outside the classroom. These students also recalled instances in which they had witnessed someone else responding to adversity in a way they believed was an expression of resilience. From my findings, I made an argument about the need for a composition curriculum focused on feminist resilience. What I have incorporated most recently is the consideration of failure associated with writing as one of the adversities students face.

In the study, the three composition teachers assigned a writing project at the end of the first unit that centered on the students' relationships to reading, writing, and language. I aimed to answer the following questions: "In what ways is feminist resilience exhibited (i.e., text, comments, behaviors, etc.)? How do gestures of feminist resilience allow students to re-script encounters and push back on their social positioning? What motivates students to enact feminist resilience? And how are the processes of enactment of feminist resilience learned?" (Trujillo, 2020). My analysis of student essays and interviews with five self-selecting participants revealed that students do not think about resilience unless they are asked to reflect upon their actions in response to adversity. I also learned through the study that students re-scripted their encounters with others through withdrawal and movement in and out of silence as resilient action. Most of the students interviewed couldn't define resilience, although felt that they knew it when they saw it. It is not uncommon to use terms without thinking about what they mean, and failure is among these commonplaces. Students also expressed a belief that resilience is learned from others and is gained through experiences rather than being a trait with which someone is born.

I found it interesting that in an interview, a student using the name J.T. incorporated failure when asked questions about resilience on two different occasions. Of the considerations of types of adversities students faced in their relationships to reading, writing, and language, I had considered issues such as being bilingual or multilingual, struggling with grammar, or not knowing how to read for comprehension, but had not focused on feelings of failing or being a failure as a writer. LaFrance and Corbett (2020) write, "In our experience, we become better writers by failing, sometimes abysmally, at the writing tasks set before us. Even so, few among us like to talk about failure, let alone admit to the ways we have failed" (p. 295). It's not explicit, but this statement accentuates the solitary nature of not just writing but failing at writing. Writing successes come pre-packaged with feeling that they are for the public, to be stuck on the refrigerator with our favorite magnet, while challenges are to be experienced in private, or turned upside down on the desk when returned by the teacher. I suspect that because writing failures are not often discussed, I was less likely to think of failing as an adversity students face in relation to writing.

FEMINIST RESILIENCE AND WRITING

While there are many ways for students to fail at writing, those that come to mind are feelings of failure when facing edits and recommendations, when writing is misunderstood, or when writing does not receive the grade or positive recognition the writer was certain they would receive. In my experience as a writing teacher, I have found that the sting of failure is most prevalent when the student has written about a personal experience and ties their writing struggles with an invalidation of the personal details they have shared.

Rather, through feminist resilience, the writer seeks neither to find ways to feel successful balancing failure, does not seek ways to escape writing or revision, nor seeks to become comfortable with feelings of failure, but instead reflects on the changes in their writing that have occurred over time and the changes their writing has brought about in the world around them. I posit that when student writers recognize themselves as agented individuals who can withdraw from their writing periodically as a way of imagining ways to recreate possibilities for the next steps, they will have an opportunity to switch the focus from what they have failed at to considering the possibilities. Through short writing prompts, I hope to create opportunities for students to reflect on their writing and the effects of the writing around them, where they recognize writing that has brought about hope and change.

While I value and have put into practice what I imagine may be all definitions of reflection that scholars in writing studies have produced over the last thirty years, I am drawn to Jeff Sommers' (2011) approach to reflection in this situation because it asks students to write about their own beliefs about writing, and their peer's beliefs about writing as well, rather than tracking their writing processes. Taking Sommers' (2011) approach into consideration, I suggest that we encourage students to think back on their own experiences and beliefs about writing for the sake of identifying enactments of feminist resilience in themselves as writers. Reflection, in this case, is about students' building awareness of what their writing has done, rather than what it has failed to do or ways they have failed at writing in the past.

I argue that feeling like we've failed at writing isn't something we're supposed to be cured of or learn to live with but something that we enter and emerge from as we practice stepping away from our failure to withdraw and rethink how we want to reengage on our own terms. We could stay in the muck of failure for a while, as Carr suggests (2013, p. 10), but we don't have to live there because we risk moving from failing as an action into failure as an identity. When writing about graduate students who dropped out of their programs, LaFrance and Corbett (2020) write, "It's only those who developed resilience—who kept writing despite the setbacks—that then moved from this place of uncomfortable confusion" (p. 303), and I extend this to posit that it is not only the traditional definition of resilience that applies here that are dependent on individual strength, but on feminist resilience, wherein the student used the resources available to them as assistance to see their way past and through their writing failures.

ADVERSITIES FACED WHEN WRITING

Some might wonder what the big deal is about receiving feedback or being able to focus on the productive side of having another person respond to writing as a way of providing a chance for revision. Per Thoune (2020), ". . . like all relationships, feedback is sometimes complicated. This is especially true when the feedback we receive tells us that we need to be and do better, that we didn't get it right, that we need to make another attempt, that we failed" (p. 54). What we write is not just about what we want to say but is about who we are and what we have chosen to share with our readers. This is surprising to some who consider academic writing to be less personal, but all writing is personal, and thus, feedback is pointed at the author's identity as much as it is on the content.

In her essay, Thoune (2020) further notes that the writer has a choice about how they will engage with feedback in a relationship where the writer can rescript how they think about failure and its role in the writing classroom. We can take Thoune's (2020) idea of failure as an opportunity for reflection on the feedback they've received and sharing our own failures as teachers in yet another direction by guiding students through writing prompts to recognize the times in their writing journeys when they have enacted feminist resilience as agented writers. Through writing prompts, students can also explore their relationship to their teachers and reviewers, who give feedback as resources rather than as their adversaries. This also helps to address Thoune's (2020) concerns about asking students and instructors to become vulnerable when asked to reflect on failures.

It is imperative to remain considerate of student vulnerabilities. A way of doing so is to remove the onus from the individual to become better writers on their own and to recognize the power of resources and community in the face of adversity. Further, by taking strategic approaches to writing that include withdrawing to re-imagine or re-consider the goals for their writing, students take an agented position in where their writing revisions go, rather than taking recommendations from feedback as instruction that they may have reasons for resisting that are not easy to immediately articulate. In a discussion of Jack Halberstam's (2011) *The Queer Art of Failure*, LaFrance and Corbett (2020) note that "Taking risks is an important piece of the growth of a writer; planning for more purposeful failures can then be a part of our intentional and strategic growth as learners and writers" (p. 300). In connection with feminist rhetorical resilience, I view planning for more purposeful failures as not only risk taking but also as a resilient response.

RESPONDING TO FAILURE

In *Mindset: The New Psychology of Success,* Carol Dweck (2006) reminds readers that failure is an action, not an identity (see also Miller, this volume). This statement makes sense and even invokes a nod from me as I read it. I say something to myself like, "Hmm. Yeah, I like that." I'd much rather say, "I failed," than say, "I am a failure." Pithy sayings like this are good and well until I get comments on a chapter I've submitted for review, and within moments, I begin to feel my shoulders tense and am overwhelmed with nausea as my eyes scan the draft, subconsciously taking count of places where the text is highlighted, my gaze sliding over the comments, some kind and productive, others not.

In "Workshopping Failure Pedagogy for Creative Writing Studies," Wally Suphap (2023) addresses common narratives supporting the idea that failure is something that we must endure to grow and experience the transformative benefits of writing. But Suphap also recognizes that "failure can also be embodied and harmful" (p. 3), drawing on the work of Carr and Micciche (2020) to extend approaches to failure pedagogy to include recognition of the harm that is felt in response to failure and that these responses are "messy," and to argue that failure is not always productive. Many of us have been taught, however, that failing is productive, and part of the formula includes persistence and even tough love.

When it comes to failing at writing, many of my students react, as Joseph Williams (1981) describes in "The Phenomenology of Error," with feelings that they must apologize or offer an excuse for errors in writing. While one or two grammar errors fall under the category of embarrassing, a handful or more are what some would consider a social error. It is possible that the written error, regardless of its size, is, as Williams writes, "located in two physical spaces, the grammar handbook and grammarian's mind, and in three experiences, the writer's mind, the mind of the reader, and the page" (p. 309). Writing failure feels as if it's multiplied like it's something we've done out of carelessness to the reader that has harmed them by misleading them or has wasted their time, and thus we need to say that we are sorry that they have been on the destructive path of our error.

On the other hand, some are taught that failure is something we have to undergo in order to realize success. Regarding success, Suphap (2023) notes that it ". . . is often defined narrowly, according to a set of standards and norms linked to capitalistic structures that valorize certain markers of success (e.g., publication bylines, social media followers, and book advances)" (p. 3). For one of the students whom I interviewed for my dissertation (2020), J.T., success and failure are directly linked.

> K.T.—Do you think you can recognize resilience when you see it in another person?
>
> J.T.—Yeah, you definitely can. You can see when a person is being put down either in the classroom or, um, just in general and how in the real world you can see where they're being put down and when they bounce back even stronger, but usually it's over a course of time. So, it's not necessarily a single event that you see resilience, but it's over, of course, of trial and error.
>
> K.T.—Right.
>
> J.T.—Failure. Keep failing. Failure, failure, and then finally success.

For this student, failure, adversity, and resilience seem to be related to one another, in that one must fail and employ resilience as a way of, at last, realizing success.

During the same interview, J.T. brought up a friend from a math class as an example of resilience. Regarding the friend, I asked:

> K.T.—Did you ever help him, or (pause)?
>
> J.T.—Yeah, we had study groups and helped each other with homework and what not.
>
> But you could tell that he was definitely—he never quit working things out. He always put a little more effort in each time he failed.
>
> K.T.—Do you think the teacher or anybody else treated him differently? Because he, like, was trying so hard?
>
> J.T.—Well, he uh, he got positive feedback from all his peers, including me, like, oh, you know, we're here to help you keep working at it, and same with the instructor. The instructor was kind of, um, he gave you the heavy hand, he wasn't like the

nicest, but what he was giving you was helpful. When he said it to you, didn't seem like the nicest thing to say, but now that I look back, he was saying those things to make you better.

K.T.—To motivate you?

J.T.—And so, yeah, the instructor didn't notice that a student was trying really hard, even though it was a challenge. It was easy to get your feelings hurt by the teacher like, yeah, it can be. I think in retrospect, it's easy to be like, yeah, they were really doing it for the best, but during the time you're like [the student grimaced at this point in the interview].

This example is an affirmation of the ways that negative reinforcements regarding failure are seen as motivators, reactions to failure, or ways that a "heavy hand" or even tough love are meant to get someone who has failed to work harder and not give up for the sake of being better. As discussed above, however, I would be the first to tell anyone that while I can see the thought process behind linking failure, resilience, and success, using negative comments or forcing success as a means of enacting resilience is neither healthy nor sustainable. In lieu, I have created writing prompts with hopes that they will serve as alternatives to focusing on failure, trying to become comfortable with failing or seeking ways to cover up the feelings that come with failure.

WRITING PROMPTS CENTERED ON FEMINIST RESILIENCE

Considering feminist resilience as rhetorical agency that continually recreates possibility, I believe that locating one's "agented actions of feminist resilience" (Flynn et al., 2012, p. 8) in the face of writing can be a productive way of responding to feelings of failure tied to writing. As a way of avoiding superficial responses to questions addressing students' recollections of times they were resilient to writing adversities, I would begin with the following 10-minute writing prompts:

- What would you consider to be a writing success?
- What would you consider to be a writing failure?
- What is the difference between failing at writing and being a failure?

The following 10-minute writing prompts would avoid asking students about their writing processes or writing failure, but to write the relational nature of writing. Agency is also addressed in the following prompts, as are opportunities for students to write about times when their writing has brought about change, hope, or allowed them to shapeshift for the sake of taking on a new identity. The prompts are as follows:

> Write about a time, or times, when you have:
> - used writing to work out a problem
> - shared your feelings with someone through writing
> - felt proud of what you've written
> - contributed to bringing about change in the world either at the local or global level—this could include song lyrics, posters, letters, homemade cards, messages, or stories
> - given your writing as a gift
> - shared sentiments of hope to another through messages in your writing
> - given them a chance to change shape through writing characters or by saying something in writing you would not say in a spoken interaction

After responding to these writing prompts, it may be productive to ask your students to write about how their definition of writing successes and failures changed. If so, how? If not, why do you think that might be? Students could also be asked if reflecting on the work that their writing has done in their and others' lives has had an impact on the way they feel about their writing when they otherwise might have felt they failed.

CONCLUSION

If becoming a better academic writer comes from practice, then I hope I live many, many more years because in over forty years of writing, I have yet to write in such a way that does not require many, many drafts. LaFrance and Corbett (2020) write: "If there is a better way to become an effective academic writer, many of us don't ever find it" (p. 295), and thirteen years into my academic experience, I feel this and silently pray it isn't true, even though I know deep down that it is. The part of me that believes I am among those who will infinitely search for ways to be a better academic writer also knows that I can find important lessons that come from my writing process while knowing that these teachings are not apparent until I have created a significant amount of distance between myself and my writing. In sum, writing failure is deeply felt, lonely, and it's possible that these feelings will continue throughout our writing lives unless we recognize that resilience in this situation can be relational rather than solitary and that we can move away from our writing to rescript encounters with our feedback, and our words. ¡Animo! dear reader, there's more. We have feminist rhetorical resilience to consider, and within, there is hope.

REFERENCES

American Psychological Association. (2023, June 14). *Building student resilience*. https://www.apa.org/education-career/k12/covid-19/building-student-resilience.

Carr, A. D. (2013, Spring). In support of failure. *Composition Forum, 27*. https://compositionforum.com/issue/27/failure.php.

Carr, A. D. & Micciche, L. R. (Eds.). (2020). *Failure pedagogies: Learning and unlearning what it means to fail*. Peter Lang.

Dweck, C. S. (2006). *Mindset: The new psychology of success*. Ballantine Books.

Feigenbaum, P. (2021). Welcome to "failure club": Supporting intrinsic motivation, sort of, in college writing. *Pedagogy 21*(3), 403–426.

Flynn, E. A., Sotirin, P. & Brady, A. (2012). Introduction. In E. A. Flynn, P. Sotirin & A. Brady (Eds.), *Feminist rhetorical resilience* (pp. 1–29). Utah State University Press.

Halberstam, J. (2011). *The queer art of failure*. Duke University Press.

LaFrance, M. & Corbett, S. J. (2020). Discourse community fail! Negotiating choices in success/failure and graduate-level writing development. In M. Brooks-Gillies, E. G. Garcia, S. H. Kim, K. Manthey & T. G. Smith (Eds.), *Graduate writing across the disciplines: Identifying, teaching, and supporting* (pp. 295–314). The WAC Clearinghouse; University Press of Colorado. https://doi.org/10.37514/ATD-B.2020.0407.2.12.

Schultz, C. (1969). *A boy named Charlie Brown - failure face scene (5/10) movieclips* [Video]. YouTube. https://www.youtube.com/watch?v=keisJRiVO-M.

Sommers, J. (2011). Reflection revisited: The class collage. *Journal of Basic Writing 30*(1), 99–129. https://files.eric.ed.gov/fulltext/EJ944156.pdf.

Suphap, W. (2023). Workshopping failure pedagogy for creative writing studies. *New Writing: The International Journal for the Practice and Theory of Creative Writing 20*(2), 244–58.

Thoune, D. L. (2020). Failure potential: Using failure as feedback. In A. D. Carr & L. R. Micciche (Eds.), *Failure pedagogies: Learning and unlearning what it means to fail* (pp. 53–62). Peter Lang.

Trujillo, K. (2020). *Enactments of feminist resilience in the composition classroom: ReScripting post-adversity encounters through writing* [Unpublished doctoral dissertation]. New Mexico State University.

Williams, J. M. (1981). The phenomenology of error. *College Composition and Communication 32*(2), 152–168.

CHAPTER 7.

TEACHING TO FAIL? THREE FEMALE FACULTY NARRATIVES ABOUT THE RACIAL AND GENDER INEQUALITIES OF SETS

Mary Lourdes Silva
Ithaca College

Josephine Walwema
University of Washington, Seattle

Suzie Null
University of California, Santa Barbara

What does it mean to fail in an inequitable culture framed by the values and metrics of student evaluations of teaching (SET)? Failure to perform well on SETs can result in some form of administrative action or sanction, such as job loss, lack of promotion, or denial of merit pay or tenure (Spooren et al., 2013; Wachetel, 1998). Not only do negative SETs have a professional and financial cost, but negative SETs can impact self-esteem, self-efficacy, and faculty morale (Boswell, 2016; Kowai-Bell et al., 2012; Wachetel, 1998). Both female faculty and female faculty of color, in particular, are disproportionately impacted by SETs. For instance, multiple studies show that students define teaching effectiveness based on gendered personality characteristics—e.g., women as nurturing and men as brilliant (Sprague & Massoni, 2005; Storage et al., 2016); female faculty are rated similarly to male faculty at the beginning of a course up until the point female faculty critique student work in the form of grades (Buser et al., 2022); and students evaluate *effective* female faculty more negatively (Boring et al., 2016) and penalize female faculty of color for both their race and gender (Baslow, 1995; Boring et al., 2016, 2017; Davison & Price, 2009; MacNell et al., 2015; Mengel et al., 2017; Pittman, 2010). As a result, female faculty and female faculty of color are compelled to play on an unequal playing field, which has multiple professional and psychological ripple effects. When administration or faculty frame negative SETs as a failure of teaching rather than as a byproduct of a racist/sexist system of evaluation, female

DOI: https://doi.org/10.37514/PER-B.2024.2494.2.07

faculty and female faculty of color must allocate additional time and resources to improve their SETs, thereby detracting from research projects, publishing, professional service and networking, and self-care.

The validity and reliability of SETs have increasingly been called into question as a measurement of teaching effectiveness (Beran & Rokosh, 2009; Boring et al., 2016; Galbraith et al., 2012; Shevlin & Banyard, 2000; Spooren et al., 2013; Uttl et al., 2017). In a seminal review of SET research, Wachtel (1998) reports research findings that confirm and challenge the validity and reliability of SETs, underscoring variables such as time delivery of SETs, class time, level of course, class size, course electivity, workload, subject area, anonymity of student raters, gender, race, age, instructor rank, and personality. With each variable, it is critical to contextualize the results. For instance, large lecture classes may correlate with higher SET scores if students have elected to take a popular course with a reputable professor, whereas a large required first-year course typically correlates with lower SET scores in comparison to smaller seminar courses. Fifteen years later, a metastudy by Annan et al. (2013) confirms Wachtel's prior findings and indicates how factors outside faculty members' control can affect SET ratings. These can include the time of day, type of room, course level, course workload, course type (required versus elective), student attendance, students' keeping up with assigned reading, and expected grade in the course. Miles and House (2015) found similar results regarding class size, class type (required versus elective), and course grade expectations. Student perceptions of SETs and their value in higher education may also influence SET scores (Spooren & Christiaens, 2017). The validity of SETs is tenuous, at best, when 30 percent of students admit to submitting false information on SETs based on their personal opinion of the instructor (Clayson & Haley, 2011). Problems of validity and reliability are exacerbated for many female faculty and female faculty of color, who have to navigate a system with inherent and ingrained biases, making experiences of institutionally perceived failure a commonplace narrative.

The reliability and validity of SETs is more pronounced for female faculty because students unconsciously evaluate their abilities and intelligence by applying different criteria. Rivera and Tilcsik's (2019) study of student ratings of instructors found that the female instructor was rated "as less brilliant than her otherwise identical male counterpart" (p. 20). Moreover, according to Storage et al. (2016), women and African American faculty were less likely to be rated or perceived as "brilliant" or a "genius" among student respondents. Relatedly, MacNell et al.'s (2015) empirical study of gender bias in an online asynchronous course with multiple sections found that students rated more harshly instructors they assumed to be female. Mitchell and Martin (2018) report similar findings in their study of two identical online courses, one taught by a female professor and the second by a male professor, with all variables held constant (i.e., course assignments, course format, and lectures). In a content analysis of student comments, Mitchell and Martin found that women were more likely to be judged for their appearance and personality and to be referred to as a "teacher" instead of "professor." Even when the male professor, on average, awarded lower grades, he received higher SET scores in comparison to his female colleague.

Evaluations based on gender are as problematic as other non-teaching criteria, but they are especially so when paired with race and ethnicity (Robinson, 2018; Reid, 2010). In underrepresented fields, women and minorities are more likely to report bias where their legitimacy is questioned (Dancey & Gaetane, 2014). On teaching evaluations, Bradley and Holcomb-McCoy (2004) report that a few Black female educators experienced "unequal treatment" and "racism" (p. 266). A study of non-white faculty by Lindahl and Unger (2010) showed that students' qualitative responses of these instructors were cruel, negative, and disrespectful, including several that, according to the authors, "were inappropriate to reprint" (p. 4). This antipathy is brought on by a variety of factors, the foremost of which is students' first impressions of instructors when based on race (Littleford et al., 2010; Roseboro, 2021; Taylor, 2021). This impression persists throughout the course, with students using it as the baseline to judge their instructors' expertise, estimations of authority, grasp of course material, and teaching style. Roseboro (2021) stresses that for Black faculty members (but also other BIPOC faculty and minority faculty), "being forced to analyze and include those course evaluations in the promotion and tenure application may, in fact, re-traumatize" (p. 57 of 190, Kindle Edition). For Roseboro, a minority instructor "requires a self-justification of one's right to be. And that prescribed self-justification reinforces the idea that one does not belong" (p. 57 of 190, Kindle Edition).

Ongoing feelings of failure and inadequacy due to SETs have psychological effects that impact professors' self-efficacy and self-esteem. In many cases, SETs may be the only feedback that faculty receive, particularly if constructive peer feedback is less available. Boswell (2016) found that participants who received positive SETs reported greater self-efficacy and confidence as professors and greater rapport with students. Boswell predicted that those with higher SET scores would most likely invest more effort to engage with students, whereas those with low SET scores may not have the motivation, affect, or resources to improve their SET scores. Negative evaluations, however, can shape professors' self-concept as it relates to teacher-student rapport (Kowai-Bell et al., 2012). Indeed, some faculty link their personal identity with negative student feedback (Arthur, 2009). Beran and Rokosh (2009) quote one instructor who described the process of SETs as "humiliating and frustrating" (p. 506). Yao and Grady (2005) found that faculty often experienced anxiety and nervousness when receiving SETs. They write that faculty reported concerns about instructors lowering standards to improve SET scores (see also Wachtel, 1998). In a separate study by Crumbley and Reichelt (2009), 53 percent of accounting professors knew someone who engaged in defensive measures such as grade inflation, grading leniency, reduction of standards, and reduction of coursework to improve SET scores. Crumbley and Reichelt state that there are monetary and administrative penalties for low SETs; however, there is no penalty for grade inflation, coursework reduction, and grading leniency, which often become professors' only option within a broken system. Moreover, in some cases, higher SETs are actually correlated with lower levels of student achievement (Galbraith et al., 2012) or with worse student performance in subsequent courses (Kornell & Hausman, 2016). When faculty reduce grading standards or coursework as a defensive measure to preserve their jobs or obtain promotion, student learning can be compromised.

In summary, female faculty, and particularly female faculty of color, often receive statistically significantly lower ratings (Baslow, 1995; Boring et al., 2016), or they often need to invest more time and energy to get the same evaluations that men do (Owen, 2019). Boring et al. (2016) write that "SET appear to measure student satisfaction and grade expectations more than they measure teaching effectiveness" (p. 10). This puts many female faculty in the untenable situation of having to decide whether to compromise their research and publications agendas (which are also required for tenure and promotion at teaching colleges) to improve their SETs or risk getting low SETs to pursue a competitive research agenda.

West-Puckett et al. (2023) challenge binary constructs of failure in which there is a defined outcome of success. Failure in this context is experienced as shameful "red marks" that we are forced to carry with us from semester to semester or from one college to the next. How do we resolve the conundrum of how and when to fail with SETs if it is not possible to succeed in all areas of academia: teaching, research, and service? Moreover, how can we benefit from failure when the system of assessment is designed to privilege certain bodies, behaviors, ideologies, and practices and marginalize or oppress others?

In the rest of this chapter, we share our personal accounts with SETs and the psychological, emotional, pedagogical, professional, personal, and health consequences of working in this culture of failure. In the first narrative, Walwema shares her experiences of shame and its heavy toll at the start of her academic career, where low SETs compelled her to withdraw from a job search. Silva writes about the shame and anxiety experienced while serving multiple leadership roles in faculty development while repeatedly receiving lower evaluations in comparison to her white male subordinates. Null describes how gendered expectations in her female-dominated field created an untenable workload and stress concerning promotion and how a critical set of SETs compelled her to stop teaching a particular course. These narratives will begin a conversation about the psychological, professional, and pedagogical consequences of navigating a field that leaves intelligent, skilled, experienced female experts constantly negotiating the conundrums of "failing" in one or more areas of their professional lives.

WALWEMA, THE RELUCTANT ACADEMIC

I embody all the attributes of foreignness. I speak differently, my outlook is global, my sensibilities are multicultural. Inhabiting these attributes has made me understand and accept the complexities and nuances of others. The position from which I operate is that of a Black woman migrant living in the United States. Here, I am constantly challenging both students and faculty about their essentialist assumptions about my identity and what it might say about me and where I am from. Occupying such a position is obviously problematic. And it is not unique to me. Thus, I acknowledge that while all of us are somewhat at the mercy of our histories, not all of us have the agency to embody the attributes of who we are and how we are perceived. I own these racialized and gendered attributes in the knowledge that I am always grounded in multiple marginalized realities.

Like other academics, I evaluate my performance based on external, often measurable criteria in the areas of teaching, research, and service. In a given year, I can enumerate the papers I have published, committees I have served on, and the work I have done on those committees; I can detail the classes I have taught and to what degree they have been successful. I can write at length the ways I have retooled aspects of the classes I have taught based on random surveys and sometimes direct solicitation of feedback from students during the course of the term. Which is why it is astounding that even with the abundance of research showing the malign nature of SETs, when it comes to decisions of hiring, promotion, retention, and tenure, colleges and universities still assign them an outsized influence. Being on the receiving end of SETs, often mean-spirited, insulting, and denigrating, with most bordering on the *ad hominem*, has induced in me a sense of failure. When I first handed out SETs at the end of my first teaching semester as a graduate student, I assumed I'd get feedback on three areas: things that went well, things that I ought to improve upon, and things that I definitely should eliminate. From that standpoint, I looked forward to using SETs to course-correct and retool. After all, I reasoned, this is the kind of feedback I gave my professors as a college student. Was I wrong! The SETs I encountered were mostly personal attacks ascribed to my race and gender. They were littered with phrases such as "does not know as much as she thinks," "she seems to care too much about writing" (I am a writing professor), and "I did not learn anything new." I was caught flatfooted. And, in the aftermath, I felt not only disengaged, as though the subject of these SETs were someone other than me but also disempowered. I felt like I had lost my agency. What is it that empowers students to act this way? How is it that they find it acceptable to hurt the human being who has interacted with them twice a week for 14–16 weeks? And why does it matter that I am a Black woman teaching mostly white students?

Prior to coming to the United States, I had never been referred to as a person of color, much less Black. Race had never been a descriptor of my identity. And it certainly was never a metric of my efficiency or the lack thereof. I was either good at what I did or was not and had to work harder to do better. With the increasing reference to my race and my gender, however, I began to wonder if being female faculty of color equates to presumptions of incompetence. Thus, even though I never thought of myself as a racial category, I soon learned that there was no escaping being multiply marginalized, no matter my qualifications. For example, what do you do with a comment that calls you "very knowledgeable" and caring "about the quality of her students" but "she does not know as much as she thinks she does" or "Women have no place teaching this class" and "she needs to assign less work." It is no wonder that these notions of difference make their way into SETs.

Scholars have found that students' first impression of their professors does influence their perception of that professor and expertise (Littleford et al., 2010). What does that mean for a person like me, who cannot disambiguate my identity? I am a person who, as James Baldwin (1997) once said, puts "my business in the street" (p. 5) the moment I open my mouth! Ironically, Baldwin (1997) observed this of the spoken English of an American living in England. Language, as Baldwin wrote, is revealing of one's "private identity" and "is capable of connecting one with or divorcing one from the larger public" (p. 5). And as a writing instructor, I may not always square my accent with my ability to teach writing because, as Littleford et al. (2010) note, students associate non-white professors with content expertise in racial courses. So, when it comes to students' conceptions of the teaching and the learning of writing and the difficulty faculty may have in presenting written feedback in ways that students perceive as constructive, confusion may ensue. And it may make its way into the hostility, anger, and resistance of SETs, some of which have had me ponder my future in the academy.

Upon going on the job market, for one of the positions I sought, I was asked for, among other things, "evidence of teaching effectiveness as measured by SETs." My heart sank. While I had acquired content and instructional expertise along with a mix of positive and negative SETs, my fixation on the negative ones won the day. No search committee, particularly one that measures teaching effectiveness by SETs, would look at my evaluations and recommend me for hire. Thus, despite my meeting all the required qualifications outlined in the job description, this additional request (not included in the job description but sent out as an additional screening mechanism) threw me off. Rather than subject myself to the rejection that I was sure would come, I withdrew my candidacy.

Teaching writing is an especially subjective endeavor, particularly when it comes to the iterative process of drafting, feedback, and revision, all of which might privilege the instructor's perspective over that of the student's. See, instructor feedback conveys the idea that there is an unarticulated standard (beyond the rubric) that has not been met. Because, as writers, we identify strongly with our writing, we can see how students' interpretation of the role of the writing instructor may have mismatched expectations about what counts as good writing. And if students' initial impression of the writing instructor presumes incompetence, they may feel the need to punish the instructor's response to their writing with stinging rebukes. Ultimately, such remarks are not a measure of teaching effectiveness because, by all accounts, the instructor is engaging in established pedagogy—the only difference being that they are gendered, racialized, or accented.

As I write this, I have been teaching for over 15 years. I have come to understand SETs as the problem we (academics) all live with (to paraphrase Norman Rockwell). I still get comments such as "She seems to know a lot." As a rhetorician, I cannot help but examine this comment for what it implies. Do students find it objectionable that someone like me, who holds a PhD in rhetoric, knows my subject matter? While my instinct is not to assign any label to these tendencies, I have nevertheless found myself puzzling over whether this comment contains some kind of coded message or if students implicitly doubt my credentials. I am not alone. Research by Smith and Hawkins (2011) shows that identity-based bias in SETs is gender-based bias (Mengel et al., 2017; Rivera & Tilcsik, 2019). Another frequent comment offered as a negative is that I am always prepared and that I come to class on time. I often wish I could go back to the class after I have read these SETs and clear up some things with students. I'd want them to know that I would never have been hired without proof of qualification, that I would not have risen to my rank without meeting the rigorous appointment and promotion processes I have undergone every two years until I earned tenure.

The truth is that academia causes some of us to internalize failure even when we are successful. Through a myriad of ways, the stress of SETs ingrain inadequacy in our lives as academics. The toll they place on our physical and mental health is real, as is their ability to induce stress and self-doubt. On #AcademicTwitter, academics have disclosed feelings of anxiety and general angst at the prospect of reading SETs. Others have decided never to read them at all. For others, SETs exact a tremendous amount of labor. Like others, to deal with harsh SETs, I have diverted time from research to revamp courses, bent over backward to accommodate students' impetuousness, and routinely apologized for students' inability to do their work on time. This constant need to accommodate while proving that I am qualified is enervating.

Seasoned and new college professors who experience the stinging rebuke of SETs have often pondered their (SETs) role in professional development, given that in other professional environments, reviews prepare the reviewee to celebrate some wins and work out approaches to tackle weaknesses. Not so with SETS. Who accounts for the cascading effects of negative ratings and the implications for career trajectory? Having tenure does not inoculate one from the negative effects of SETs, perhaps because of the very human need for validation. And for me, who occupies a place that defines the boundaries of race, gender, and foreignness, the effects can be precarious.

SILVA, FIRST GENERATION IMPOSTOR

If there was a point system for the imposter, I would lose one point for the handful (sometimes two) of low SETs I receive each semester, one point for being a woman in higher education, one point for being part of Generation 1.5, one point for having elementary school teachers who scared my parents into speaking English with us, another point for the spankings I got for leisure reading, and the last point for attending a poor rural high school with science textbooks copyrighted two generations prior. I always had some good excuse for each perfect report card or accolade. Even my becoming a writing professor was sort of a fluke. Students who fail the verbal portion of the SATs don't go on to become writing professors, so I assumed. After two terminal degrees, a master's, two certificates, and, of course, tenure, there is little to apologize for; however, my inability to see myself reflected in my professors and colleagues left me believing that my endless questions and lifelong pursuit for knowledge were evidence of my outsider status.

My parents immigrated to this country in 1965 without a high school education. They labored under the California sun, enduring back-breaking work while raising six children, including my severely handicapped sister. We eventually thrived within the agrarian communities of the valley where immigrant families have long lived in the margins with limited access to literacy resources, such as literacy sponsors, public libraries, and well-staffed and fully stocked schools (Brandt & Deborah, 2001). My academic trajectory as an overachiever paralleled my path as a first-generation daughter raised by austere Catholic parents who did not hesitate to use shame, criticism, and corporal punishment to mold me into a loyal, obedient child. From these parallel worlds emerged my very own internal critic.

Imposter syndrome is chronic across all demographics. According to an article published by the American Psychological Association, imposter syndrome was first coined in 1978 by psychologists Suzanne Imes and Pauline Rose Clance (Weir, 2013; see also Teagan Decker, this volume). They describe it as feeling "like a fraud" and attributing one's success to luck. The phenomenon is most common among successful high achievers. According to Hutchins and Rainbolt (2016), tenured and tenure-track faculty also experience the imposter phenomenon, in which the highest reported cases were tenure-track faculty. Emotional exhaustion as an outcome of the impostor syndrome was reported by both tenured and tenure-track faculty. It was first believed that only women experienced this problem. In the last two decades, researchers have discovered that men and some minority groups are also impacted significantly by the imposter syndrome. For faculty of color, it is challenging to develop and sustain "a scholarly identity" because faculty often internalize the prejudicial messages about their minority group (Dancy & Gaetane, 2014, p. 367).

Callie Edwards (2019) is a Black female scholar who shares her experiences overcoming the imposter syndrome at a predominantly white male university. She writes:

> Rooted in the ideologies of privilege and oppression, both phenomena ignite a sense of otherness and probate the dominant metanarrative. Whether they feel as though they do not belong (i.e., imposter syndrome) or they feel as though they must prove they belong (i.e., stereotype threat), some marginalized groups are hyperaware of how they are bothered, and this awareness influences how they navigate spaces. (p. 20)

Individuals from marginalized groups often feel they have to hide or alter their true selves to fit in. Since I have worked at predominantly white, affluent institutions of higher education for the past 17 years (i.e., doctoral program and current college), I have had to perform *better* the role of the nurturing, compassionate, accommodating *mother* rather than the strong-willed, firm but understanding matriarch. In my community, women speak their minds in a manner that often appears abrasive to outsiders. The more we care, the more amplified our commitment. The more I care about my students' growth as writers, learners, and thinkers, the less nurturing I may appear. Hence, the more I have to hide my authentic self.

Both Edwards (2019) and I lacked positive representations of female leaders within education, and, similar to Edwards, who had a stuttering problem as a child, I stuttered at times in stressful academic situations. Also, because English was not my first language, I struggled to pronounce certain English words during my primary and secondary education, which made me the butt of many cruel jokes. Even during my college years, I had a male mentor who mocked me when I stuttered. I endured his emotional abuse for a couple of years because I was enamored by his intelligence, confidence, and modest beginnings. Thus, when the occasional SET comment about my pronunciation surfaces, it is a painful reminder of the emotional abuse I endured most of my life regarding the way I speak.

Moreover, writing never came easy for me. It still doesn't. I assume that academics of privilege have fewer doubts than me and labor far less to write. But I followed in my parents' footsteps and did what made the most sense: I worked and worked. For my parents, hard work meant more cows and more land. For me, hard work meant straight A's, a tenured job, and the compulsion to quadruple my disciplinary knowledge to leave no doubts in colleagues, administrators, and students. Failure as a child was not an option if I wanted to avoid abuse, and failure on the tenure track and as a tenured professor was loss of income, access, and opportunity.

For years, since I was a graduate student in predominantly white institutions of higher education, I worked alongside white male colleagues who boasted about neglecting their responsibilities in the classroom while receiving positive SETs. Despite the additional hours I invested weekly to meet with students one-on-one, provide ample feedback on drafts, or develop course materials to scaffold gaps in student knowledge, each semester, there was always a handful of students critiquing my pronunciation, mocking 1–2 grammatical errors on an assignment sheet, or questioning my intelligence. When I tutored and taught in California over 20 years ago, which has a large Latinx community, I mainly received high SET scores, established a positive rapport with students, and felt a strong calling in my work. In recent years, the call to purpose barely persists, like a phantom limb.

It's one thing to endure the criticism of student evaluations in the privacy of your office, but when your department chair, administrative assistant, executive committee, and dean have to read these evaluations each semester, then it's a constant *public* reminder that you DO NOT BELONG here. The experience is tantamount to public shaming. In the humanities, our culture of failure presumes that educators and scholars must be accountable for their individual behaviors and actions. We normalize the daily grind of teaching, research, and writing and only take notice of fellow colleagues when someone publicizes a publication, promotion, or award; otherwise, successes remain private, unlike industries that commonly publicize to internal and external audiences sales reports and share values as indicators of individual and collective success. Failures may be reported similarly, and for many industries (e.g., information communication technology), the culture of failure is changing, in which knowledge workers, influencers, and innovators are encouraged to embrace failure in order to progress and remain competitive in a rapidly changing market. In the humanities, however, our personal failures as writers, researchers, instructors, and community members are kept in the vault of secrecy (Brown, 2015). When we choose to learn from our failures, we may seek the support of a trusted colleague, counselor, or confidant or attend professional development events, but for the most part, Brown states, we internalize our failures as our shame. And our vault of secrets and silence is pried wide open annually when administrators and fellow colleagues evaluate or question our performance and competence off a single data point—SET.

In a biased system of assessment that privileges certain bodies, personality characteristics, and manners of speech, the only option left for those who do not benefit from such a system is to assimilate. Ibram X Kendi (2019) writes that assimilationist discourse is racist and sexist because we believe that a marginalized group should change and that there is something inherently wrong with this group. If I'm going to succeed and learn from my failures within this biased system, the only option left for me is to assimilate "better" and embody "better" the figure of the nurturing, accommodating professor who speaks "better" standard American English. When the great American success story of the leather-patched academic features values such as hard work, grit, curiosity, and a bit of ingenuity, we naively presume that a life committed to such values would result in success. No amount of hard work, intelligence, or grit equates to higher SET scores. The truth involves a somber acceptance of systemic racism and sexism in higher education manifested in multiple forms, including the standardized evaluation of teaching by students. Most SET surveys are not designed to improve the quality of the course and teaching; rather, they provide an anonymous public platform for students to voice their perceptions, assumptions, and biases about the professor or instructor, regardless of whether they are positive or negative.

The long, arduous journey to tenure nearly broke me. When I first arrived at my current place of employment, I was denied merit pay due to mediocre SETs in non-elective courses, even though I had completed exemplary accomplishments in research and service. When I petitioned my rejection to the department chair, I asked, "Based on the minimum qualifications for merit pay ("excellence" in service, research, AND teaching) and the inherent bias of SETs, how is it possible for me to ever be eligible for merit pay? He dodged the question and simply encouraged me to try again. I never bothered. I knew it was impossible for me to meet their bar of "teaching excellence." After years of steady improvement in my SETs, I put forth my tenure file to the All-College Tenure Committee. My departmental tenure committee was not confident in my ability to acquire tenure and suggested that I withhold my tenure process another year. I felt both rejected and humiliated. I ignored their recommendation and submitted my file anyway to the All-College Tenure Committee, which unanimously approved my tenure file. Although my department intended no harm, their doubts left me questioning my place in the department.

After I received tenure, my department chair raised several concerns about a handful of negative SETs from each course, questioning my competence and commitment to teaching without viewing any of my curricular materials or visiting my classroom. In an email, he provided a rationale for rejecting my research grant application for $3000, arguing that my research pursuits detracted me from teaching well. The same chair later raised concerns to the Executive Committee about my interests in the Writing Center Director position, doubting my ability to work with students, even though I had successfully collaborated with students multiple times in the past. With each rejection, failure after failure, it was clear my department did not want me there.

A friend once told me, "Now that you have tenure, you don't have to worry about those evals anymore. They can't fire you." True. They can't fire you. But they can deny you merit pay, promotion, research opportunities, and social validation. They can ensure that within a punitive, biased system of assessment, no amount of professional development and self-improvement will free you from feeling like a failure.

NULL, RUNNING AROUND LIKE MOTHER HENS WITH OUR HEADS CUT OFF TO AVOID THE DREADED LOW SETS

As a female professor in an almost all-white and all-female department that prepares students for the majority-female and service-oriented profession of K-12 teaching, I find that even when I do all the work of developing extensive course materials, providing communication through multiple channels, being available almost to the point of being on call 24-7 and identifying and responding to students' needs that are often far beyond the scope of the class—sometimes at the cost of meeting other professional goals—I still risk being penalized with lower SETs if students didn't feel like I did enough to meet their expectations, which are often gendered.

For example, last year, I volunteered to teach an additional one-credit course for incoming freshmen, which required investing a great deal of time into creating a new curriculum, creating a shell on our course management system (CMS), continuously revising the curriculum and CMS shell to adapt to ongoing new requests from the program committee, and working with students to accommodate a variety of needs around attendance, homework completion, accommodations for life events, etc. I'd thought I had managed all of this well until I received course evaluations that weren't just negative but downright snarky. I had brought snacks on the day we did SETs, and one student even complained about the snacks (apparently, she did not like Diet Snapple). I was baffled as I read evaluations that I have never gotten in my other classes, such as, "My teacher was too abrasive and rude for me to develop any feelings stronger than contempt and dislike for her." Or, "My professor was extremely scattered, confusing, and mercurial." I racked my brain to try to identify anything I might have said or done to make one or more students feel this way but was left unsure about when I might have given them that impression. I realized I was being evaluated on personality, likeability, and delivery rather than on whether I had taught the content the program committee had asked me to teach.

The evaluations made me feel like I had failed on multiple levels. I had failed to teach the course well, failed to read my students' feelings and needs as I'd taught the course, and failed to give my students what they needed. When several students ended the term on academic probation, I wondered whether a negative experience in my class had been a factor, and I felt like I had failed to set them up for a successful college experience. Also, since quite a few of my colleagues had received rave reviews about their courses, I couldn't help but internalize the failure as something that was specifically wrong with me or with my teaching.

Although the sane part of my brain told me that I was probably obsessing more than I should about comments that a couple of eighteen-year-olds might have written without giving it too much thought, I also felt like my college's SET and promotion processes almost required me to worry about the possible ways their words could affect my career. I received these evaluations the term before I was required to submit my post-tenure review and the year before I planned to submit my application to be promoted to Full Professor. The SETs were from a new program that administrators at our college were looking at closely. The negative SETs were from the most recent term, which members of the tenure committee might be most likely to read. Despite twelve years of strong evaluations, I felt like I now had a stain on my record. Plus, I would have to spend extensive space within the two pages allowed for my Teaching Reflection discussing these low reviews, which would give me less space to discuss my numerous teaching accomplishments, including teaching 16 different courses, the innovative partnerships I'd established with middle and high schools, or the fact that I had helped found two master's programs. Colleges' use of SETs for evaluation can often mean that a few negative course reviews risk supplanting years of accomplishment.

It was especially galling that documentable evidence of the quality of my teaching carried far less weight than a few eighteen-year-olds' perceptions and recollections of the course. While students' perceptions of the course are certainly an important data point and are information I use when I re-design courses each term, over-reliance on this data to the exclusion of other data creates a biased and unreliable faculty evaluation system. Even when faculty members can demonstrate evidence of extensive preparation, communication, assessment, and student responsiveness through our CMSs, emails, and logs of discussions with students (35 for that one class of 14 students over a period of 8 weeks), administrators and tenure committee members often rely on SETs because they take less time to read and have the deceptive appearance of being objective data.

SETs create a "customer service" culture in which students expect frequent exceptions and accommodations, and these expectations particularly fall on faculty within female-dominated fields (Annan et al., 2013). Particularly when I was pre-tenure, I felt compelled to "accommodate" additional needs and expectations in the hopes that my additional work would be acknowledged on my SETs at the end of the term. Instead, I found there was not a clear correlation between doing more and getting better SETs. While saying "no" to additional requests is almost a guarantee of getting a low SET, agreeing to make accommodations that may not have even been asked of a male faculty member is not a guarantee that I will get higher ratings. In fact, the correlation is often negative; students who require the most time and accommodation are more likely to give lower evaluations. The student I bent over backward to help may forget to do the SET, may give me average ratings since they simply expected female faculty members to do this additional work, or may still give me a negative evaluation if they felt like all of my accommodations still weren't accommodating enough. It often feels like the expectations created by SETs leave me with no clear pathway to prove pedagogical effectiveness.

Other scholars have found that what I've described is not atypical for female faculty. Owen (2019) writes, "Investing more time in teaching comes at a price, often decreasing the amount of time available to spend on scholarly activities that are crucial for successful tenure, promotion, and salary reviews." She further explains that constantly striving to meet this higher standard "can encourage a counterproductive downward spiral for some female faculty and faculty of color because it requires those from underrepresented groups to make a greater investment in teaching in order to receive ratings similar to those received by those who aren't subject to this bias." El-Alayli et al. (2018) describe these expectations made of female faculty as "academic momism" (p. 137), in which female faculty are expected to do the additional emotional labor of being more available, nurturing, accommodating, and supportive. In my department, I call this common practice of doing a lot of additional work to maintain the levels of clarity, availability, and responsiveness expected of female faculty "running around like mother hens with our heads cut off." This additional academic and emotional labor can often take up hours (or even days) of additional work each week—time that is often required on an "on call" basis, which further fragments our schedules. These extra time and energy costs can reduce our productivity in other areas and even our quality of life as it eats into our weekends and evenings. Nevertheless, the additional teaching labor required of female faculty is a non-promotable task (Babcock et al., 2022) that is rarely recognized within our institutions and doesn't usually help us with promotion (Hiller, 2020). Given these expectations, while male faculty members may encounter predictable, manageable, and straightforward pathways toward tenure and promotion, female faculty members may encounter an asymptotic curve where it's impossible to fully reach the institution's definition of "successful" teaching, service, and research.

In the case of my optional one-credit course that created such low SETs, I reflected on the many ways I could have done a better job, and I wrote a whole list of ideas for re-designing the course that incorporated my students' feedback. Then, I decided that the benefits of teaching an optional class for a new program were not worth the costs. The extensive time investment in developing the course, making constant changes, and responding to extensive student needs—combined with feeling like I'd been penalized for the effort—made the decision easy. I concluded that other faculty might better be able to serve students in that program.

As a white, tenured professor who is also the child of a professor and from an extended family where everyone has college degrees, I want to acknowledge my privilege navigating academia and acknowledge that I didn't experience the same kinds of significant departmental, administrative, or job search limitations that my co-authors did. Working with my colleagues on this chapter made me realize how frequently female faculty make these types of choices, often in areas that have bigger potential effects on their career trajectories. These decisions often end up creating losses for the institutions that over-relied on SET data and for those institutions' current and future students.

CONCLUSION

Many colleges encourage their faculty to shift their pedagogies to growth and asset models of student achievement, and yet they employ SETs, which can implicitly rely on a deficit model—most strongly for faculty members who are women and/or people of color. Colleges encourage faculty to be thoughtful about gender bias and racial biases and to guard against all the subtle ways they can impact classroom cultures and students' learning, and yet they subject their own faculty who are women and/or people of color to evaluation tools, which they KNOW are subject to racial and gender bias. Moreover, if the feedback faculty members are supposed to use isn't reliable, valid, or actionable, how can faculty members use this feedback to improve their own teaching, and what does this process say about how much the institution really values effective teaching?

SETs create the illusion that teaching can be measured objectively. But the literature shows—and our experiences underscore—that objectivity is a fiction. Kowai-Bell et al. (2012) quote an Education professor's thoughts about SETs, who stated that SETs are not an "objective assessment of instructional skills;" rather, SETs measure *how* students "perceive the teacher makes them feel as a learner and an individual" (p. 348). To persevere in an inequitable system of evaluation that privileges white, heteronormative males and disadvantages, professionally and psychologically, female faculty and female faculty of color (as well as male faculty of color), semester after semester, we are compelled to rework and edit the narrative script for students so that they *perceive* and *feel* that learning took place, independent of the evidence of meeting learning outcomes. Chan et al. (2014) write that SETs should focus on student learning outcomes "as opposed to improving only the students' perceptions of the teacher" (p. 286). McMurtrie (2024) writes that colleges and universities continue to administer SETs because the "current system is also easy—and cheap." In sum, SET oversimplifies the complexity of student learning and the instructor-student dynamic and reduces it to a numerical value or Yelp review.

Failure can be generative for faculty who have supportive networks and time to reflect on and implement what they've learned and who have the experience and expertise to contextualize failure without feeling overcome by it (Jungic et al., 2020; Laksov & McGrath, 2020; Timmermans & Sutherland, 2020). And failure can be "sideways" if there were paths that led to new and healthy ways of knowing, being, and emoting (West-Puckett et al., 2023). But none of the conditions that make failure a springboard for growth are in place in most colleges' SET systems. Although people learn the most in the short term from successes and from positive feedback (Eskreis-Winkler, 2020), SETs do not consistently highlight successes, nor do they make room for learning. Even when SETs report positive feedback, they are subject to the same biases as negative SETs, such as feedback based on personality and appearance. In response to negative, baffling, or even spurious feedback, faculty may lose motivation or seek to avoid the issue (Eskreis-Winkler, 2020). In addition, the current system, as it is used by most colleges, doesn't usually provide the structures or opportunities for the support, reflection, contextualization, or guidance toward growth that can make failure meaningful and help faculty grow (Jungic et al., 2020; Laksov & McGrath, 2020; Timmermans & Sutherland, 2020). Instead of engaging in a generative meaning-making process, faculty usually end up reading and processing their SETs on their own (perhaps with a glass of wine) and may end up feeling more isolated (Laksov & McGrath, 2020). As Timmermans and Sutherland (2020) wrote of "failure" in academia:

> Failure is individualised and privatised (Gill, 2009). We are called upon to develop resilience—a quality enabling us to withstand the impact of failures and to persevere. However, the burden of overcoming failure is a solitary pursuit and responsibility. We are not further connected to and lifted up by the communities and cultures in which we work. We are not reassured that failure is a normal dimension of being human. (p. 44)

Such isolation can make faculty feel concerned that they are the only ones getting low evaluations or that their lower evaluations indicate deficits in their teaching ability. It can make SETs feel like something we need to hide, gloss over, mitigate, or even avoid rather than as useful feedback that can help us grow into more effective teachers.

Although managing feelings of failure from low SETs can affect both male and female faculty, the fact that women and people of color (particularly female faculty of color) are more likely to get low SETs—even when they put more time and effort into their courses—suggests that those faculty are more likely to feel isolation, depression, anxiety, and mental exhaustion. The additional time and energy burden imposed by an endless process of improving their courses can negatively affect productivity in other areas, catching women and, particularly, women of color in a "counterproductive downward spiral" in which they are compelled to spend more and more time on their teaching in order to earn scores that their white, male colleagues may be able to earn without so much additional effort (Owen, 2019). Or, as with workplace bullying, continuous negative feedback can cause instructors to disengage, and disengaged instructors aren't as likely to invest extra time or energy innovating their practices, engaging with students or colleagues, or improving their institutions (Hollis, 2015).

When used for hiring, tenure, and promotion, SETs undermine the efforts of universities and colleges to diversify their faculty and teaching staff. Job applicants may preemptively remove themselves from a job search due to worries about low SETs (Walwema), remove themselves from consideration for directing their campus' Writing Center (Silva), or stop teaching an optional course (Null). Consequently, colleges and universities lose the diverse faculty they proclaim to value; female students and students of color lose access to representative faculty members; all students lose exposure to talented faculty who may challenge their thinking and cultivate their skills; and last, our research fields lose the scholarly contributions and narratives of female faculty and faculty of color.

This is not a call to implement SETs better or create a more generative or more reflective process with a cohort of colleagues. This is not about creating better questions on more "observable" behaviors because even those are subject to bias (Boring et al., 2016; MacNell et al., 2015). However, there are other, better ways for instructors to collect and use feedback from students that would be more meaningful. Chan et al. (2014) argue that SETs "should be part of an overall strategic plan that provides reliable triangulated evidence from different perspectives for the improvement of teaching and learning" (p. 286). There are more reliable forms of data instructors can use to demonstrate their teaching effectiveness. For example, faculty members could collect formative student feedback at different points throughout the term as an ongoing reflective practice.

One study revealed that this type of formative feedback improved SET scores at the end of the term (Winchester & Winchester, 2014). Formative feedback allows faculty to apply students' feedback when it can benefit their students; moreover, non-anonymous feedback in the form of student learning reflections offers more meaningful and actionable commentary about the course that benefits students and instructors mutually (Youssef, 2012).

We live in the age of data. Why do colleges rely on a 1960s-era evaluation tool (Wachtel, 1998, cited by Uttl et al., 2016) in the age of email and spreadsheets, plus CMSs that compile data analytics of all course activities (e.g., analytics of site usage by students and instructors, feedback to students, announcements, and email correspondence)? While not all college faculty are comfortable with this level of record retention and even (some might say) surveillance, personnel evaluations that rely on more objective criteria tend to be less biased toward women (Jirjahn & Gesine, 2004). Perhaps one option might be to allow faculty a broader range of choices about what they submit in their evaluation portfolios, such as records of course observations from other instructors, administrators, or faculty; records of interactions with students; student artifacts; course materials; CMS analytics; or other forms of data, including formative and summative course evaluations. Such a process could allow faculty members to provide a more complete picture of what they have achieved and could provide options that could mitigate bias. Hobson and Talbott (2001) broadly define the scholarship of teaching as "the ideology, pedagogy and evaluation of teaching" (p. 26). Based on this definition, the examination of teaching should include a variety of teaching evaluation methods. However, in plenty of instances nationwide, the overreliance on SETs by administrations and search committees has derailed and stalled the career paths of faculty and graduate students.

As long as SETs remain in place, we are forced to endure anonymous attacks, aggregate binders of data to justify our contributions to our department and discipline, knowing full well that our colleagues who benefit from SETs do not have to do the same, and exhaust limited emotional resources and time to appease dissatisfied students and colleagues. If we're going to change this culture of failure that presumes that faculty could learn something of value from discriminating comments about their teaching, it must start with policy changes and drafting a new narrative about teaching and the dialogic and dialectical relationship between faculty and students.

REFERENCES

Annan, S. L., Tratnack, S., Rubenstein, C., Metzler-Sawin, E. & Hulton, L. (2013). An integrative review of student evaluations of teaching: Implications for evaluation of nursing faculty. *Journal of Professional Nursing, 29*(5), 10–24. https://doi.org/10.1016/j.profnurs.2013.06.004.

Arthur, L. (2009). From performativity to professionalism: Lecturers' responses to student feedback. *Teaching in Higher Education, 14*(4), 441–454. https://doi.org/10.1080/13562510903050228.

Babcock, L., Peyser, B., Vesterlund, L. & Weingart, L. (2022, October 5). Female faculty: Beware the non-promotable task—Mentoring, committee work, and other campus service disproportionately burden women. *The Chronicle of Higher Education*. https://www.chronicle.com/article/female-faculty-beware-the-non-promotable-task.

Baldwin, J. (1997). If Black English isn't a language, then tell me, what is? *The Black Scholar: Ebonics, 27*(1), 5–6.

Baslow, S. A. (1995). Student evaluations of college professors: When gender matters. *Journal of Educational Psychology, 87*(4), 656–665. https://doi.org/10.1037/0022-0663.87.4.656.

Beran, T. N. & Rokosh, J. L. (2009). The consequential validity of student ratings: What do instructors really think? *Alberta Journal of Educational Research, 55*(4), 497–511.

Boring, A., Ottoboni, K. & Stark, P. (2016). Student evaluations of teaching (mostly) do not measure teaching effectiveness. *ScienceOpen Research, 0*, 1–11. https://doi.org/10.14293/S2199-1006.1.SOR-EDU.AETBZC.v1.

Boring, A., (2017). Gender biases in student evaluations of teaching. *Journal of Public Economics, 145*, 27–41. https://doi.org/10.1016/j.jpubeco.2016.11.006.

Boswell, S. S. (2016). Ratemyprofessors is hogwash (but I care): Effects of Ratemyprofessors and university-administered teaching evaluations on professors. *Computers in Human Behavior, 56*, 155–162. https://doi.org/10.1016/j.chb.2015.11.045.

Bradley, C. & Holcomb-McCoy, C. (2004). African American counselor educators: Their experiences, challenges, and recommendations. *Counselor Education and Supervision, 43*(4), 258–273. https://doi.org/10.1002/j.1556-6978.2004.tb01851.x.

Brandt, D. & Deborah, B. (2001). *Literacy in American lives.* Cambridge University Press.

Brown, B. (2015). *Rising strong: The reckoning. The rumble. The revolution.* Random House.

Buser, T., Noemi, P. & Wolter, S.C. (2022). Willingness to compete, gender and career choices along the whole ability distribution. *Experimental Economics 25*, 1299–1326. https://doi.org/10.1007/s10683-022-09765-8.

Chan, C., Luk, L. & Zeng, M. (2014). Teachers' perceptions of student evaluations of teaching. *Educational Research and Evaluation, 20*(4), 275–289. https://doi.org/10.1080/13803611.2014.932698.

Clayson, D. E. & Haley, D. A. (2011, Summer). Are students telling us the truth? A critical look at the student evaluation of teaching. *Marketing Education Review, 21*(2), 101–112.

Crumbley, D. L. & Reichelt, K. J. (2009). Teaching effectiveness, impression management, and dysfunctional behavior. *Quality Assurance in Education, 17*(4), 377–392.

Dancy, E. T & Gaetane J. (2014). Faculty of color in higher education: Exploring the intersections of identity, impostorship, and internalized racism. *Mentoring &*

Tutoring: Partnerships in Learning, 22(4), 354–372. https://doi.org/10.1080/13611267.2014.945736.

Davison, E. & Price, J. (2009). How do we rate? An evaluation of online student evaluations. *Assessment & Evaluation in Higher Education, 34*(1), 51–65. https://doi.org/10.1080/02602930801895695.

Edwards, C. W. (2019). Overcoming imposter syndrome and stereotype threat: Reconceptualizing the definition of a scholar. *Taboo: The Journal of Culture and Education, 18*(1), 18–34. https://doi.org/10.31390/taboo.18.1.03.

El-Alayli, A., Hansen-Brown, A. A. & Ceynar, M. (2018). Dancing backwards in high heels: Female professors experience more work demands and special favor requests, particularly from academically entitled students. *Sex Roles, 79*, 136–150. https://doi.org/10.1007/s11199-017-0872-6.

Eskreis-Winkler, L. (2020, May-June). Maybe failure isn't the best teacher. *Harvard Business Review.* https://hbr.org/2020/05/maybe-failure-isnt-the-best-teacher.

Galbraith, C. S., Merrill, G. B. & Kline, D. M. (2012). Are student evaluations of teaching effectiveness valid for measuring student learning outcomes in business related classes? A neural network and Bayesian analyses. *Research in Higher Education, 53*(3), 353–374. https://doi.org/10.1007/s11162-011-9229-0.

Hiller, J. (2020, August 11). After working 50 unpaid hours this week, I fear for my job. *Times Higher Education.* https://www.timeshighereducation.com/blog/im-working-50-unpaid-hours-week-and-i-fear-my-job?fbclid=IwAR27112k45FAPS9NOIhx6FBo3wjRxGNhU7BKTeClDo4TemkJkBdREUAobJo.

Hobson, S. M. & Talbott, D. M. (2001). Understanding student evaluations: What all faculty should know. *College Teaching, 49*(1), 26–31. https://doi.org/10.1080/87567550109595842.

Hollis, L. P. (2015, April-June). Bully university? The cost of workplace bullying and employee disengagement in American higher education. *Sage Open, 52*(2), 1–11. https://doi.org/10.1177/2158244015589997.

Hutchins, H. M. & Rainbolt, H. (2016): What triggers imposter phenomenon among academic faculty? A critical incident study exploring antecedents, coping, and development opportunities. *Human Resource Development International, 20*(3), 194–214. https://doi.org/10.1080/13678868.2016.1248205.

Jirjahn, U. & Gesine, S. (2004). Gender, piece rates and wages: Evidence from matched employer-employee data. *Cambridge Journal of Economics, 28*(5), 683–704. https://doi.org/10.1093/cje/beh027.

Jungic, V. J., Creelman, D., Bigelow, A., Côté, E., Harris, S., Joordens, S., Ostafichuk, P., Riddell, J., Toulouse, P. & Yoon, J. (2020). Experiencing failure in the classroom and across the university. *International Journal for Academic Development, 25*(1), 31–42.

Kendi, I. X. (2019). *How to be an antiracist.* One World.

Kornell, N. & Hausman, H. (2016, April 25). Do the best teachers get the best ratings? *Frontiers in Psychology, 7*, 570. https://doi.org/10.3389/fpsyg.2016.00570.

Kowai-Bell, N., Guadagno, R. E., Little, T. E. & Ballew, J. L. (2012). Professors are people too: The impact of informal evaluations of professors on students and professors. *Social Psychology of Education, 15*(3), 337–351. https://doi.org/10.1007/s11218-012-9181-7.

Laksov, K. B. & McGrath, C. (2020). Failure as a catalyst for learning: Towards deliberate reflection in academic development work. *International Journal for Academic Development, 25*(1), 1–4. https://doi.org/10.1080/1360144X.2020.1717783.

Lindahl, M. & Unger, M. (2010). Cruelty in student teaching evaluations. *College Teaching,* 58(3), 71–76.

Littleford, L. N., Ong, K. S., Tseng, A., Milliken, J. C. & Humy, S. L. (2010). Perceptions of European American and African American instructors teaching race-focused courses. *Journal of Diversity in Higher Education, 3*(4), 230–244. https://doi.org/10.1037/a0020950.

MacNell, L., Driscoll, A. & Hunt, A. (2015). What's in a name: Exposing gender bias in student ratings of teaching. *Journal of Collective Bargaining in the Academy,* Article 52. http://thekeep.eiu.edu/jcba/vol0/iss10/52.

McMurtrie, B. (2024, February 6). Teaching evaluations are broken. Can they be fixed? *The Chronicle of Higher Education.* https://www.chronicle.com/article/teaching-evaluations-are-broken-can-they-be-fixed.

Mengel, F., Sauermann, J. & Zölitz, U. (2017, September). Gender bias in teaching evaluations [Discussion Paper Series, No. 11000]. Institute of Labor Economics (IZA), Bonn.

Miles, P. & House, D. (2015). The tail wagging the dog: An overdue examination of student teaching evaluations. *International Journal of Higher Education* 4(2), 116–126. https://doi.org/10.5430/ijhe.v4n2p116.

Mitchell, K. M. & Martin, J. (2018). Gender bias in student evaluations. *PS: Political Science & Politics,* 51(3), 648–652. https://doi.org/10.1017/S104909651800001X.

Owen, A. (2019, June 24). The next lawsuits to hit higher education. *Inside Higher Ed.* https://www.insidehighered.com/views/2019/06/24/relying-often-biased-student-evaluations-assess-faculty-could-lead-lawsuits-opinion?utm_source=naicu.

Pittman, C. T. (2010). Race and gender oppression in the classroom: The experiences of women faculty of color with white male students. *Teaching Sociology,* 38(3), 183–196. https://doi.org/10.1177/0092055X10370120.

Reid, L. D. (2010). The role of perceived race and gender in the evaluation of college teaching on RateMyProfessors.com. *Journal of Diversity in Higher Education, 3*(3), 137. https://doi.org/10.1037/a0019865.

Rivera, L. A & Tilcsik, A. (2019). Scaling down inequality: Rating scales, gender bias, and the architecture of evaluation. *American Sociological Review,* 84(2), 248–274. https://doi.org/10.1177/0003122419833601.

Robinson, J. (2018). *Through their eyes: A grounded theory study of resilience for Black women in counselor education* [Unpublished doctoral dissertation]. The University of Texas at San Antonio.

Roseboro, D. L. (2021). Dismantling the architecture of "good" teaching. In L. U. Taylor (Ed.), *Implications of race and racism in student evaluations of teaching* [Kindle edition] (pp. 43–66). Lexington Books.

Shevlin, M., Banyard, P., Davies, M. & Griffiths, M. (2000). The validity of student evaluation of teaching in higher education: Love me, love my lectures? *Assessment & Evaluation in Higher Education, 25*(4), 397–405. https://doi.org/10.1080/713611436.

Smith, B. P. & Hawkins, B. (2011). Examining student evaluations of Black college faculty: Does race matter? *Journal of Negro Education 80*(2), 149–162.

Spooren, P., Brockx, B. & Mortelmans, D. (2013). On the validity of student evaluation of teaching: The state of the art. *Review of Educational Research, 83*(4), 598–642. https://doi.org/10.3102/0034654313496870.

Spooren, P. & Christiaens, W. (2017). I liked your course because I believe in (the power of) student evaluations of teaching (SET). Students' perceptions of a teaching evaluation process and their relationships with SET scores. *Studies in Educational Evaluation, 54*, 43–49. https://doi.org/10.1016/j.stueduc.2016.12.003.

Sprague, J. & Massoni, K. (2005). Student evaluations and gendered expectations: What we can't count can hurt us. *Sex Roles, 53*(11–12), 779–793.

Storage, D., Horne, Z., Cimpian, A. & Leslie, S. J. (2016). The frequency of "brilliant" and "genius" in teaching evaluations predicts the representation of women and African Americans across fields. *PloS One, 11*(3), Article 0150194.

Taylor, L. U. (2021). Their voices must be heard. In L. U. Taylor (Ed.), *Implications of race and racism in student evaluations of teaching* [Kindle edition] (pp. 17–40). Lexington Books.

Timmermans, J. A. & Sutherland, K. A. (2020). Wise academic development: Learning from the 'failure' experiences of retired academic developers. *International Journal for Academic Development, 25*(1), 31–42.

Uttl, B., White, C. A. & Gonzalez, D. W. (2017). Meta-analysis of faculty's teaching effectiveness: Student evaluation of teaching ratings and student learning are not related. *Studies in Educational Evaluation, 54*, 22–42.

Wachtel, H. K. (1998). Student evaluation of college teaching effectiveness: A brief review. *Assessment & Evaluation in Higher Education, 23*(2), 191–212, https://doi.org/10.1080/0260293980230207.

Weir, K. (2013). *Feel like a fraud*. American Psychological Association. https://www.apa.org/gradpsych/2013/11/fraud.

West-Puckett, S., Caswell, N. I. & Banks, W. P. (2023). *Failing sideways: Queer possibilities for writing assessment*. Utah State University Press.

Winchester, T. M. & Winchester, M. K. (2014). A longitudinal investigation of the impact of faculty reflective practices on students' evaluations of teaching. *British Journal of Educational Technology, 45*(1), 112–124. https://doi.org/10.1111/bjet.12019.

Yao, Y. & Grady, M. L. (2005). How do faculty make formative use of student evaluation feedback? A multiple case study. *Journal of Personnel Evaluation in Education, 18*(2), 107–126. https://doi.org/10.1007/s11092-006-9000-9.

Youssef, L. S. (2012). Using student reflections in the formative evaluation of instruction: A course-integrated approach. *Reflective Practice, 13*(2), 237–254. https://doi.org/10.1080/14623943.2011.626031.

PART 3.

SHORT (BUT BITTER/SWEET) NARRATIVE SNIPPETS OF FAILURE

It can sometimes be tricky determining the who? what? when? where? why? and how? questions of any given failed performance. The contributors to Part Three offer short narratives of failure from multiple intersectional angles and points of view. These authors take a good look in the mirror with accounts of their own experiences with failure. Contributors provide personal and professional snapshots of situations where it's sometimes difficult to pinpoint precisely why and how a failed performance occurred.

Teagan Decker, in **Chapter 8**, "Imposter, Performer, Professional," continues the personal narratives of professional women, started in Chapter 7, as she looks back on her time as a graduate student experiencing haunting imposter-syndrome feelings. In **Chapter 9**, "Self-Sponsored Writing & Academicized Space in FYW (Or, A Failure in Three Moves)," Tyler Gillespie presents a narrative of their failed Instagram essay assignment to explore failure as an important pedagogical moment, as well as to illustrate their trajectory of digital writing pedagogy in FYW (with a few examples from their former students). William Duffy, in **Chapter 10**, "The Afterlife of Unfinished Writing," narrates their coming to terms with something most writing teachers never talk about even though many of us are intimately familiar with it: all the writing we start but never finish. And in **Chapter 11**, "In Pursuit of Industry Knowledge: Always Learning by Often Failing," Michal Horton looks back on their failures to find a job, to pay the bills, to stay positive, and asks, "When is failure valuable?" The author illustrates how, in their personal life, they have adjusted the paradigm, recognizing failure as a re-orienting process—one redirecting them toward experiences that can be meaningful even if not "successful."

Sean Fenty, in **Chapter 12**, "Opening Doors to the Ivory Tower: Helping Students Feel Welcome to Engage in Academic Discourse," tells the story of a former student of theirs who, as a photographer, explored spaces fraught with real peril to life and limb, fueled by the adrenaline of discovery, but as a writer, he switched from writing about his true passion, because he was afraid he'd fail. And in **Chapter 13**, "Standardized Test Writing and the Fear of Failing," Elizabeth Blomstedt reflects on their own experience learning to write in high school in the shadow of No Child Left Behind and examines how that experience influences how they approach teaching writing and critical thinking to today's college students. Jerrice Renita Donelson and Anicca Cox, in **Chapter 14**, "Failure to Launch? Theorizing Rhetorics of Rejection from Graduate Student Perspectives," attempt to explore the terrain of rejection-as-failure by examining the development of their own relational, affective, and community-oriented perspectives in processing realities essential to daily grad-life.

In **Chapter 15**, "The CV of Failure: Making Rejection Visible and Cultivating Growth Mindsets in Doctoral Writers," Dana Driscoll shares their CV of Failure, where they include failed dissertation topics, failed degree programs, and article and grant rejections, offering the "story" behind the publications. Laura Decker, in **Chapter 16**, "Reaping What You Sow: Reframing Academic Rejection as a Community Garden for Writing Studies," reframes academic rejection, using their own narrative as a non-tenure track faculty in writing and describing the way they worked to understand their labor for others' success as a sort of tending to the collective garden of writing studies. In **Chapter 17**, "Using X as Applied Learning in a First-Year Writing Classroom," Jeffrey Jackson laments how their intended goal of making Twitter a vehicle for applied learning in their course never advanced from the embryonic stages. And Mario D'Agostino rounding out Part Three with **Chapter 18**, "'Trust the Process:' Dissertation Gatekeeping, Failure, and Graduate Student Writing," builds on their troubled dissertation-defense experience to highlight the emotive work of writing, as well as the importance of building relationships that support graduate student writers.

CHAPTER 8.

IMPOSTER, PERFORMER, PROFESSIONAL

Teagan Decker
University of North Carolina, Pembroke

I was the assistant director of the writing center when I applied to the PhD program in English Language and Rhetoric in 2002 at the University of Washington, Seattle. I felt lucky to be accepted. During the application process, however, I worried a bit over whether my application was as competitive as those of my new classmates. Since I already worked for the English department as a professional staff person, I had a niggling feeling that my application had been accepted based more on familiarity and the understanding that I wouldn't need funding than on the quality of my materials. And so the anxiety over my writing and my self as an academic began.

Of course, this type of anxiety is not uncommon or new among professionals. In 1978, psychology professor Pauline Clance and psychologist Suzanne Imes wrote in *The Impostor Phenomenon Among High Achieving Women* that "Despite outstanding academic and professional accomplishments, women who experience the imposter phenomenon persist in believing that they are really not bright and have fooled anyone who thinks otherwise" (p. 241). The impostor phenomenon (more commonly called the impostor syndrome) has been documented as a continuing problem for women and people from working-class backgrounds ever since.

On her website, Valerie Young (2023), author of *The Secret Thoughts of Successful Women* (2011), gives readers an opportunity to consider whether or not they are suffering from impostor syndrome by taking this short quiz:

1. Do you secretly worry you're not as bright, capable, or qualified as everyone "thinks" you are?
2. Do you chalk your accomplishments up to luck, timing, connections or computer error?
3. Do you believe "If I can do it, anybody can"?
4. Do you agonize over the smallest flaws in your work?
5. Are you crushed by even constructive criticism, seeing it as evidence of your ineptness?

6. When you do succeed, do you secretly feel you fooled them again?
7. Do you worry that it's just a matter of time before you're "found out?"

Looking back now on my time as a graduate student, I remember precisely those feelings. I was from a low-income background, the first in my family to attend college, and a single mom on welfare and food stamps while working toward my BA and MA degrees. While in my doctoral program, my husband drove to the food bank once a week to ease the burden on our income. I often felt deeply frustrated that I would have to wait and work for so many years before earning my PhD and finally earning a middle-income salary. My gender, background, and financial status all pointed to a person with impostor syndrome: someone who doesn't feel that they fit in, who doesn't feel that they deserve what they have worked for.

TAKING MY QUALIFYING EXAMS AND THE THREAT OF UNMASKING

I did well in my PhD courses and even managed to publish seminar papers as articles. But, as I was studying for qualifying exams, I confessed to one of my committee members fears that the oral exams would "unmask" me, that, without the structure of a course where I could maneuver to please the instructor, I would reveal that I had no idea what I was doing. The committee member then told me, "It's normal to feel that way. I feel like an impostor every day." She was a successful, fully tenured, and well-published professor. Even with this sympathetic advice, I remained unsettled about the prospect of representing, through writing, nearly a year's worth of learning over the course of a weekend. The week prior to exam weekend found me beset by various ailments. One day, I would come down with a cold; the next day, the flu would threaten. After prompting the anxious specter of sitting for exams while sick in bed, the mysterious ailment would disappear overnight. The pre-exam anxiety played itself out in time for the actual work of writing, and I felt satisfied (although still worried until the feedback came in) with my performance.

The feedback, when it did arrive, was overwhelmingly positive and went a long way toward curing me of impostor syndrome. When it came time for oral exams, I was confident and comfortable; the committee was an interested and sympathetic audience who asked me to expand on the themes I had touched on in the written exams. They had tough questions, of course, but the tough questions were asked with the expectation that I would answer them well—and I did. When the exam was over, they presented me with wine, flowers, and hugs—along with my official candidacy.

THE JOB INTERVIEW PERFORMANCE

But, of course, before I could move from my exams (and dissertation) to a professorship, I had one more major trial to endure, one more test of the impostor syndrome to overcome: the job search. I found myself fully marshaling all of my authorial powers up to that point—updating CVs down to the minute, putting together the teaching portfolio, sample assignments, sample course syllabuses, meticulous cover letters and statements of teaching philosophy, and spell-checked email responses . . . Then needing to present the person behind the pen and paper.

My written application materials generated quite a lot of interest, and my schedule quickly filled up with interviews. None of them seemed to go well, however. I wasn't able to present myself in person as well as I did on paper. I couldn't summon up the level of self-presentation needed to show interviewers that I was worth inviting to a second (on-campus) interview. After suffering through the post-interview weeks with no callbacks, I applied to a late-advertising university and was asked to do a phone interview. Determined to finally show my true worth to a hiring committee and quite aware that my "regular" self wasn't communicating that worth, I borrowed another persona for the interview. As part of my dissertation work, I had conducted a research interview with an administrator at the University of Washington, Sheila Edwards Lange. Lange struck me as the most poised, articulate, intelligent, and professionally passionate person I had ever met. Listening to the tapes of the research interview, I realized I could *be* Sheila Edwards Lange for my own job interview.

And, somehow, it worked. The hiring committee invited me to a campus interview where I continued to perform this poised-and-articulate self and subsequently was offered a position. I deliberately took on a false persona, put on a mask, performed as an impostor. Or, perhaps, I used Lange's persona as a tool to bring the polish of my written self to my in-person self, to give me the confidence to behave as if I were qualified for, because I *was*, in fact, qualified for, an academic appointment. Either way, an actual physical job contract came in the mail a few months later.

QUESTIONING THE IMPOSTER SYNDROME

Clance and Imes are reportedly dismayed by the way their 1978 work has been used to pathologize the experience of women in the workplace and would prefer that their "phenomenon" had not morphed into a "syndrome" in popular culture (Jamison, 2023). In fact, the whole idea of imposter syndrome has come under scrutiny. Ruchika Tulshyan and Jodi-Ann Burey (2021) have pushed back against the pathologizing of women's experiences and questioned the imposter syndrome's ubiquitous status as a diagnosis of insecurity and self-doubt. In their article "Stop Telling Women They Have Imposter Syndrome" (2021), they argue that "imposter syndrome puts the blame on individuals, without accounting for the historical and cultural contexts that are foundational to how it manifests in both women of color and white women. Imposter syndrome directs our view toward fixing women at work instead of fixing the places where women work."

Could the failure of my job interviews have been the fault of the nature of the interviews themselves? Looking back now, sixteen years later, I remember the uncomfortable and unfamiliar feeling of wearing a suit (that I bought at the local thrift store). Of walking into upscale hotel suites (as was the practice at that time) to meet with committee members. Of feeling off guard and wrong-footed in the face of unanticipated questions. And while some of this is a matter of me having a hard time rising to the occasion, job search committees could take some steps to accommodate those who might be less adept at this particular professional hurdle. A colleague of mine recently interviewed for a position where all questions were provided at least a week in advance. As someone who also struggles with interviews, he appreciated the opportunity to think and prepare and felt confident going into the interview.

IMPOSTER(S) FOR LIFE

A large part of my education has been to learn to accept success as well as failure, to manage feelings of inadequacy and self-doubt and to nurture feelings of confidence and self-assuredness. My experiences are in some ways similar and in some ways very different from many other people's, but if I can offer anything from my experience, it is perhaps that the life of the academic necessarily is the life of an impostor—one who is continuously posturing, masking, unmasking, borrowing, building confidence, suffering through insecurity.

Maybe my background has formed an identity that is especially prone to imposturing, or maybe my background has led me to more acutely question the legitimacy of my own persona. I've pushed my way through hurdles, sometimes blindly, with what seems like sheer force of will, using whatever tools and personas I find at my disposal.

In the end, though, what I have learned from these experiences is not how to stop being an impostor but how to more successfully perform my professional identity in satisfying, exciting, productive ways both on the page and in the flesh.

I may never truly be cured. And maybe I don't need to be.

REFERENCES

Clance, P. R. & Imes, S. A. (1978). The impostor phenomenon in high achieving women: Dynamics and therapeutic intervention. *Psychotherapy: Theory, Research and Practice, 15*(3), 241–47. https://mpowir.org/wp-content/uploads/2010/02/Download-IP-in-High-Achieving-Women.pdf.

Jamison, L. (2023, February 6). Why everyone feels like they're faking it. *The New Yorker*. https://www.newyorker.com/magazine/2023/02/13/the-dubious-rise-of-impostor-syndrome.

Tulshyan, R. & Burey, J. (2021, February 11). Stop telling women they have imposter syndrome. *Harvard Business Review*. https://hbr.org/2021/02/stop-telling-women-they-have-imposter-syndrome.

Young, V. (2011). *The secret thoughts of successful women*. Currency.

Young, V. (2023, June 13). Imposter syndrome quiz. *Imposter Syndrome Institute*. https://impostorsyndrome.com/infographics/impostor-syndrome-quiz/.

CHAPTER 9.

SELF-SPONSORED WRITING & ACADEMICIZED SPACE IN FYW (OR, A FAILURE IN THREE MOVES)

Tyler Gillespie
Ringling College of Art and Design

1.

This story starts with a breakup.

After my first love dumped me, I moved from Florida to Chicago because I needed a change. My college friends lived in the Windy City, and its winter matched my mood. I moved in with an activist who organized a monthly body-positive dance party at a local bar. Through her, I became friends with a group of queer artists and writers. We tried to both write and dance away the cold as we later hosted poetry readings and made zines together.

My roommate and then I started a queer artists' collective. We called it Failed Attempt. We celebrated failure, celebrated the act of trying. In *The Queer Art of Failure* (2011), Judith (Jack) Halberstam says queers fail "exceptionally well" and posits that "under certain circumstances failing, losing, forgetting, unmaking, undoing, unbecoming, not knowing may in fact offer more creative, more cooperative, more surprising ways of being in the world" (p. 3). Our collective set out to reimagine a way of being. We centered moments deemed failures by a society focused on success.

This story won't spend too much time in the theoretical. But I want to acknowledge concepts of failure as connected to material conditions. It can prove difficult for our students to reframe failure. Many associate it with traumatic experiences—the team they didn't make, the grade they didn't get. My experiences as a queer writer and teacher inform the ways I think about who gets to fail and in what capacity. Success, a type of survival. Only certain kinds of people can fail safely. A writing classroom provides a space to expand who gets to do so.

The collective I started with my roommate failed along with our friendship. I moved into a new apartment and applied for an editorial role at the

DOI: https://doi.org/10.37514/PER-B.2024.2494.2.09

fancy magazine I wrote for in the city. I didn't get this position. I then did what so many before me have done in times of existential crisis: I applied to graduate school.

2.

This story discusses a failure in grad school.

During grad school, I taught first-year composition. I wanted to bring a platform many students used socially into the classroom. I asked them to write an Instagram essay. I figured if students liked to use Instagram, then it would help foster their writing in class as well.

Use hashtags, I told them. *Emojis, too*!

I thought my class of "digital natives" would get excited about the assignment. But I was wrong. They didn't get into it, and it seemed to be one of their least favorite assignments of the semester. Aside from some functional issues, I identified two main problems: (1) not everyone used or wanted to be on Instagram, and (2) those who used Instagram didn't want the requirement to use it for class.

Youngjoo Yi and Alan Hirvela (2010) assert that sites of self-sponsored writing can, at times, provide students with spaces to vent about schoolwork and find community with peers. Their research subject enacted a different persona online in her role as a student. She seemed shy in class, but the "exasperation boiling beneath her calm exterior needed a release in order for Elizabeth to maintain (i.e., regulate) a reasonable degree of equilibrium in her life" (Yi & Hirvela, 2010, p. 104). This self-sponsored writing allowed her to negotiate her life outside of class.

Students often produce meaningful writing outside the classroom. The incorporation of these sites into the curriculum acknowledges a range of literacies. But it can be tricky. Students play with language and identity through self-sponsored writing. We don't want to transform them from fun to her class assignment. If it's an assignment, then that means there's a grade attached to it. This shift can change how students view and use an important site for their writing lives.

I've had much better results discussing social media posts as text to "understand students' writing activities and digital literacy practices within digital environments" (Buck, 2012, p. 36). I've taught a Twitter thread as a literacy narrative. I've asked students to analyze rhetorical situations of social media posts. I've also given students sites of self-sponsored writing for their assignments, but I don't require it.

The twenty-four-hour writing log assignment makes connections from self-sponsored writing to our class. I often ask students to document a full day of their writing across all platforms. These platforms range from composing an email to sending a message on Snapchat. Students usually turn in pages of data. We can then use this data to introduce discussions of writing practices. We also talk about rhetorical situations. I ask if they'd write a text message to their mom in the same way they'd write it to their best friend.

Kevin Roozen (2012) urges us to create first-year writing (FYW) curriculum design that incorporates the inclusion of self-sponsored writing without making them seem like precursors to the actual writing of the academy. He says it's important for us to frame why the "weaving together of multiple literate engagements is a key element of literate development throughout the lifespan" (p. 123–124). I've had the most success when I can weave together their literate engagement into our classroom by giving them the option—and not the requirement—to utilize their self-sponsored writing sites.

3.

This story moves back to the beginning to end with a conclusion.

After graduate school, I moved back home to Florida. I currently work as a FYW specialist at a private art college. This semester, I brought zines with me into class.

I first collaborated on "Failed Attempt" zines in Chicago a decade earlier. I had just wanted to make some cool stuff with my friends. Now, those failures have become useful experiences for my FYW students. I can talk about my self-sponsored writing of zines as a form of collaboration, experimentation, and multimodal writing. I can also talk about their tradition of queer activism and DIY publishing in marginalized communities.

In a unit on research, I discussed zines as a potential genre for their research. They circulate in communities and to a particular audience. I asked students to think about how effective arguments in zines would look different than in an academic research paper. The use of zines in curriculum can challenge the status quo. They create alternative discourse and models for "a variety of vehicles for meaning making" (Lonsdale, 2015, p. 12). The genre allows for discussion of meaning-making activities as embedded in specific contexts.

Because of this, assessment strategies prove a major concern. Requiring zines might reduce their potential for self-sponsored writing. The genre has roots in punk music and counter-culture movements. Their use in a classroom, to some, may even be antithetical to the genre's original purposes. Tobi Jacobi (2007) suggests zines shouldn't receive grades because of their roots in self-sponsored discourse and suggests a more appropriate assessment model would be for students to establish "shared goals and expectations rather than genre expectations" (p.

48). This process can take a long time, sometimes a full unit or a semester-long project. Instructors must consider these and other implications when using zines in their classrooms.

My students this semester liked zines as a genre, but not one of them made one for their research project. I'd given them the option of delivering their research in three different genres: (1) a traditional academic paper, (2) an op-ed, or (3) a creative project. I've written in all three genres. Their differences presented productive discussion of genre, writing conventions, and audience. I assumed the art school students would choose the creative option, but yet again, I was wrong. Most of them chose the traditional research paper or op-ed format (there's probably a further case study in there somewhere).

The students' other classes required them to complete visually creative projects. Some wanted a break. They also wanted to further develop confidence in their academic writing skills or try a new genre in the op-ed.

None of my students composed a zine, but I don't consider this a failure as I might have done earlier in my career. Students showed interest in the genre, but, for various reasons, didn't want to make one for our class. That doesn't mean they won't create one on their own later. Their future selves might make zines to process a move or build community or one day talk about the generative possibility of failure in a classroom of their own.

REFERENCES

Buck, A. (2012). Examining digital literacy practices on social network sites. *Research in the Teaching of English 47*(1), 9–38. https://doi.org/10.58680/rte201220670.

Halberstam, J. (2011). *The queer art of failure.* Duke University Press.

Jacobi, T. (2007). The zine project: Innovation or oxymoron? *The English Journal 96*(4), 43–49.

Lonsdale, C. (2015) Engaging the "othered": Using zines to support student identities. *Language Arts Journal of Michigan, 30*(2), Article 4. https://doi.org/10.9707/2168-149X.2066.

Roozen, K. (2012). Comedy stages, poets projects, sports columns, and Kinesiology 341: Illuminating the importance of basic writers' self-sponsored literacies. *Journal of Basic Writing 31*(1), 99–132.

Yi, Y & A. Hirvela. (2010). Technology and "self-sponsored" writing: A case study of a Korean-American adolescent. *Computers and Composition 27*(2), 94–111. https://doi.org/10.1016/j.compcom.2010.03.005.

CHAPTER 10.
THE AFTERLIFE OF UNFINISHED WRITING

William Duffy
University of Memphis

In my office, there is a cheap metal cart that is an unencumbered 4-foot roll from my desk. Each drawer in the cart holds the drafts of unfinished writing projects. Specifically, this cart is for writing that has a material history traceable through conference presentations, journal submissions, seminar papers, and similar occasions when writing gets "finished" for a spell before further development. This cart is for writing that has been iterated and shaped but still needs attention; it's been temporarily suspended; it needs time to marinate. These drawers aren't for failed or abandoned writing. As Stephen King would call them, these are trunk projects—manuscripts you put aside until the time is right to complete them.

Composition instructors are trained to understand that writers develop by learning to navigate the processes through which writing itself develops. Writers-writing move through recursive processes of drafting, revising, and editing. Flip open a stack of English Language Arts or First-Year Writing textbooks, and you'll likely see a variety of conceptual models that enact the "writing is a process" dictum. Prewrite, write, rewrite. Brainstorm, outline, draft, revise, edit. Freewrite, excavate, situate. One single pedagogical resource for legal writers incorporates these four different acronyms to explain the writing process: RAFT, MEAL, ARMS, CUPS (Sneddon, 2020). I don't know what these mean.

So some process curriculums are acronymed, some rhyme, some are hard to describe. Most process curriculums try too hard.

Some of my unfinished writing is stored in digital files. Many I keep on a third-party server "in" the cloud. Other files I keep on my devices, which themselves are backed up in (or is it on?) the cloud. Bruno Latour (2011) helped me understand that whether paper or pixels, the material traces of writing are, in fact, material even if we give infrastructure airy names. So, while not physically within reach, these files have a material significance, a material *weight*, even if I can't feel their materiality. These folders store writing projects I've started but haven't articulated to the extent I have those cart manuscripts. A lot of writing in these folders are single, one-page documents with only a few lines of notes.

DOI: https://doi.org/10.37514/PER-B.2024.2494.2.10

These one-offers have an excess of ellipses, like I'm signaling to myself that these ideas can be developed later. All that matters is securing a basic mold of the thing before the weather gets it.

~~~

When I say process curriculums try too hard, what I really mean is that they are too presumptive about the life cycle of a writing project. Specifically, they presume the conception and delivery of *something* more or less *finished*. There is a presumed finality, that is, an ending. While I've vacillated in my own definitions and representations of the writing process, I've lately grown more interested in coming to terms with something most writing teachers never talk about, probably because they were never taught how to talk about it even though most of us are intimately familiar with it: all the writing we start but never finish.

Some unfinished writing I keep bundled in a tattered file folder that I've sorted through each time I've moved offices. These are projects I've abandoned but still feel the need to possess in their final unfinished forms. I don't have plans to return to these manuscripts, but obviously, they hold value to me. One is a seminar paper from grad school that offers what I still think is a novel rhetorical interpretation of Margery Kempe's penchant for crying. But I can't imagine returning to this manuscript, but neither can I imagine throwing it out. These manuscripts are material evidence of labor that I don't want lost.

I get it, though. From a programmatic perspective, can writing programs practically accommodate the presence of unfinished writing? Composition courses are, by default, shaped around synthetic writing experiences complete with predesigned exigencies, constraints, and assessments. But as a writer myself, I've learned that I can't finish every writing project I start. Sometimes work or family demands take priority. Sometimes, I lose interest. Sometimes, the reason is much simpler: I can't finish. Chalk it up to writer's block or any of its related aphorisms (*the well's run dry, you hit a wall*), but these trials are more complicated than that. Sometimes, self-doubt has something to do with it, a felt sense of inability or lack of preparedness. But mostly, I simply hit the limits of what I know/can articulate. To put this another way, I get to a point when I don't know how to get the piece where it needs to go, and that's if I know where it's going, which isn't always the case.

~~~

While I've happily abandoned some projects, others have proven much harder to give up. They have a claim on my thinking. But isn't this true of all writers? That's why I'm writing this now: to give myself the space to consider how to account for all this unfinished writing. As a writing professor, however, I must admit I hope this inquiry proves useful pedagogically. I'm not interested in building a pedagogy for unfinished writing; I simply want to put voice to the presence of something that we should talk about more publicly, more often.

By the way, I've written at least five different versions of this essay. I considered including a list of all the writing I haven't finished, but the list kept growing. That I'm having trouble finishing this piece—the topic of which is unfinished writing—is an irony I'd rather not take as artifice. But here we are.

If I had to frame this essay like I would a more conventional academic piece, I'd begin with a grammatically strong but conceptually abstract claim, something like *All writing has an afterlife*. Then I'd explain when I publish an article, for example, that piece of writing takes on a life as others read it, think about it, reference it. It lives as lines on my CV, a record in a yearly report, and as a thing that I can share with others. Some of my writing has had a quieter afterlife, like the paper I wrote that won "Co-Third Place" in an essay competition during my junior year of college. But what about all the writing we start but don't finish, writing that we *want* to finish but can't, writing that compels us with its potentiality? What about writing that wants to be written, that is? This writing has an afterlife too. In fact, I'd wager that for some writers, their unfinished writing is more imminent than the writing they've finished.

"There has never been a scholar who really, as a scholar, deals with ghosts. A traditional scholar does not believe in ghosts—nor in all that could be called the virtual space of spectrality," notes Jaques Derrida (2006, p. 12). I'm not sure about this. If we consider the specter of unfinished writing, what scholars lack are sanctioned spaces to embrace these ghosts as ghosts. Hauntology, Derrida's territory here, "does not ask 'to be or not to be'; it claims instead the simultaneous playfulness of 'to be and not to be'" (Rahimi, 2021, p. 4). Unfinished writing is and is not.

~~~

But finished writing is and is not, too, depending on the context. As John Gallegher (2020) observes, "While print writers have in some ways always dealt with the afterlife of their texts, such as novelists going on book tours or journalists going on television to discuss an article, the internet, and social media have greatly intensified this afterlife, as well as made the activities of this afterlife extremely heterogeneous" (p. 4), a point he makes in reference to the ways writers can and do update their writing after it has already gone public. But I share Gallegher's point because the technological affordances writers increasingly have at their disposal make it harder to forget about or otherwise discard writing they won't finish.

It can be gauche, but sometimes I like it when writers talk about their writing as if it has a life of its own. I get it. Sometimes, it's helpful to hold up our writing at a remove, especially the writing we haven't finished, and treat it like it's something foreign or inexplicable. Such a method can help us think about the place we have let this unfinished writing occupy in our attention. That's why I think we have to live with our not-yet-writing, walk around with it, carry it upstairs each night, and put it to sleep. But this not-yet-writing might also turn into the always-writing or, more accurately, the always-not-writing you're doing.

As someone who grew up in religious circles, I can't not channel the proverbial wisdom from Ecclesiastes about the ubiquity of change. For every writing there is a season of loving and hating, killing and healing, rending and sowing. There is a season for birth, for renewal, and there is a season for death, for letting go.

Indeed, some unfinished writing haunts us from the grave. Such unfinished writing is both a burden and a blessing for the ones on whom the responsibility for its care now rests. I'm thinking of a former student, Mattie, and the stack of papers she cradled in her lap. She was in my office to discuss how to finish the novel her daughter started before she died. Mattie was auditing the course, she explained, to gain confidence. "I have to finish Sasha's book," Mattie said.

~~~

Sometimes, I tell my students that writing can't be learned; it can only be practiced. It's an aphorism that applies to any disciplined activity, of course, but I like this claim because procedural knowledge rarely translates into incorporated knowledge—the knowledge that grows from lived experience. Experience is what tells me unfinished writing can be no less real and no less immediate than the writing we've finished. Experience is what tells me unfinished writing is stubborn in its insistence that the potential of the thing is worth the burden of writing it.

What is the value of coming to terms with our unfinished writing? For me at least, it matters that there are things we can always return to if we choose, even if this returning is a chimera, a useful fiction we deploy to convince ourselves that the well isn't dry, that writing is, really and truly, a process.

REFERENCES

Derrida, J. (2006). *Specters of Marx*. Routledge.
Gallagher, J. (2020). *Update culture and the afterlife of digital writing*. Utah State University Press.
Latour, B. (2011). Networks, societies, spheres: Reflections of an actor-network theorist. *International Journal of Communication, 5*, 796–810.
Rahimi, S. (2021). *The hauntology of everyday life*. Palgrave MacMillan.
Sneddon, K. J. (2020). More than IRAC: Acronyms to support the writing process. *Perspectives: Teaching Legal Research and Writing, 28*(1), 26–31.

CHAPTER 11.
IN PURSUIT OF INDUSTRY KNOWLEDGE: ALWAYS LEARNING BY OFTEN FAILING

Michal Horton

Baylor University

I am a PhD of just a few years, with a faculty position teaching writing in a business school. I've nurtured company relationships that bring internships to my students. I've stepped into an Advisory Head of Communications role at a tech start-up, which keeps me relevant and involved in industry. I wouldn't say I've "made it," as my career is still quite new, but it is finally heading in the direction I wanted it to go. Just a few years prior, life was disrupted by financial instability: Having left the security of my graduate stipend to pursue industry work, I finished my dissertation with nickels and dimes in my bank account, months of job rejections, and much pessimism about my professional future.

Now that my career is coming back together, it would be easy to package my failures in clichés. *Failure is an essential ingredient to success; I overcame and persevered against all odds; The hard times built character that made me who I am today.* These trite expressions do ring true, but they also ring hollow because they premise failure's value on its relationship to success. When I was mid-failure, when I feared getting lost in the gaps on my resumé, I realized the precariousness of failure's value. I never heard it said, but I did find it loudly implied that people value failure when it is coupled to success in a "happily ever after" narrative. The fairytale ending told in a failure-to-success paradigm is a popular refrain, one in which Failure is cast as the villain that needs to be overcome so that Success can win the day. Yet, failure itself is a valuable life process and an invaluable way of learning. Failure has brought me insight and knowledge that success could not, making it the true heroine of my story—one I will tell in reverse.

Fall 2020-Fall 2022. I am in my third year as a Clinical Assistant Professor teaching business communication, a course that represents the meeting ground between academia and industry that I long pursued. I enjoy the teaching emphasis my role as clinical gives. I find my teacherly ethos taking distinct shape and motivating my scholarship. While I have by no means arrived at the pinnacle of my career, I see that my efforts are bearing fruit for students and for myself. In my first two years, I developed partnerships with start-up companies to create an internship pathway in my course; I have become Advisory Head of Communications at a start-up company to stay engaged in industry; I have developed meaningful relationships with students and colleagues, which have initiated new projects and fostered an excitement for my work life. My career is becoming what I dreamed of—a blend of intellectual rigor and industry impact.

Spring 2020. Now, let's go backward. As an adjunct and doctoral candidate on the job market, my first campus visit approached while I had about $300 in my bank account. I needed to buy a suit, but I also needed to keep enough money for groceries. The JC Penney sales rack produced something passable, and I accessorized it with the bluff that life was not falling down around me, though indeed, it seemed to be. When I went into the job talk for my current position, I had an agonizing 20 months behind me: lots of work, little pay, utter failure. The day of the interview felt surreal as if it was happening around me but not to me. I moved through it on a cloud, performing well enough to get the first offer. It was my top pick, so I signed the contract and withdrew my name from other interviews, which included some for tenure-track positions. I wanted the clinical role because of its location in a business school, where I could activate the ideals of the humanities in a context where those ideals are very much needed. I believed then, as I do now, that the humanities matter across disciplinary contexts, so I set out to do cross-disciplinary work.

Fall 2019. At the beginning of this academic year, I took an adjunct position along with tutoring hours, writing work, and a local coordinator role at an academic exchange program for high schoolers. I was also hitting the job market, which, as everyone knows, is "itself a full-time job," and I was in the thick of dissertation writing. My head was spinning with the clutter of daily to-do lists, and despite the exhaustion of working hard and working always, the financial payoff consistently fell well below my monthly expenses. I am no outlier in feeling the pinch of working for the privilege of working, of taking on side jobs so that I could advance my long-term career dreams. The strain of output, the discouragement of no measurable or guaranteed return, posed a haunting question, "What if my failure does not lead to success; is it still valuable?" While I had reached the threshold of financially viable academic employment, I hadn't yet crossed over it. I had the wearied feeling of free climbing up a steep rock face, nearing the top, with intense awareness of how far I could fall back down.

Spring and Summer 2019. Prior to my adjunct role, I worked a part-time, remote customer service position. Every second of my shift was monitored, recorded, and ranked. The intensity of big corporate, low-level jobs like this one filled me with new respect for the hourly employees carrying companies on their backs like so many ants burdened by a load well over their body weight.

As a customer service associate, I observed company communication from the ground floor, and I realized how much companies run on writing, an insight that fed my hunger to bring academia and industry meaningfully together in my own career. At this time, I was also taking contract projects for start-ups, even when the pay was meager. I found the rate of exchange worthwhile because I was still gaining experience, and more than anything, I wanted to take my industry experience another step forward. I was in a season of choosing between gas and grocery money, physically and emotionally spent, but still pursuing experience over income with the belief that a larger payoff would come in time.

Fall 2018-Spring 2019. From August to April, I was desperately applying to jobs (any and all jobs), meanwhile maxing out my credit cards. Networking with start-ups got me a $600 project—the only income I made during these months. Still, the work was fascinating, and I was excited to find it required a process that my academic training had prepared me for. I was contracted to research provisional patent applications and help draft one, a process much like writing an academic argument. Patents parallel academic research closely. They require writers to: (1) research existing and like inventions; (2) put prior patents into comparison, a kind of patent lit review; (3) place the company invention into a milieu of prior patents yet also show how it is distinct. These kinds of genre-parallels were common in my freelancing and kept me wanting to learn more.

Summer 2018. I have now arrived at the catalyst of my failure, the first domino to fall and set off a chain reaction of failures: I received a job offer from a start-up tech company, one I had connected with through an internship program. I jumped at this opportunity to take my skills into the workforce, with the long-term goal of ultimately bringing the experience back into my academic research. I was set to begin in data enhancement and then move into technical writing, documenting the standard operating procedures for the company's data entry process as an entry point into higher-level work. In my graduate program, I met with my dissertation committee to plan the process of finishing my PhD remotely so that I could begin my new position. I withdrew from comparable and promising job applications. I forfeited my instructorship. I moved states. And the job vanished. We had drawn up the contract, and the board approved my salary when a hiccup with a partnering company dissolved the income for my position and the need for it altogether.

In the months leading up to the job's appearance and disappearance, I had been researching "alt-ac" or alternative academic pathways for humanities degrees as part of my work as a research assistant.[1] I was also looking into the

---

1   Though Bethany Nowviskie coined "alt-ac" on Twitter in 2009 (Rogers, 2013), the concept of alt-ac and the application of work in humanities to other industries has been around much longer. A notable mismatch in PhD production and available academic positions arose

relevance of humanities degrees in other industries, in contexts completely outside of academia. The research greatly interested me, as I soon found that this area was ripe for work. I noted many bold claims about the relevance of the humanities, like Stephen R. Yarbrough's (2001) statement that "Few industries in the contemporary world could not benefit from the kind of cultural expertise a doctorate in English represents. The fact that those industries are often unaware of those benefits simply illustrates how thoroughly we have hidden our light under a bushel" (106). Such arguments seemed to abound yet stayed largely in the preliminary. They emphasized the potential marketability of PhDs in the humanities, but they maximized on ambiguity. For instance, Christine Kelly (2016) writes: "[T]here are so many options outside academe where you can be your own boss and create a job that fits what you want" (para. 9). This sounded great to me. But what did having "so many options" mean—both in terms of career preparation and in terms of actual career choices?

Kelly Anne Brown (2017) points out that we still know very little of what becomes of those who pursue intellectual work outside of academia or who pursue non-professorial academic work (para. 1). I wanted to search these unknowns out; I wanted to get to the other side of these speculations and find a navigable pathway from rhetoric and composition into industry writing, one that other enterprising graduate students like myself could follow. I suppose I envisioned a kind of "how to" article emerging from the experience, one guiding students and programs into successful connections in industry (I'm chuckling at my own naivete, even as I proofread this essay).

Toward A Healthier Ever After. I tell my story in reverse because professional narratives take this structure. Our resumés and CVs move from present to prior experience. Our LinkedIn pages do the same. Where you are right now is a priority for most professional audiences, which is a scary reality when you aren't anywhere significant. Somewhat dangerously, the question, "Who are you?" has become conflated with, "What do you do?" For two years, I did nothing of measurable significance or of immediate monetary value. As a result, I felt like I had no measurable significance.

I steadily worked on projects that brought me to a promising starting point, finally finding the synthesis of industry and academia that I initially set out for. What I do right now is exhilarating and rewarding to me. What I didn't do for so long permanently changed my perception of failure and my perception of myself. I didn't find a straightforward path into industry, one that others could neatly follow. I found that the process is much more complex and highly

---

in 1969: "At the 1969 convention, this system was overwhelmed by the large and still growing wave of PhDs and doctoral PhD candidates who arrived in Denver to compete for what had suddenly become a contracting number of professorial positions" (Laurence, 2017, para. 3).

individualized. I also didn't find my value or happiness when I started succeeding, but rather, the pressures of failure produced the profound insight that I have inherent value, and so does failure. I realized that I shouldn't tether my value or my identity to success, but I should embrace failure as always bringing knowledge and, therefore, always enhancing the value I can add to the next classroom lecture or company project.

Interestingly enough, I am now immersed in entrepreneurship, which celebrates failure. In start-up world, failure needs to happen quickly so that learning can happen quickly, and as a result, I have learned to link failure to learning, which has shifted my valuation of it. I need to learn, so I need to fail. Meanwhile, my failures also lead to very interesting opportunities and experiences. In my current role as Advisory Head of Comms, I develop internal and external company communications. I have written SOPs, go-to-market strategies, technical summaries, web copy, investor pitches—the list is endless and ever-growing, so I'll stop there. I am now in an environment where I can be learning and practicing my learning continually. Of course, my learning always comes with a series of missteps and setbacks, all of which increase my knowledge even more and enhance my performance on the next iteration. To always be learning means to often be failing.

REFERENCES

Brown, K. A. (2017, May). Beyond the numbers: plotting the field of humanities PhDs at work. *Profession*. https://profession.mla.hcommons.org/2017/05/26/beyond-the-numbers-plotting-the-field-of-humanities-phds-at-work/.

Kelly, C. (2016, July 6). Stop resisting nonfaculty careers. *Inside Higher Ed*. https://www.insidehighered.com/advice/2016/07/07/phd-candidates-should-consider-careers-other-faculty-essay.

Laurence, D. (2017, April). Outside the box: Occupational horizons for modern language doctoral programs. *Profession*. https://profession.mla.hcommons.org/2017/04/07/outside-the-box-occupational-horizons-for-modern-language-doctoral-programs/.

Rogers, K. (2013, August). Supporting humanities careers and scholarship beyond the tenure track. *Scholarly Communication Institute*. https://libraopen.lib.virginia.edu/downloads/6h440s441.

Yarbrough, S. R. (2001). The aims of graduate education in English: A few thoughts about survival. *South Atlantic Review* 66(3), 101–107.

CHAPTER 12.

OPENING DOORS TO THE IVORY TOWER: HELPING STUDENTS FEEL WELCOME TO ENGAGE IN ACADEMIC DISCOURSE

Sean Fenty
Binghamton University

Faded jeans and worn-out Converse shoes jutting out from a Midtown Manhattan rooftop. The image looks like it was taken just as the photographer jumped, but I know it wasn't because he was sitting next to me, eyes locked on the pages I was reading, anxiously awaiting my response. I was enthralled by this account of an urban explorer, a photographer who documented abandoned and dilapidated places made beautiful by his friends, graffiti artists back in his old home, Algeria, and his new one, New York. I couldn't stop reading and looking at his photographs, showing me secret dark spaces, illuminated through rays of light from holes in ceilings revealing glimpses of the graffitied walls. This was one of the most interesting personal essays I had ever read, and I knew the ideas in it could also be the basis for an exceptional academic argument.

Imagine my disappointment when, six weeks later, after weeks of development, this young man turned in an essay about the well-worn topic of the inequities in the American prison system. As a photographer, he explored spaces fraught with real peril to life and limb, fueled by the adrenaline of discovery, but as a writer, he switched from writing about his true passion because he was afraid he would fail.

I turned to the reflections I had students write about their academic argument drafts, hoping for an answer there for why Sami (pseudonym) switched topics after weeks of developing an ambitious research agenda on the nature of graffiti as an art form that gives voice to the oppressed and marginalized. Instead, I saw a breakdown of his interest in the inequities of mass incarceration and his writing process for his new essay, with no mention of the abrupt topic switch. I waited until after our next class meeting to ask Sami if he had time to talk about his essay. I had known Sami for months before this conversation. Prior to the spring first-year writing class he was currently taking with me, Sami was in two

DOI: https://doi.org/10.37514/PER-B.2024.2494.2.12

previous courses I designed that were offered exclusively to Education Opportunity Program (EOP) students—one in the fall and one as part of a bridge summer program. Sami's work in those previous classes highlighted his unique background and perspectives as a recent immigrant navigating, both figuratively and literally, the new spaces he found himself in, learning a new language, adapting to a new culture with a different dominant religion and the reality that he was now surrounded by many who feared and misunderstood him as a young, Arabic man raised Muslim. There was no discernible anxiety coming from Sami as he accepted my invitation to walk with me back to my office for our conversation, just a subtle smirk that let me know he knew what I wanted to talk about.

Unusually, our classroom was in the same building as my office, so the walk was a short one filled with small talk. Once in my office, I asked Sami why he had switched from a topic I knew he was passionate about, and I was excited to read about, to one he had expressed no prior interest in or personal connection to. I had already made some assumptions about how our curriculum may have led to Sami's decision to switch topics to something safer. Just a couple of weeks before reading his essay draft, I'd learned that the Director of our Writing Program, and the only ladder faculty member in our program, was leaving the university, and she expressed that she no longer wanted our university to use the curriculum I had helped her develop in my role as Associate Director. I had spent the previous two years developing a custom textbook for a standardized version of this first-year writing course, and I was grappling with the reality that we would no longer be using that textbook and that we would have to develop a new curriculum over the summer. Because of the uncertainty around our program's future, and my own future in it as a WPA, the decisions about where to take our curriculum next weighed heavily on me and I could not help but think of Sami's situation in light of my own doubts about our curriculum.

Had our assessment practices, which were informed by post-process theories emphasizing finding a balance between focusing on teaching writing processes and acknowledging the need to assess writing products as socially significant texts (McComiskey, 2000), caused a fear of failure that made Sami switch to something safer? Did our curriculum put too much weight on finished products by assigning 80 percent of the course grade to the final portfolio? Did these grading practices encourage students to avoid challenging research agendas? Would switching from a quality-based rubric to labor-based grading practices have helped Sami be less afraid to pursue his research agenda and more comfortable writing about a subject that was breaking new ground (Inoue, 2014)? I continue grappling with questions like this about our standardized curriculum now that I am director of our program, and I am sure these issues played a role in Sami's switch in topics. But these were not the issues Sami focused on when he opened up to me in my office. Instead, Sami articulated another frustration that led him to switch topics. He confessed that he simply did not think he could make his argument about what this art meant to him and his friends within the genre conventions of academic writing that we had been covering in class. Our curriculum was largely based on genre theory, and we spent a lot of class time discussing genre awareness and the differences in conventions and expectations among personal, civic, and academic genres of writing (Bawarshi, 2003; Devitt, 2004). Sami had successfully been able to write within the conventions of the personal essay, but he did not feel he could do so within what he believed were the confines of academic discourse.

As previously mentioned, Sami had written a spectacular personal essay. In it, he described his adventures exploring abandoned, often dangerous, places. In Algeria, he had explored every abandoned place he could get to—a school, a hospital, a police station, a mental institution, an abandoned military base. In New York, his love for exploration led him to old subway stations, derelict buildings, even bandos and trap houses, all with camera in hand, trying to capture the images he found, making new art with his friends using steel-wool photography with graffiti-art backgrounds. He had exposed me to a world I had not previously known. As anyone who has read hundreds of student essays a year knows, finding one that does this is rare and special. I wanted to learn more about Sami's art and his ideas about what it meant. While our curriculum at the time did not require students to maintain a consistent research agenda throughout the semester, after receiving my feedback on his personal essay, Sami seemed excited to explore his ideas by writing about them in a researched academic argument.

But as he attempted to transition from the personal writing he had done in his previous assignment, and in his previous writing classes, to the academic writing he was being asked to do for this assignment, he felt he could not make his argument relying heavily on synthesizing academic sources he did not think really fit his argument. Inherent flaws in the curriculum had encouraged Sami to avoid pursuing a research agenda that was not already well-researched and extensively discussed in existing scholarly sources. I had failed him by not helping him see that it is precisely when we find a dark place where academics have not yet shed sufficient light that we must explore and show with our writing what we believe others should be seeing. In my efforts to help him become familiar with the conventions of academic discourse, I had failed to help him see how his voice could fit within existing academic conversations.

At that moment, I realized the underlying issues of our situation were the same ones at the heart of the constructivist versus expressivist debate between David Bartholomae and Peter Elbow decades prior. The assignments Sami had done in our summer and fall classes were largely informed by expressivist ideals, but the course he was now in was a standardized course that had recently been created to directly address specific concerns from upper administration about the preparedness of first-year students to engage in academic discourse. The expectation in this course was for Sami to begin learning to mimic the language of scholarly writing. In short, while Sami's previous courses had been informed largely by expressivist ideals, such as those put forth by scholars such as Elbow (1973), who argued that writing should belong to students and teachers are better off largely getting out of their way, the course he was now in, following institutional mandates, and the theoretical perspectives of our program director, took an academic initiation approach. Bartholomae (1985) argued that a student such as Sami has to find "some compromise between idiosyncrasy, a personal history, on the one hand, and the requirements of convention, the history of a discipline, on the other. He must learn to speak our language" (p. 135). Despite my best efforts, my teaching had gotten in Sami's way by focusing too much on making him try to "speak our language" instead of showing him how his language and his ideas could be brought into existing academic conversations about his chosen topic.

Sami was an urban explorer who wanted to bring the beauty he found in abandoned places to light for a larger audience, but did not feel he could connect his passion with the academic conversations he was finding, and he felt the way he wanted to explore this topic did not fit the genre conventions for academic writing we had covered in class. His frustrations with the difficulties of adapting to the conventions of academic writing made me reflect not only on my own teaching but also on the theoretical underpinnings of our standardized curriculum. Potentially making major alterations to our curriculum at the time was an intimidating possibility to consider. The curriculum's development had been led by respected scholars in the field, and as a result of their work, our program had won the Conference on College Composition and Communication's Certificate of Writing Program Excellence. Contemplating the risk of failure in deviating from the established path of our program as a non-tenured, non-ladder faculty member helped me appreciate the fear of failure Sami must have felt when he decided to play it safe and stick with a well-established topic that he knew he could write about easily.

Ultimately, our remaining faculty found what we believed was an approach that was consistent with the mandates of our program's foundation and respectful of what had made it successful but adaptive to the needs of our students, like Sami, who needed more support and encouragement in finding a way to bring themselves into academic discourse communities. Part of these changes involved adjusting our assessment practices to make it safer for students to experiment in their writing processes on their way to finished products. We considered that genre awareness did not need to lead to total conformity of established genre conventions. We could allow students to expand the boundaries of academic writing to be more inclusive of personal experience and family history (Rankins-Robertson et al., 2010; Hindman, 2001). We were able to develop from sociocultural and postcolonial theories practices that help students to cross boundaries between discourse communities without positioning them as deficient and needing to conform fully to the conventions of an existing community for them to transition from being considered outside of that community to being accepted within it (Viete & Le Ha, 2007).

But I did not get a handle on a better approach in time to help Sami switch topics back to his passion that semester. Instead, after discussing his practical concerns, given our established standardized curriculum at the time and our model of collective portfolio grading that meant his work would be evaluated not just by me but by others trained in following our shared rubrics, Sami stuck with his newer, safer topic and continued to develop his draft for his portfolio. His primary frustration was in trying to reconcile how he wanted to share his truths within the limitations I had identified as the genre conventions of academic writing.

I learned that what we lose in setting such limitations is the willingness of students like Sami to shed their light on the secret, dark spaces they have found. We potentially lose their unique perspectives if we do not allow students like Sami to push the boundaries of academic writing by openly approaching their research agenda from personal experiences that they can weave into current academic discourses, allowing them to bring a part of themselves into their research so that their work becomes more than simply a synthesis of established ideas found in scholarly sources.

Thankfully, my failures in making Sami feel safe to explore his initial research interests did not end up derailing his success. He went on to earn his degree and graduated excited to begin his post-college journey. But, to my knowledge, he never ended up writing about urban exploration and graffiti in an academic essay. It is this realization that leads me to continue to grapple with the best ways to teach students the conventions of academic writing while also ensuring they feel safe and welcome in entering academic discourse communities.

Because I know it is a loss for both those communities and the students in my classes if I do not help foster a sense that it is safe for them to explore the corridors of the ivory tower, bringing something of themselves along the way to help connect existing academic conversations to their experiences.

REFERENCES

Bartholomae, D. (1985). Inventing the university. In M. Rose (Ed.), *When a writer can't write: Studies in writer's block and other composing-process problems* (pp. 134–165). Guilford Press.

Bawarshi, A. S. (2003). *Genre and the invention of the writer: Reconsidering the place of invention in composition.* Utah State University Press.

Devitt, A. J. (2004). *Writing genres.* Southern Illinois University Press.

Elbow, P. (1973). *Writing without teachers.* Oxford University Press.

Hindman, J. (2001). Making writing matter: Using "the personal" to recover[y] an essential[ist] tension in academic discourse. *College English, 64*(1), 88–108.

Inoue, A. (2014). Theorizing failure in US writing assessments. *Research in the Teaching of English, 48*(3), 330–352.

McComiskey, B. (2000). *Teaching composition as a social process.* Utah State University Press.

Rankins-Robertson, S., Cahill, L., Roen, D. & Glau, G. (2010). Expanding definitions of academic writing: Family history writing in the basic writing classroom and beyond. *Journal of Basic Writing, 29*(1), 56–77.

Viete, R. & Le Ha, P. (2007). The growth of voice: Expanding possibilities for representing self in research writing. *English Teaching: Practice and Critique, 6*(2), 39–57.

CHAPTER 13.

STANDARDIZED TEST WRITING AND THE FEAR OF FAILING

Elizabeth Blomstedt
University of Southern California

I encountered my biggest writing failure during my prospectus defense for my doctoral dissertation, a teacher-research study of how college students experience and approach writing as a result of writing primarily for standardized tests in K-12. A member of my dissertation committee told me my proposed project was not intellectually daring enough and suggested that this was partially because I was the product of the standardized testing culture I sought to study and critique. If I had been taught an approach to writing that centered on critical thinking and valued exploration, perhaps I would have been able to come up with a more interesting plan for my dissertation project.

This was a hard piece of feedback to swallow, in part because of the truth it contained. It's not a coincidence that all of my writing failures are from college or graduate school. I grew up in Texas public schools during the No Child Left Behind era, and thus, being "good at writing" meant I was good at producing an essay that fulfilled the requirements of any standardized writing test I encountered: the TAAS, TAKS, PSAT, AP, SAT, and GRE. The clarity of my communication was valued more than the quality of my ideas on each of those exams, in part because each took place in a closed, timed environment that severely limited my ability to engage in invention or create an argument that *could* fail. I was tested on my ability to write a test essay, and I usually succeeded.

My stellar performance on these exams can be credited to the majority of my writing instruction centering on how to replicate a formula that would guarantee my success on them. In ninth grade, our pre-AP English teacher taught us exactly how she wanted us to write essays: the five-paragraph method, including an introduction with a thesis statement at the end, three body paragraphs whose topic sentences consisted of "thesis + reason," and a conclusion that restated your argument. We were also taught an eight-sentence paragraph with exact proportions of evidence and analysis. I used that formula on the practice AP exam essays we wrote in class (called "timed writings"), but I was also evaluated on how well I used it on the handful of essays we wrote and revised (the "non-timed writings"). It was that formula that earned me passing scores on my AP

DOI: https://doi.org/10.37514/PER-B.2024.2494.2.13

English exams, which in turn got me credit for first-year writing classes at the University of Texas at Austin. By giving me credit for college writing courses based on my performance on a 50-minute timed AP exam essay, I assumed this formula would prepare me well for writing in college.

But it didn't. The formula failed me. It did not prepare me well for the diverse genres I encountered, nor did it give me the critical thinking skills I needed to succeed on my college writing projects. The first time it failed me was in a required essay for my US history class. The details of the prompt are fuzzy, but I knew they included direct instructions to make an argument. I didn't know how to make an argument in a *history* paper. History was static, either a list of correct answers on a multiple-choice TAKS test or a well-organized timed essay on the AP US History exam synthesizing the factors that led to the Great Depression. One could not create an argument *about* history. And what would that even look like in five-paragraph format? How could I "thesis + three reasons" that argument?

Standardized test writing is writing with guardrails. For many students, failure happens only when you venture outside of the box you were told to stay within. "Real" writing—writing for real audiences, contexts, and purposes—has no guardrails. Failure is a real possibility in real writing, and this explains why students may cling to formulaic, test-friendly writing over exploring new writing processes and forms.

I didn't understand that until I took a Principles of Rhetoric course, my first required lower-division class for my rhetoric and writing major. I learned that all texts were not slight variations of the ideal essay (a five-paragraph argumentative essay with topic sentences at the beginning of each paragraph, a one-sentence thesis statement, and ample transition words sprinkled throughout). Instead, I learned texts were shaped to meet the rhetorician's purpose for a specific audience within a given context. I was excited. And I was scared.

When we're asking students to step away from the formulas they learned in the past, we are asking them to risk failure in a way they have rarely been asked to do in their writing lives. That's a big ask. As Ruth Mirtz (this volume) conveys, testing has greatly shaped how today's writers think about writing failure; its high-stakes nature has created a greater fear of failing that prioritizes a "safe," formulaic final product above pursuing daring arguments.

And these stakes are the highest for student populations with the least amount of privilege. You would not be surprised to learn that my students who have the most extensive experience with writing outside of the testing environment are those who went to private schools or well-funded public schools. While students in AP classes do often focus heavily on exam prep, my dissertation research revealed that students who did *not* take advanced courses often take English classes that focus more heavily on passing statewide exams whose prompts ask simpler questions than those on the AP exam. Other students, often low-income and non-white students, attend college prep charter schools that focus almost exclusively on college entrance exams, touting their scores on those exams as signs of educational effectiveness. Multilingual international students often spend months preparing to take the Test of English as a Foreign Language (TOEFL), which includes timed writing, to be granted admission to American universities. While writing primarily for standardized tests hurts all students, it can be particularly harmful to students who have seen success on standardized test essays as their "ticket" into higher education; these students see "failure" on writing projects as keeping them from accessing the life they desire, and yet, adhering to these formulas in college will limit their success in college and beyond. Helping students move from the five-paragraph essay to a more intellectually daring and rhetorically flexible approach to writing is an equity issue in our classrooms.

I'll end with a few ideas for how we can start to help our students begin overcoming their standardized-test-induced fear of writing failures. If we lack understanding of how destabilizing this risk of failure can be, our students may not take us up on the opportunity to explore what writing can be outside of these formulas. We must take an empathetic approach, beginning by considering how we guide students to reflect on their past writing experiences. One of the most harmful things we can do to our students is declare everything they learned about writing in K-12 useless and ask them to start from scratch—that's overwhelming and inaccurate. Instead, we can contextualize their past experiences using the same tools that will prepare students to discern the appropriate approaches to different writing scenarios. I start my classes by guiding students through a written reflection on a five-paragraph essay they wrote in the past, asking them to consider the audience, purpose, and context of this five-paragraph essay and why those factors led them to use this form. We then discuss their experiences and thoughts; I share some of my experiences as an AP grader, explaining how the five-paragraph formula facilitates speedy evaluation. We then consider which writing habits, principles, and skills might transfer well to other environments, like paragraphs having a single controlling idea.

Second, we must structure our courses in a way that allows failure to be generative, not devastating. I have worked with the concept of growth mindsets in first-year writing courses, encouraging students to see failure as an opportunity for growth rather than an indictment on their permanent writing abilities, but most students did not fully embrace this notion until I made a major shift to my course structure: adopting a labor-based grading contract. Popularized most recently by Asao Inoue (2022), these contracts guarantee students grades for completing coursework rather than averaging grades awarded on major writing projects submitted throughout the semester, thus allowing students to submit ambitious writing projects without fear of being evaluated in a way that will harm their overall grade in the course. With grading contracts, students feel freer to explore new approaches, knowing that failure will not harm their GPA. Standardized testing is emblematic of the achievement-oriented, grade-obsessed culture of our education system, and grading contracts combat that by making space for failure in education.

Lastly, we must create opportunities for students to reflect meaningfully on the failure they encounter in their writing processes. My students apply their growth mindsets by writing responses to the written feedback they receive from me on their first writing project, acknowledging places where they failed and considering what they've learned from those specific failures. I also guide my students to reflect critically on their writing *process*, not just their written products. For standardized tests, most students are taught to engage in minimal prewriting and to dive into replicating an essay formula immediately. I teach students the process of invention and spend time in individual paper conferences considering where their ideas led to dead ends or "failures" and what that taught them about the argument they're making. Integrating failure as a part of a successful writing process is pivotal for students who have viewed writing primarily as producing a specific product with minimal consideration to the process they engage in to generate ideas and produce effective reader-based prose.

That piece of feedback from my prospectus defense is my biggest writing failure, and so I share it with my students. I know many of them are in the same boat that I was once in: champions of standardized testing who now find themselves in a brave new world of critical thinking and strange genres. It surprises them to know that I was once the captain of that boat, crashed it into some rocks, had to swim to a deserted island, build myself a new boat, and find a better land, one where writing failures of all kinds (including terrible metaphors) are welcome.

REFERENCES

Inoue, A. B. (2022). *Labor-based grading contracts: Building equity and inclusion in the compassionate writing classroom* (2nd ed.). The WAC Clearinghouse; University Press of Colorado. https://doi.org/10.37514/PER-B.2022.1824.

CHAPTER 14.

FAILURE TO LAUNCH? THEORIZING RHETORICS OF REJECTION FROM GRADUATE STUDENT PERSPECTIVES

Jerrice Renita Donelson
University of Michigan, Dearborn

Anicca Cox
University of New Mexico, Valencia

Early one spring semester, we struck up a conversation in the writing center where we both worked as graduate consultants. Jerrice was in the process of revising one of her qualifying exams, and Anicca had just gotten a journal rejection after two rounds of revision.

As we conversed, we began to understand we were both living in exhausted places related to our perceived rejections and failure. Our initial conversations and those that followed revealed that one of the most difficult parts of our experiences was a lack of space to talk about them openly with peers or mentors, in part because of shame but also in part because of the difficulty of relational understanding from those in "different" professional locations than ourselves.

For example, Jerrice mentioned going to a trusted advisor and receiving what she perceived as "good" advice, but from the vantage point of a well-established scholar in the field who, though they offered some perspective, couldn't *really* relate to the challenges of scholarly failure from the precarious standpoint of a graduate student. On the other hand, Anicca had mostly kept her own failure a secret, working to keep narratives of it away from a competitive graduate cohort in our widely celebrated program, very much for fear of judgment or for stepping beyond the bounds of her graduate student role as an older returning student. The result of our conversations, detailed in this chapter, was that we began to conceptualize a peer-centered, relational model for support, which we constituted through our experiences as writing center tutors. We contend that writing center theory and training provide a valuable model for these relational support structures.

DOI: https://doi.org/10.37514/PER-B.2024.2494.2.14

And so we began, together, to unpack and make meaning of our own internalized narratives related to scholarly failure within the context of our graduate community. Carmen Kynard (2012) suggests that for graduate students, sending an article out "means that students will have to go out on a limb and do what graduate students seldom do: let go of fear and insecurity . . . in other words: allow themselves to risk getting their work rejected" (n.p.). We found together that it is vital to have fellow travelers if we are to live *with* fear and insecurity and maintain the stamina it takes to persist in our work.

We begin here in an effort to map how we both built strength and resilience by leaning on our conversations and relationship. We mean to take off where LaFrance and Corbett (2020) leave us (they say grad students need to be trained to fail) and extend their argument to make a claim for the need for a community-oriented approach to failure that builds resilience. As Tellez-Trujillo (this volume) notes, "Resilience isn't solitary, nor maintained without community." So then, a community approach, built in writing center pedagogies, led us to begin learning what we will call the "rhetorics and etiquette of failure." We suggest that orienting toward failure, not alone, but together, can be a source of strength for our continued professional work.

To explain this orienting, we engage our own experiences in story form below and trace the ways we, as writing center fellows and practitioners, drew from peer support strategies mirrored in our writing center work to bolster one another across programmatic milestones, setbacks, and workplace contexts.

ANICCA

Our conversation began because Jerrice was working on a proposal she wanted me to look at. Then, she told me she was revising a graduate exam, and she began to consider out loud why returning to the document was so emotionally difficult to do. I realized how familiar these feelings were to my own, as an older student and as someone who was prepared for graduate school in some ways and woefully underprepared in others. Particularly, I related to her experience as someone who carries a perpetual outsider identity in academic spaces tied to working-class identity.

I told her how I'd worked on an article and how embarrassed, how ashamed I felt about not getting it in. I told her how, for weeks, I had poured over revisions. How I'd submitted it to a flagship journal in our field at the encouragement of a professor. I told her how, in the absence of faith in myself, I'd revised and worked to catch every sentence-level error over and over and over, something I would caution other writers against but found myself doing obsessively, trying to make it perfect, to prove my belonging.

I shared the feedback I'd gotten. The first round of reviewer comments was both helpful and not. One reviewer (unknowingly, of course) used a previous article I'd contributed to as an example to compare to my current one, as they pointed out every flaw in my current work. The other, a generous, well-known name in the field, noted that she, too, was unconvinced (but really wanted to be) and needed an argument. I told Jerrice how confused I was because the professor who told me to submit it had promised that it was "ready for publication." I told her how hard it was to revise multiple times only to get rejected and how I'd lost faith in the piece itself.

This is what began our friendship, bonding over the ways in which we made sense of our failures and how the particular social location we found ourselves in made it difficult to seek help. We wondered together if faculty, whom we had gone to for advice, simply couldn't help us because, by all measures, they had achieved the kind of success we were apprenticing ourselves to. Because our shared work was located in a writing center, we began to ask ourselves what it would look like if we took all we knew about the writing center as a space for dismantling hierarchies and analyzing power and for dynamic relationship building across experience, as a model for helping one another through rejection and failure.

And so, we began to do that. It took years. But, somehow our friendship, built in peer feedback, taking place in our writing center, was a tool we were building together to persist, to get back up and keep believing our voices matter.

Now, living in different states, we continue to make sense of our failures and rejections, so normal in academic life—in the classroom, in our scholarship, in our mentoring, in our professional next steps—and to bolster one another. That work revolves around understanding one another's goals just as we do with writers in consultations and considering the role of our positionalities, experiences, and orientations as integral to our relationship with the field and our own work.

As returning students and professionals with different racial identities, research interests, and experiences, we continue to find a path through listening, recasting, mapping, and sharing resources. Our relationship is a place where it is safe to cry, to crack jokes, to talk shit, and keep on going through it. Through the continuous moments of rejection, we somehow fostered a community where our failures are not visceral but moments for reorientation.

JERRICE

I recall during my comprehensive exams, where the experience of rejection reverberated my feelings of failure after my initial submission was returned "needing revision." Upon my eager request to receive feedback, my chair quipped, "you did what many grad students do in these exams" apparently signaling my errors were common rhetorical choices made among grad students.

While the statement may have been factual, its ethos sliced through my ego like a corroded machete as each word chopped away at what little confidence remained. I already suffered from interminable doubt in my ability to display "acceptable" scholarly performance. I was sure my contrary perspectives would most certainly impede any success I might have. My chair was unaware of the impact the feedback had or how it caused a very real disorientation. It wasn't until later, in a creative writing space we worked in together, where I shared the embodied experience, that she learned what I was feeling was unbridled failure.

Since I was a child, the mantra of radical belief to become "the best you can because you can" was etched within the marrow of my identities. But it now seemed in contrast to my experience. The ambiguity of what I had done or hadn't done sent me reeling down a rut of despair where I festered in silence and isolation.

I occasionally re-emerged from my mental station when I decided to meet with a few of my committee members. Even as I was confident they'd see me, I became convinced it was only to ingeminate the knifing I'd already received, so I entered with my heart in hand, hoping doing so would lessen any further damage to my already incapacitated soul. I asked for advice on how to proceed after describing what I felt as hollowing failure, only to hear a dismissive response to my anguish: "Rejection is part of the process."

As I sat there pondering how my inquiry went unanswered, I reorientated the question, asking point blank, "How do you recover from rejection?" My press caused the molecules in the room to shift momentarily as I listened to conflated moments of rejection offered to explain its necessity. I sauntered away from this encounter, wondering why the rhetoric of rejection has some sort of expected "etiquette," where admitting or revealing a discourse of disorientation is met with hushed tones.

This ponderance became an utterance when hearing of Anicca's article rejection, which she shared only after offering me comfort and encouragement. It was after hearing her attempt to rationalize her own rejection that I encouraged her not to—and to instead name it as she feels it because it was absolutely ok to do so. It was here where our kinship birthed friendship spearheaded by our questioning the lack of support and guidance grad students are provided for instances of rejection. We began to ask: How do we, as grad students, rising scholars, and job seekers, navigate moments of rejection, which can quickly become embodied, by representing failure as an experience that is professional but also lives in the personal?

THEORIZING RHETORICS OF REJECTION AND FAILURE

As mentioned in the introduction to this collection, failure has and can be theorized in a number of important ways for writing studies, and we aim to build on those important works. We find particular resonance in Judith Halberstam's (2011) work on failure. Like Halberstam, as we discussed writing this article, we found ourselves returning over and over to non-scholarly references from popular culture for diverse and abundant representations of failure and rejection, as well as models of relational responses to it. Popular culture is a rich ground from which to explore the multitudinous aspects of theorizing failure. We turned to those texts as models of relational approaches in order to theorize our own experiences of rejection and failure. Below are some brief vignettes that we discussed in our personal conversations about rhetorics and etiquettes of failure and rejection.

In an episode of *The Loud House*, a Nickelodeon cartoon, two sisters grapple with rejection and failure while inadvertently competing for the same accomplishment (Sullivan & Marshall, 2018). The older sister finds herself simultaneously advising her younger sibling on how to handle the emotions of a rejection over a piece of writing, coaching her to resubmit, *and* losing her own perspective on relational support when the younger sister receives an opportunity she herself sought out. It's complicated, y'all. In graduate programs, we often find ourselves in real or imagined competition with people we love, champion, and support. So then, we wondered, what happens when we are challenged and where our own locations leave us lost? How do we support one another anyway? And what if past rejections inflame moments of failure that have yet to be resolved?

Another example we discussed was in a Chuck Lorre comedy series, *Mom*, where one of the characters experiences failure through a series of program rejections (Lorre et al. 2017–2018). Much like Anicca, they are too embarrassed to tell anyone but eventually disclose to someone near. The response: The listener confesses to being unable to offer any advice.

This too, was familiar territory. What do we do when, sometimes, the only answer is to sit with this, with the discomfort? It is those moments that we can bear witness, rather than needing to work to resolve our embodied feelings of despair around rejection-as-failure much as Jerrice coached Anicca to do. Instead of rationalizing, *feel*.

Finally, in yet another example within a Chuck Lorre series, a married couple, both academics and researchers, find that their theory has been disproven. Reeling in their individual despair at the moment of their own nuptials, they find each other at the same location—rejection-as-failure. Here, we learn that rejection and failure can coexist, can show up even amidst our collaborative moments, yet can be processed together in intimate and familial ways.

Though in many ways, some of these examples eventually highlight some humorous aspects of rejection and failure or use humor to approach a painful subject (something academics have difficulty doing in those moments), they also serve to familiarize and normalize the discomfort of rejection and failure—to make it palpable. We believe that is what our community, graduate student-mentor relationships, and connections can make available. In writing center relationships, where feedback is critical and reciprocal, we meet each other exactly where we are, whether drafts are imperfect or imagined. We, as a community of writers, begin to build together a working theory that coheres and disperses in the moments we are together.

We build rhetorics and etiquettes together in these precise moments. We do so collaboratively and collectively as we ask questions, witness, and work to provide continuity across ideas and texts together. In other words, by responding to internal and/or external perceptions of rejection, whether feedback or doubt, we develop behavioral practices with one another that are not built from the outside but rather develop in relationship. So often, helpful advice in moments of rejection and failure is unhelpful for that very reason; it comes from the outside, or above, from a mentor.

We instead argue that working together as peers in these moments is a valuable space from which to live with, learn from, and persist through our embodied and professional experience of rejection, failure, and, ultimately, progress.

REFERENCES

Halberstam, J. (2011). *The queer art of failure*. Duke University Press.

Kynard, C. (2012, December 6). Race, publishing and rhetoric of rejection. *Education, Liberation & Black radical traditions for the 21st century: Carmen Kynard's teaching & research site on race, writing, and the classroom.* http://carmenkynard.org/rhetoric-of-rejection/.

Lorre, C., Gorodetsky, E. & Baker, G. (Writers) & Widdoes, J. (Director). (2018, March 1). Pudding and a screen door (Season 5, Episode 13) [TV series episode]. In C. Lorre, E. Gorodetsky, N. Bakay, G. Baker & W. Bell (Executive Producers), *Mom*. CBS.

LaFrance, M. & Corbett, S. J. (2020). Discourse community fail! Negotiating choices in success/failure and graduate level writing development. In M. Brooks-Gillies, E. G. Garcia, S. H. K. K. Manthey & T. G. Smith (Eds.), *Graduate writing across the disciplines: Identifying, teaching, supporting* (pp. 295–314). The WAC Clearinghouse; University Press of Colorado. https://doi.org/10.37514/ATD-B.2020.0407.2.12.

Sullivan, K. (Writer) & Marshall, K. (Director). (2018). Teachers union (Season 3, Episode 14) [TV series episode]. In C. Savino, M. Rubiner & K. Marshall (Executive Producers), *The loud house*. Nickelodeon Studios.

CHAPTER 15.

THE CV OF FAILURE: MAKING REJECTION VISIBLE AND CULTIVATING GROWTH MINDSETS IN DOCTORAL WRITERS

Dana Lynn Driscoll
Indiana University of Pennsylvania

When I began teaching an advanced research writing class for doctoral students at Indiana University of Pennsylvania, I had difficulty conveying to my students the role of failure, revision, and persistence in professional academic publishing. As an experienced faculty member who publishes, failure and rejection are simply part of the process, and my experiences are hardly unique. Studies of writing for publication in the field routinely point to the need to address failure and engage in complex revisions (Wells & Söderland, 2017; Söderland & Wells, 2019; Tulley, 2018; Gallagher & Devoss, 2019). But to graduate students and new faculty under pressure to publish, rejection and revision present serious challenges that cross lines of self-care, identity, and self-esteem and may encourage imposter syndrome (Driscoll et al., 2020).

I see at least four factors that make "rejection as part of the process" difficult to convey to doctoral students. First, students don't see the process behind published pieces they are reading in their courses. They read the best versions of articles and books in the field, versions that have undergone rigorous revision and peer review. The messiness, failure, resubmission, reworking, and general struggle of the process that created the article or book are invisible to them. Even if they conceptually understand this, the invisible nature of the process makes it difficult for them to fully grasp.

Second, doctoral students are used to being the best at what they do, and, for many, being the best translates into straightforward and successful writing processes. Doctoral students aspire to grad school while still in their undergraduate careers, likely performing at the very top of their majors and maintaining high GPAs. This striving towards excellence continues as they work through

DOI: https://doi.org/10.37514/PER-B.2024.2494.2.15

their graduate coursework. For many, writing isn't necessarily easy, but it is often immediately successful in the contexts they have done it in the past in that they work hard, get good grades, and move on to the next paper. Rarely in coursework do they have the opportunity to experience failure, persistence, and revision to the extent that they will when they pursue professional publishing. These observations have been borne out in my data exploring both expert and emerging scholars writing for publication in the field (Driscoll, forthcoming).

Third, successful publication and successful dissertation writing is extraordinarily high stakes and is critical to job market success and graduation. This puts graduate students in a tenuous position with any publications, difficult feedback, or rejections they may face and contributes to overall graduate student fragility during these very difficult times (Smith et al., 2019).

Finally, success as students may lead to unproductive relationships with struggle and failure, relationships shaped not only by their own educational experiences but by the larger institutional frameworks in which they study. Psychologist Carol Dweck (2008) identifies two underlying theories of learning that shape how people approach struggle and failure. Fixed mindset learners may attribute failure and success to their own intelligence; thus, a failure of any kind is a deep challenge to their self-esteem and identity and causes the learner to shut down or avoid the situation rather than persevere. Growth mindset learners see failure and struggle as part of the natural process of learning and embrace failures as a chance to grow and succeed. To be successful as professional academic writers, students need to embrace a growth mindset with their writing. Dweck has argued that we can model and teach toward growth mindsets (see also Miller, this volume)—and I have found that the "CV of Failure" presented here is an excellent way to do just that.

Given all of the above, I began looking for ways to demonstrate to my students that getting rejected and having to do many rounds of revision was simply a "normal" part of the practice of professional academic publishing. Talking to them about it or sharing examples from my own experience didn't seem to be enough. A year or two after my course, I would often find myself dealing with a crisis in my office as a graduate student had a meltdown over an article rejection or a dissertation committee member's comments. I had to somehow help "normalize" this idea of failure and struggle in a way that sunk in, and that demonstrated that failure wasn't a reflection of their intelligence or ability—it was just part of the process.

I came across an article in the Guardian (2016) discussing how Princeton Professor Johannes Haushofer published his "CV of Failure" on Twitter. His CV of Failure included degree programs he didn't get into, grants that weren't funded, and rejections from academic journals. Soon, other faculty in other disciplines began publishing their own CVs of Failure. I thought the idea was brilliant and incredibly courageous, and I worked to transform my CV into a CV of Failure to share with my students.

In my CV of Failure, I include failed dissertation topics, failed degree programs, and article and grant rejections. I tell the "story" behind the publications and offer a timeline behind each of the entries on my CV. To see how it works, here are a few sample entries from my CV of Failure.

Education

Ph.D. in English—Primary area: Rhetoric and Composition, Purdue University, May 2009

Secondary Concentrations: Writing Program Administration, Empirical Research Methodology

Third Dissertation: *Pedagogy of Transfer: Impacts of Student and Instructor Attitudes.* Linda Bergmann (Chair), Irwin Weiser, Shirley Rose, and Anne Beaufort.

Second Dissertation Topic: Studying RAD research in Composition. I found a study too similar after attending CCCC the year I was selecting my dissertation topic, and so I switched topics. Even though I didn't pursue this as a dissertation, two years later after graduation, I did engage in an extremely successful collaboration with Sherry Wynn Perdue looking at RAD research in writing centers.

First Dissertation Topic: Explorations of the Sapir-Whorf Hypothesis with regards to Environmentalism and Linguistic Choices (dropped after I could not find a director, leading me to be mastered out of my first Ph.D. program in Linguistics and join the field of Rhetoric and Composition instead).

Publications

****Driscoll**, D. L. & Yacoub, O. (2022). Threshold genres: A 10-year exploration of a medical writer's development and social apprenticeship through the patient SOAP note. *Written Communication,* Vol. 39(3) 370–39. https://doi.org/10.1177/07410883221090436

This was probably the hardest article revision I have ever undertaken. We originally submitted a much larger study with more data, but reviewers told us to narrow it. We focused on the case study, abandoning 1 year of data analysis and rewriting 50 percent of the article. We got additional feedback from reviewers (revision 2) and then the editor (revision 3). It was accepted, and later, won the 2022 Association for Writing Across the Curriculum and The WAC Clearinghouse Best WAC Article or Chapter Focused on Research Award. Revision pays off!

Driscoll, D. L., Leigh, R. S. & Zamin, N. (2020) "Self Care as Ethical Professionalization: A Case of Doctoral Education in Composition Studies." *College Composition and Communication* (CCC), Vol 71(3) 453–480.

Rejected from one journal (without review for issues of audience and genre), revised and submitted to *CCC*. Accepted with revision at *CCC*.

Driscoll, D. L., Gorzelsky, G., Wells, J., Hayes, C. & Salchak, S. (2017) Down the rabbit hole: Challenges and methodological recommendations in researching writing-related student dispositions. *Composition Forum 35*.

Failed portion of our larger multi-institutional and grant funded study. We tried to code data unsuccessfully for three years. I was ready to walk away from this part of the project. Then my co-author Gwen (Gorzelsky) suggested we needed to study the failure, so we did a systematic analysis of what happened over a three-month period. It was fascinating and illuminated reasons for the failure. As first author, I had 50 percent of the original article already written and had to do a full rewrite. Accepted with revisions.

Driscoll, D. L. (2014). Clashing values: A longitudinal study of student beliefs of general education, vocationalism, and transfer of learning. *Teaching and Learning Inquiry* Vol. 2.1. pp. 21–37. https://doi.org/10.2979/teachlearninqu.2.1.21

Rejected from two journals prior to submission to *TLI*. This rejection process took 2 years while I was on the tenure clock. *TLI* gave me a Revise and Resubmit, then Accepted with Revisions. The process took 4 years and had 6 major revisions before publication.

As you can see from my own CV of Failure entries above, the CV of Failure is a powerful and transformative teaching tool that shows graduate students the realities of the work and writing that faculty do. It helps normalize failure and shows them that successful faculty frequently struggle and fail—and that's ok.

The CV of Failure is a two-part lesson, useful for any advanced writing course for graduate students. Towards the end of the course, I share my CV of Failure and introduce them to mindset theory. To do this, I start the class by bringing in my regular CV and asking the students to read over it. I ask them what they see when they read my CV, and they usually respond with comments surrounding my success as a scholar. I ask them how often they think I fail or get rejected, and they tell me it is obvious that I rarely get rejected. Then I hand them my CV of Failure. I have them read over it and, again, ask them to comment. They are often shocked by how often I get rejected and how many revisions I need to make.

The second part of this class shifts to mindset theory. For mindset-shifting work, I have doctoral students read a piece I wrote with a co-author on growth mindsets, writing transfer, and graduate writers (Powell & Driscoll, 2020). The data in this piece suggests that mindsets toward feedback shape both short and long-term writing outcomes in two graduate writers. After we discuss the article, I ask them to get in groups and create a list of positive qualities that can help shift to growth mindsets. These often include things like accepting that failure and struggle are part of the process, practicing persistence, working to not link academic success to self-esteem, recognizing that tough comments can improve writing, developing resiliency, and practicing self-care.

In a following class, I bring examples of in-progress articles that are undergoing revision. These examples include rejection letters, feedback, and my revision notes. I talk to them about what I'm struggling to do or where I am stuck and how I hope to get out of the difficulty. The important thing here is not just showing them the pieces that reflect in-progress academic discourse but also modeling non-emotional and growth-oriented engagement with revision. I talk about these rejections and failures matter-of-factly, sharing how they help me grow in new ways, improve my work, and are an opportunity to see my work from a new angle. I talk about my emotions and how I deal with frustration, feedback I am unhappy about, and anxiety. I show them, through drafts with track changes, how much of my original work is often revised before it finds publication. We talk about strategies for shifting mindsets, such as walking away from their work for a time if they are angry or upset and also putting themselves in the position of the reader or having another person read through the comments. As a homework exercise, I encourage them to engage with my own comments on their drafts in a similar manner.

The end goal with these activities is creating academically resilient members of our discipline that have growth mindsets and that can thrive in the face of failure and struggle. Through the CV of Failure, modeling a growth mindset, and sharing examples of real-life rejections and revision processes, doctoral students can see how struggle and failure are normalized processes and are simply part of academic life. While mindsets can't be shifted overnight, repeated engagement with these ideas, especially as they move into dissertation writing and writing for publication, can foster growth. By reframing failure, rejection, and struggle as opportunities for growth, they can engage in more productive and successful writing processes long term.

REFERENCES

Driscoll, D. L. (forthcoming). *Becoming an expert writer: Threshold concepts in writing for publication*. The WAC Clearinghouse; University Press of Colorado.

Driscoll, D. L., Leigh, R. S. & Zamin, N. (2020). Self-care as ethical professionalization: A case of doctoral education in composition studies. *College Composition and Communication 71*(3), 453–480.

Dweck, C. S. (2008). *Mindset: The new psychology of success*. Ballantine Books.

Gallagher, J. R. & DeVoss, D. N. (Eds.). (2019). *Explanation points: Publishing in rhetoric and composition*. Utah State University Press.

Guardian staff (2016, April 28). CV of failures: Princeton professor publishes resumé of his career lows. *The Guardian*. https://www.theguardian.com/education/2016/apr/30/cv-of-failures-princeton-professor-publishes-resume-of-his-career-lows.

Powell, R. & Driscoll, D. L. (2020). How mindsets shape response and learning transfer: A case of two graduate writers. *Journal of Response to Writing, 6*(2), 42–68. https://scholarsarchive.byu.edu/cgi/viewcontent.cgi?article=1002&context=journalrw.

Smith, S., Hunter, D. & Sobolewska, E. (2019). Getting in, getting on: Fragility in student and graduate identity. *Higher Education Research & Development, 38*(5), 1046–1060. https://doi.org/10.1080/07294360.2019.1612857.

Söderlund, L. & Wells, J. (2019). A study of the practices and responsibilities of scholarly peer review in rhetoric and composition. *College Composition and Communication, 71*(1), 117–144.

Tulley, C. E. (2018). *How writing faculty write: Strategies for process, product, and productivity*. Utah State University Press.

Wells, J. M. & Söderlund, L. (2018). Preparing graduate students for academic publishing: Results from a study of published rhetoric and composition scholars. *Pedagogy, 18*(1), 131–156.

CHAPTER 16.

REAPING WHAT YOU SOW: REFRAMING ACADEMIC REJECTION AS A COMMUNITY GARDEN FOR WRITING STUDIES

Laura Decker
Nevada State University

The grower of trees, the gardener, the man born to farming, whose hands reach into the ground and sprout, to him the soil is a divine drug. He enters into death yearly, and comes back rejoicing. He has seen the light lie down in the dung heap, and rise again in the corn.

– Wendell Berry

In the spring of 2019, I set myself on the course for professional success. I was in my final year of my doctoral program—a program through which I had worked as a full-time student while also teaching as a full-time, non-tenure track lecturer at a nearby college and serving as a WPA of a writing-intensive course pilot program. I had just won my department's Teaching Excellence award, an honor made even sweeter by being the first non-tenure track faculty member to win it. My energy and optimism were never higher.

Over the next six months, I planned for my future successes by submitting numerous grant applications, a nomination packet for a prestigious state-wide teaching award, my first empirical article for publication, and I even applied for a tenure-track position in my own department—all while finishing my dissertation. I envisioned myself smiling as I opened all those congratulatory emails the next spring, and I gleefully imagined the moment when I would add "Assistant Professor" to my email signature.

I was meticulous in my planning and perfect in my process. In December 2019, after all my grants, articles, and applications had been sent out, I celebrated the coming success with my husband on our back patio, under the moonlight, beneath the bare limbs of our desert oaks.

You can guess what happened next. I received rejections for everything.

Well, not everything. I did receive one small travel grant, though, because of COVID-19, the conference was canceled and so the grant was never fully realized (which was disappointing at the time but inconsequential now, knowing the full scale of the virus's impact). Importantly, the virus and quarantining efforts would also thwart my dream job, to which I had been invited for a campus interview but which had then been frozen by human resources. I had successfully finished my PhD program, which, of course, felt great. And although it hadn't been on my list of "academic successes," I had given birth to my second child, a lovely, sweet baby who slept on my lap while I defended my dissertation on Zoom. While those successes were real, failing to earn more of those grants, publish my article, receive an offer for my dream job, and win that teaching award still hurt incredibly.

However, on reflection, I realize that even in all those other failures, I had been successful. When I submitted my package for the teaching award in the fall of 2019, I had also put together a nomination package for one of our graduating writing studies seniors for the student version of the award, and they received it along with all the notoriety it brought and the money that would certainly turn out to be important as they began their doctoral work in rhetoric and composition.

At about the same time, I submitted my application for the tenure-track position in my department. I had also submitted a letter of recommendation for a colleague for the endowed chair of writing at a university back in her hometown, near her family. Although my own job-search was stuck in COVID limbo, hers continued and she would go on to accept her dream job.

And when I received word that my article would not be published at that time, little did I know that another colleague had her article accepted and that she credited me in one paragraph for guiding her toward contract grading—an honor for her, as it was her first peer-reviewed publication, and an honor for me because I had led her to a transformative practice that she had something meaningful to share about with the larger writing studies community.

It seems that for each opportunity that hadn't produced for me, an opportunity had produced for someone else—and I had a small hand in those successes.

In 2018, professor and scholar Max Perry Mueller wrote about the inevitability of rejection in academia. In "Grow Your Own Rejection Garden," he dissects the genre of the "How to Get Over Academic Rejection" article—popularized by *The Chronicle*, *The Professor is In*, and other academic online hubs. He spends much of his analysis looking at how the genre offers guidance on overcoming professional rejection, specifically through finding opportunity for growth from rejection, and most importantly to Mueller's article, self-care around rejection.

Mueller (2018) goes on to describe how, after being rejected from his dream job, he began a tradition of anticipating rejection and weaving it more profoundly into his professional life. For each rejection he receives, he purchases a small plant and visualizes that "with nurturing," the plant "will sink deep roots into its soil and grow tall branches, leaves and flowers reaching toward the sun." In short, he uses his professional rejections to create a literal rejection garden. He often gifts these plants to colleagues, citing cultural wisdom and empirical research on the construct of happiness, that happiness comes from focusing on the wellbeing of others rather than on ourselves. Mueller's literal rejection garden is a beautiful and proactive way to deal with the feelings of failure that are written into our jobs.

Going back to 2019 and 2020, it's clear that while I wasn't planting a literal rejection garden like Mueller, I was indeed cultivating a metaphorical one. Looking back at all the rejection I had, but all the success my writing studies colleagues and students had, I was able to reframe my feelings of rejection in terms of how my labor was fruitful for others, and it hurt a little bit less. In short, I could see the work I had done as contributing to a community garden of writing studies. Though my plants failed to produce that year, even with my meticulous planting, watering, and weeding, I had been simultaneously invested in the gardens of my colleagues and students, and theirs bore fruit. Our community garden had been successful.

The rejection I took on that year had felt devastating initially, and even realizing how I had a hand in the success of my colleagues and students didn't magically make that pain disappear. As we all know, professional rejection hurts to the core, and, at times, it's hard to separate that rejection from our own personal worth. In "Why Is Academic Rejection So Very Crushing?" educator and academic writing coach Rebecca Schuman (2014) argues that the deep pain of academic rejection is due to our academic self-conceptions or the notion that those of us working in academia do so because we see our teaching, writing, and research as the embodiment of who we are at our core. So, a rejection of our professional self is a rejection of our personal self. Schuman herself describes a particular moment of academic rejection in which she hoped to die by some terrible accident and be done with it all.

Schuman's (2014) confession is a reminder that the pain of failure and academic rejection is very real, and it's not a topic that's often discussed. Retrospectively, I wonder about all the faculty who helped me along the way. What failures were they experiencing while they prepared me for my first conference presentation or while they wrote letters of recommendation for my graduate studies? My memory is void of conversations about academic failure in general, and I only remember learning about their professional work in the context of publications and presentations—all typical forms of academic success. How might we further cultivate success for our colleagues and students if we had more open conversations about failure? How might we address the issue of rejection and crushing academic self-conceptions if we allowed those topics to come to light more often?

Reframing rejection and failure as part of a larger task of building a community garden in the field of writing studies won't bring an end to rejection or the pain that comes with it. But, as Schuman (2014) notes, "The goal should not be to avoid rejection in a profession where rejection is unavoidable. The goal should be to address the core existential issues that make said rejection so painful." If those elders and scholars are correct about happiness—that it comes from tending to the well-being of others—then focusing on tending to the community garden of our field should, at the very least, help us bear the pain of failure when we encounter it, which we unavoidably will. And having more discussions about failure should help others bear the pain, as well.

Importantly, the repercussions of failure are different for each of us and for our students, depending on our identities and how we are positioned in our institutions. As a white, able-bodied, cisgender faculty member, my failures are rarely attributed to my demographic characteristics, which makes failure a little easier to handle, perhaps, and I have few *-isms* beyond a mild language disorder that challenge my work, potentially offering more opportunities for my success. However, if I choose to tend to my colleagues' and students' gardens while tending my own, then it should follow that our community garden will be more diverse, too, and any good farmer knows that a monoculture is bad for crops. In truth, interplanting, or planting crop varieties that complement each other, may be easier or more difficult depending on where we do our academic work. At my own institution, our mission is to teach and serve what we identify as "the new majority," a racially, culturally, and linguistically diverse and primarily first-generation college student body. For me, at my institution, with the privileges that my identity imbues, reframing rejection and failure as a community garden not only brings me a little more happiness when I fail, but it also feels like an important ally move.

Jean Giono (1985), in the novella *The Man Who Planted Trees* (accompanied by Michael McCurdy's breathtaking wood engravings), tells of a man who planted trees in a mountain range without any requirement to do so, eventually planting an entire forest, which in turn offered small villages the opportunity to thrive in valleys that were once too rocky, dry, and windy to be hospitable. The man's work is tedious and takes decades to come to fruition, and the man encounters failures along the way, but in the end, he is successful. In the closing paragraph of the book, Giono writes of that man:

> When I reflect that one man, armed only with his own
> physical and moral resources, was able to cause this land . . .

to spring from the wasteland, I am convinced that in spite of everything, humanity is admirable. But when I compute the unfailing greatness of spirit and the tenacity of benevolence that it must have taken to achieve this result, I am taken with an immense respect . . .

Of course, Giono's description is of a fictional man who plants an entire forest on his own. Academics are not called to do that kind of solitary work, as the pursuit of knowledge and the development of practice rely on collaboration and discussion. But the larger application of Giono's story is this: Academic failure and rejection are inevitable to our work. There will always be pain when our grant applications are turned down or when an editor passes on our proposals. But if we focus on more than just our work, if we also tend to the work of our colleagues and students, if we can reframe failure as a community garden, we just might plant a forest.

REFERENCES

Berry, W. (2011). *Farming: A handbook*. Counterpoint Press.

Giono, J. (1985). *The man who planted trees*. Chelsea Green Publishing Company.

Mueller, M.P. (2018, June 5). Grow your own rejection garden. *Inside Higher Ed.* https://www.insidehighered.com/advice/2018/06/06/how-deal-positively-rejection-academe-opinion.

Schuman, R. (2014, June 2). Why is academic rejection so very crushing? *The Chronicle of Higher Education.* https://www.chronicle.com/article/why-is-academic-rejection-so-very-crushing/.

CHAPTER 17.

USING X AS APPLIED LEARNING IN A FIRST-YEAR WRITING CLASSROOM

Jeffrey L. Jackson
State University of New York, Cortland

"There's a bug in my class!" After all my planning and research, a bug that flew through an open window in my first-year composition class introduced my students to tweeting in the classroom. That inconspicuous message was also a precursor of a semester-long struggle to get students to expand their understanding of the online platform, which would hopefully prepare them to communicate with a larger world. My goal of using X in the classroom to prepare students for online service learning, useful in a post-pandemic world, would soon be abandoned due to pedagogical shifts and eventually online learning beginning in March 2020.

Rather than adopt this practice for use during the COVID-19 pandemic, I shifted to a more traditional service-learning model the following semesters. However, having reviewed the course, presented the results at a conference, and studied my methodology and results, I better understand how I could have made the project more viable. As the Northeast region of the United States shifts from the pandemic phase of COVID-19, there are now renewed opportunities to engage once again with service learning.

LITERATURE REVIEW

SERVICE LEARNING

Gray et al. (1998) document the many benefits of service learning, including helping students remember more course information, earn better grades, and enjoy their classes more. Waldstein and Reiher (2001) argue that service learning encourages students to actively learn because there is greater participation within the classroom and the surrounding community. These opportunities only increase as online learning becomes more normal, according to McGorry (2012), who writes: "As more students begin to explore online education alternatives and institutions increase service-learning offerings, there will be greater opportunities to incorporate service learning into the online curriculum" (p. 48).

McGorry's research also addresses the intersection of service and online learning. They ask, "Can an online learning experience deliver the same benefits to students and organizations as it does in a traditional classroom setting" (McGorry, 2012, p. 45). Even though they found "no significant difference in outcomes between the online and face to face models" (McGorry, 2012, p. 45), Nellen & Purcell (2009) report a gap in research concerning service learning online.

X, Formerly Known as Twitter

The online message platform X is often used in the classroom to foster communication and learning. It is a low-stakes entry vehicle that provides as much or as little interaction as needed between instructor, student, and outside entities. X fosters student-to-student learning, which indicates to students which concepts are important (Blessing et al., 2012) and serves as a gateway to writing in a larger context while simultaneously allowing students protection due to their anonymity (Young, 2009). Blessing, Blessing, and Fleck (2012) note when used in class, tweets can provide an avenue for students to disengage due to distractions and that students who read class-content tweets retained the information more than students who did not read said tweets.

Course Goals

Rather than have students immediately begin online service learning, I decided to slowly immerse them in online communication via X. The four initial goals I created were: (1) create public discourse that would still be anonymous, (2) foster low-stakes online interaction with people not in the classroom, (3) allow them to write in the "real world" where the results were less predictable than in the classroom, and (4) help students understand which concepts were important (Blessing et al., 2012).

METHODOLOGY

Anonymous discourse would allow the students to become comfortable communicating with people both in and out of the course. While I knew which X names they used, the other students did not. Online discussions of coursework and readings would serve as low-stakes interaction, though there was always the chance that an unknown person would respond, which eventually happened.

Finally, through instruction and formative feedback, students would begin to understand which concepts were important. As it turned out, most students had only a basic knowledge of X and would need time to get acclimated to the platform. Those who had accounts rarely tweeted when not in class. As a group, they reported at the beginning of the semester that they were anxious about interacting with people outside of the course.

However, in addition to these short-term goals, my long-range plan had three components as it was designed to transition from online communication within the classroom to online service learning. They included (1) the first semester would be a test to navigate the challenges of acclimating students to online communication with strangers, (2) connection to a local organization to partner with, and finally (3) in coordination with a local partner, agree to an online format that would allow students to gain real-world experience.

Next, I sought to foster a sense of larger community by using the hashtag #cortlandwrites to connect students in my courses with students across campus and even community members in the town of Cortland, New York. Every tweet students sent would incorporate that hashtag. At the very least, it allowed students in multiple sections of the same course to find all course content tweeted by using that hashtag.

However, to do that, I would have to ensure the students were comfortable with using the platform. I had used X in the classroom before, however not for the purpose of introducing students to applied learning. My goal was to have them write on the open web to begin conversations and experience interaction with people outside the classroom. Armed with this research, it seemed possible to use online communication to prepare students to interact with local communities online. It also appeared reasonable to slowly prepare students for this communication using the composition classroom as a test bed.

RESULTS

The results reported by Blessing, Blessing, and Fleck (2012) represent my results in the classroom. X served as a platform to help students interact with course material. It also served as a tool for impromptu formative assessment, which is excellent for helping to evaluate student learning (Black & William, 1998) and can enhance student performance (Lunt & Curran, 2010). However, interactions with users outside the classroom provided either humor or anxiety for students. Additionally, it proved difficult to keep students focused on the material at hand. They would tweet about non-course subjects, such as bugs in the classroom.

LESSONS LEARNED

X was not the correct platform to train students to interact online. The strength of the platform in the classroom, being disconnected from others, is also the weakness since it did not provide interaction with anyone in the local community. Communication through an organization's website would have helped to foster understanding of the organization.

In later semesters, I would partner with the campus cupboard so that students could learn firsthand about providing services to fellow students who were food insecure. That experience was primarily face-to-face, and students wrote about and reported positive results.

TRANSITION TO APPLIED LEARNING

There are several takeaways from the semester. First, the focus must be on connecting to and engaging with the organization. Online communications will become more comfortable for students when they know the people on the other end of the platform. Second, online communications, irrespective of platform, should be between students and the organization and only include secondary audiences when appropriate.

CONCLUSION

My project proved to be unviable in part because I chose to slowly introduce my students to online communication in the hopes that once they had that skill set, we could expand to incorporate community partners. This was the opposite of what I should have done. Any instructors pursuing a combination of in-person and online service learning should consider the order of operations. While the research shows that online service learning is not only viable but effective, instructors should consider combining in-person with online communication. Although X is still an effective platform to communicate online, the rise of alternate social media such as Instagram, TikTok, and others presents new avenues of engagement with local communities and organizations that seek to interact with students and instructors to provide real-world experiences.

REFERENCES

Black, P. & Wiliam, D. (1998). Assessment and classroom learning. *Assessment in Education: Principles, Policy & Practice, 5*(1), 7–74. https://doi.org/10.1080/0969595980050102.

Blessing, B. B, Blessing, S. B. & Fleck, B. K. B. (2012). "Using X to reinforce classroom concepts." *Teaching of Psychology, 39*(4), 268–271.

Gray, M. J., Ondaatje, E. H., Fricker, R. D., Geschwind, S. A., Goldman, C. A., Kaganoff, T., Robyn, A, Sundt, M., Vogelgesang, L. & Klein, S. P. (1998). *Coupling service and learning in higher education: The final report of the evaluation of the Learn and Serve America, Higher Education Program.* RAND Corporation.

McGorry, S. Y. (2012). No significant difference in service learning online. *Journal of Asynchronous Learning Networks, 16*(4), 45–54.

Lunt, T. & Curran, J. (2010). "Are you listening please?" The advantages of electronic audio feedback compared to written feedback. *Assessment and Evaluation in Higher Education, 35*(7), 759–769. https://doi.org/10.1080/02602930902977772.

Nellen, A. & Purcell, T. (2009, August) Service learning and tax: More than vita. *Tax Adviser 40*(8), 550–552.

Waldstein, F. A. & Reiher, T. C. (2001). Service-learning and students' personal and civic development. *The Journal of Experiential Education, 24*(1), 7–13. https://doi.org/10.1177/105382590102400104.

Young, J. R. (2009, November 27). "Teaching with X: Not for the faint of heart." *The Chronicle of Higher Education,* 56, A1-A11.

CHAPTER 18.

"~~TRUST THE PROCESS~~": DISSERTATION GATEKEEPING, FAILURE, AND GRADUATE STUDENT WRITING

Mario A. D'Agostino
Nova Southeastern University

DISCLAIMER: MY FAILURE NARRATIVE

The largest takeaway from my failure narrative is that while what transpired was challenging in the moment, I understand through the benefit of hindsight that what took place *needed* to happen. I am grateful for the individuals who worked tirelessly with me on my project (including my partner and inspiration, Janine Morris). The individuals that comprised my committee are devoted educators and *great people*, and I understand that I would not be where I am today as a researcher and practitioner had it not been for their support during the direst stages of my project. As I write this narrative of failure, *my failure*, I understand that the extensive revision process that ensued after my defense postponement was necessary.

MY FAILURE NARRATIVE—WHAT HAPPENED?

It has taken some time for me to arrive at a place where I could write about this experience. To go back through saved emails, the external committee member's report and memories that fill the gaps around these evidentiary items was not easy. By every barometer of measure, you would classify my dissertation experience as a bad one. My PhD journey began in 2010 at a university in Ontario, Canada. After completing my required coursework, passing my major and subfield dissertation examinations, and engaging in a lengthy four-year writing process, I completed a draft of my dissertation in 2017 and, having submitted this draft to my committee, received support from *nearly* all committee members that the draft was defensible. A defense date was established for October 2017.

DOI: https://doi.org/10.37514/PER-B.2024.2494.2.18

To say that I was ecstatic to move to the final stages of this process would be an understatement. Of course, like most students in this situation, I was terrified, given what lay ahead. My institution's defense process was perhaps a bit more punitive than other institutions in the sense that the defense committee consisted of a three-person advisory committee, an on-campus external adjudicator from outside my home department, an off-campus external adjudicator, and a moderator from the home department who also possessed the ability to ask questions about the dissertation and the claims made within. For months leading up to the defense—and while my draft was under review with the off-campus external—I met with members of my committee regularly and was assured that the project was "good" and that the defense was "merely a formality." I recall one member of my committee specifically stating that "while the dissertation wasn't the best, it was certainly good enough to pass;" as such, I had, in their words, "nothing to worry about." These assurances, while much appreciated, did not pacify my anxiety, and, like most students, I spent months preparing for the defense (both my partner and I brainstormed potential defense questions and held numerous one-on-one meetings where she would pepper me with questions to better prepare me for this process).

It was within two weeks of my scheduled defense date when all this preparation was rendered meaningless. Thinking back, I remember this day so vividly, and what transpired on that date will live with me forever. I received a missed call from my advisor, who rarely ever called. Rather than immediately calling this person back, I assumed it was a mistake on their end but decided to check my email to see if there was any further correspondence. There, at the top of my inbox, was an email earmarked with high importance, and the contents within stated that I should call this person immediately. Trembling, I scanned my contacts for my advisor's number and called. They answered quickly and got straight to the point: The review from the off-campus external was back, and this person absolutely eviscerated the project, eating the *entire* meal and leaving no crumbs in their assessment of the work. While on the call, my advisor kindly sent the external's report. The opening line read: "This thesis 'cannot come to examination.' Overall, it does not demonstrate the research techniques, scholarship, knowledge of the subject, or appropriate level and quality of discussion and argumentation needed to meet the requirements of a doctoral degree." The conversation between my advisor and I went as you might expect it: somber and polite in its origins, though once the gravity of the situation set in, my tone in the conversation devolved from subtle and confused to a place where the pauses in my speech were replaced with some variation of the f-word.

I was blindsided. More than this, however, I was angry and frustrated. I kept asking my advisor how/why the external's report carried so much weight in determining my defense fate. Moreover, if the claims this person made in their opening statement were true, how was none of this brought to my attention during the extensive reading, writing, and revision process that took place the previous four years? There were no easy answers to these questions, and, in hindsight, it was probably unfair of me to confront my advisor with them at that point. Unfortunately, the power that the off-campus external possessed—a *major* influence in the process that wasn't exactly made clear to me during the course of my writing—set off a series of events that led to my defense date being postponed to October 2019. In that time, the expectation fell on me to make extensive and global changes to the work.

Adding another layer of stress and anxiety to the situation is that in the months leading up to my initial defense date in 2017, I was able to secure a Visiting Assistant Professor position, pending defense. While I was ultimately able to remain in this position, staying put meant that the revisions needed to be completed ASAP. I was fortunate to have an institution and department chair who believed in me throughout this challenging process, though their support did not mitigate the pressure that keeping this job added to an already stressful situation. I'll spare the reader here from the site-specific changes that took place during my eighteen-month revision process. In October 2019, almost two years to the date, I successfully defended the thesis and was able to graduate with my PhD in 2020. What I want to make clear, however, is that this is *my* failure narrative, and the defense postponement fell on my shoulders. I produced the work, and it simply wasn't good enough. And while I wish I could have avoided the extensive revision process that took place, this process has led to several learning lessons that inform my teaching, advising, and scholarship in my current position in higher education.

THE LARGER TAKEAWAYS—WHAT FAILURE TAUGHT ME?

My failure narrative taught me many important lessons: (1) failure is *not* equitable; (2) privilege plays a tremendous role in an individual's ability to overcome failure, regardless of what the myths surrounding 'hard work paying off' have previously taught us; and (3) failure in the writing process underscores the importance of revision and how one must wholly commit to this exercise if they are to complete their project. Allison Carr and Laura Micciche (2020), writing in *Failure Pedagogies*, investigate equity and privilege in the writing process, questioning ". . . [f]or whom is failure a real end rather than an opening to generative possibilities?" (p. 3). The authors note that "the relationship between failure and success . . . has long played a role in bootstraps ideologies pervasive within American progress narratives" (Carr & Micciche, 2020, p. 1), and they similarly wonder whether every person who fails is granted equal access to the same "generative" opportunities to persist? Gillespie's discussion of failure linked to material conditions in this collection, and an individual's ability to "fail safely," extends Carr and Micciche's discussion further. Within the myths of American exceptionalism, however, the widely held misconception is that any person can achieve impossible feats so long as the individual in question is willing to *put in the work*. *Putting in the work*, in itself, carries additional emotional weight and cultural baggage linked to dominant white culture, where the archetype for perseverance is most commonly white bodies who harbor a commitment to hard work and self-reliance.

Carr and Micciche's (2020) line of questioning is significant not simply because it helps undermine these myths of progress, but because, viewed through the lens of higher education, it forces educators to question whether all failures are created equally. That is to say, are educators ensuring that the students they advise, and who may misstep in their thesis/dissertation process, are afforded the same opportunities as other students to amend and reconcile this situation? Are educators performing the critical work of undermining the "beliefs, attitudes, and actions . . . that support or perpetuate racism in . . . unconscious ways" (Smithsonian, n.d.) in the counsel they provide their graduate students? Teagan Decker, in this collection, writes a narrative of failure from a graduate student perspective that offers an insightful look into the kinds of issues (e.g., various socio-economic stressors, imposter syndrome, to name a few) current graduate students are experiencing and that we, as advisors, should be cognizant of in advising their work.

The final takeaway from my failure narrative connects with Darci Thoune's (2020) writing on *failure potential*. In "Failure Potential: Using Failure as Feedback," Thoune (2020) notes that a student's ability to use failure productively points to their "failure potential" and their capacity to learn from their mistakes. Thoune (2020) writes that, for some, ". . . failure could exist as an ending point," while for others, it could function "as a form of feedback . . . for students and instructors, failure provides us with information at a crossroads in the writing process that will likely affect future writing practices and performances" (p. 54). On one level, Thoune points to the provisionality of failure and how one's ability to use feedback productively can sometimes be linked to their subject position. She extends this conversation in the essay, noting that feedback should always be conveyed with words of encouragement in order to not shut the writer down and turn them away from the revision process. On another level, however, and extending my previous statement, Thoune's quotation offers important insight into the role that *failure potential* plays in the revision process and how educators must be upfront about this process with their graduate students.

Looking back at my narrative of failure, while the situation was incredibly challenging in the moment as it unfolded, I know that I was extremely fortunate to be granted the opportunity to revise the work and to get it to a place where it could be defended. In the months after the postponement, my committee was extremely generous with their time, providing appropriate feedback as I worked on my revisions. Borrowing a line from Carr and Micciche (2020), I understand that in my situation, failure opened itself up to "generative possibilities" (p. 3), and this is not always the case for individuals who find themselves in a similar situation. Making failure equitable is something that currently informs my advising, and interpersonal communication plays a vital role in this process. That is to say, understanding who the student is on a human level, their background, how they respond to feedback are critical; keeping these items at the forefront of one's counsel can help level the playing field, so to speak, to ensure that failure is not a result of a privileged situation.

The other important aspect to achieving equity in failure coincides with Thoune's (2020) central argument: Failure can be productive when students embrace feedback and the larger, more extensive changes that need attention. Driscoll's piece in this collection extends this conversation further, noting the important role that failure can play in our writing and revision processes. Driscoll specifically urges practitioners to normalize failure with graduate students so they may better see its potential. Failure is not an endpoint; rather, it is an act that can be super generative and is something we *all* struggle with (and should be made visible to others). In my situation, I had a tremendous committee that was patient with me and who offered encouraging advice that made the long process of revision palatable and something to look forward to. In this case, *failure potential* stemmed from an understanding that revision is not simply a matter of accepting track changes, nor does it mean inserting a word or two here and there within the document to amend sentence-level concerns. Rather, larger issues present in the draft often need major attention, and having these conversations with students early on is critical. Students should be made aware that no person submits the *perfect* draft. Revision is a process that everyone goes through, and it is vital to be upfront with students so that they are aware of what this process looks like (and the time it takes to complete). Avoiding these sometimes-difficult conversations is a disservice to graduate student writers.

MINOR TAKEAWAYS—WHAT FAILURE ALSO TAUGHT ME?

Making Clear Departmental Expectations. Perhaps the biggest "minor" takeaway from my narrative of failure is ensuring that departmental expectations for a thesis or dissertation are clearly defined and communicated to the student. As

I noted above, it was not entirely clear to me that if a dissertation draft did not pass the off-campus external examiner's reading, then the student would not pass and would be out of the program. When I meet with students about joining their project as an advisor, in our initial conversations, the expectations for completing the thesis are clearly defined, and students are assigned readings from the department that explain the following: what the thesis/dissertation process looks like; what a timeline for completion looks like; what will happen if the thesis/dissertation isn't completed within the two academic-year window; what the defense portion looks like; what it means to pass with revisions; and what it means to fail the defense.

Being Aware of the Power Dynamic Between Advisor and Student. Ultimately, the advisor makes the final call on whether a project is ready to go to defense, and this can sometimes lead to an unequal power balance within that relationship. Ironically, during my actual dissertation defense, one of my advisors noted that I wrote my second chapter on the novel *The Brief Wondrous Life of Oscar Wao* (Diaz, 2008) and, since my writing of the chapter, the author of the text had been accused of sexual harassment and verbal abuse towards women. My advisor thus asked how I would envision teaching this text, given these accusations. What my advisor was ultimately referring to was the incredible power that instructors often hold in their class and their ability to pick and choose what they teach and to augment some facts while potentially glossing over others. In this case, those accusations are now a part of the story when teaching the novel (especially since so many of the characters depicted within the text outwardly promote a specific brand of toxic masculinity, making it difficult to ignore the connections between fiction and reality). Since my defense, my advisor's question is one I have turned over multiple times in my mind, in part because I want to ensure that I am doing justice to the curriculum I teach and the students I advise. As educators advising a long-standing writing project, we need to be aware of the power we yield and the gatekeeping that comes with this counsel, ensuring that the relationship between advisor and student is more equitable.

How Punitive Should the Process Really Be? The final minor takeaway from my failure narrative has pushed me to have a candid conversation about how punitive the super-punitive dissertation process needs to be. I want to be careful with what I'm writing here, in part because aspects of the process are necessary and important. Students need to demonstrate the research techniques, subject knowledge, and line of argumentation appropriate for a thesis/dissertation. In addition, there is an adequate level of research that students must engage in. These are items that, for me, are non-negotiable; understanding how to research and write in the humanities is critical. Still, though, some processes are more punitive than others. Oftentimes, the decision to allow a student to defend comes from the number of burning academic hoops they have jumped through, lending credence to the notion that these processes should be reconsidered and, if necessary, revised on the administrative level.

REFERENCES

Carr, A. D. & Micciche, L. R. (2020). Introduction: Failure's sweat. In A. D. Carr & L. R. Micciche (Eds.), *Failure pedagogies: Learning and unlearning what it means to fail* (pp. 1–7). Peter Lang.

Diaz, J. (2008). *The brief wondrous life of Oscar Wao*. Riverhead Books.

Thoune, D. (2020). Failure potential: Using failure as feedback. In A. D. Carr & L. R. Micciche (Eds.), *Failure pedagogies: Learning and unlearning what it means to fail* (pp. 53–62). Peter Lang.

Smithsonian National Museum of African American History & Culture. (n.d.). Being antiracist. Retrieved December 12, 2023, from https://nmaahc.si.edu/learn/talking-about-race/topics/being-antiracist.

AFTERWORD.
FAILURE: A DWELLING

Allison D. Carr
Coe College

This will be a bit of a wandering reflection.

A few nights ago, having some trouble falling asleep, I reached for my phone. Usually, when I can't sleep—a rare and therefore all the more bothersome event—it's because I can't quiet my mind. My word for it is spiraling. Maybe you know this feeling. My therapist tells me when I am spiraling, I should write down whatever it is that my brain won't let go of.

"Let it go."

She says this will calm my mind by reassuring me that my thoughts will be waiting there for me when I need them.

I love my therapist, but the first time she suggested this, it sounded so stupid to me—and something about my spiraling is that often I have very good ideas and insights mixed in with all the annoying worry—and so for the years we have been together I have not taken this advice for fear, I suppose, of cutting off the opportunity to have an idea. But a few nights ago, having some trouble falling asleep, spiraling, I reached for my phone. I thumbed open the Notes app and wrote:

> All the ways I feel inadequate
>
> Weird to be the most cited person in a book
>
> Failing my students
>
> Systems failing me
>
> Everything everywhere all at once
>
> Push more unsettled discomfort
>
> It will be fine

A summary of the spiral, notes toward a writing project that has been weighing on me for months. I fell asleep.

∼∼∼

I am, I must admit, a bit uneasy about the title of this volume, which could be read as reifying the success/failure binary that most work on failure in our field has been, in one way or another, trying to deconstruct. Still, as I reflect upon the chapters within, upon the range of other engagements with failure over the last decade, and maybe especially upon my own work on this subject—I get it. There would simply not be a market for this book if deconstructing the binary were as simple as turning one's attitudes 180 degrees. It is the nature of the dominant narrative to dominate, and the success/failure binary is wholly baked into our profession, our society, our economy, our self-concepts. If anything, this volume is a testament to just how difficult it is to break out of this model for reasoning, and I admire the work these authors have done to expand and complicate our relationship with the binary: as a dyad and with each individual term.

In an interview with Shane Wood for *Pedagogue*, describing the way my thinking on failure has changed over the last decade, I said, "I'm less committed to [failure] as a concept that . . . is portable" (Wood, 2022). The more time I spend with the idea of failure, the more I sense that the deep *meaning* of this term is too context-specific and contingent to hold scholarly significance. It both sticks and slips. Or as Karen Tellez-Trujillo (this volume) puts it in her chapter: "As a commonplace, failure means something different to everyone and each relationship with failure has developed in a unique way . . . It is not uncommon to use terms without thinking about what they mean, and failure is among these commonplaces." At the same time—maybe because of all this sticking and slipping—there is something shimmery here. Alluring. People *want* failure *to mean*, to carry meaning, for the same reason I wanted failure to mean when I first began writing about it: We want to feel that our struggle is not a waste. That our bad feelings are not indulgent or vain or shameful or weak. The idea of failure helps to hold this, and us. If we can name it, we can know it, find community in it.

The range represented by the chapters in this volume underscores my hunch. All of us—self included—use this word as if its meaning is shared, yet, *except for its relational opposition to success* (a fixed narrative that supersedes any individual's consent to be shaped by it), there is no unifying meaning for "failure" here, though there is a great deal of difficulty, struggle, challenge, fuckups. Failing, and being failed (by others, by processes, by systems, by chance), the term offers a fleeting coherence. I make this observation not as critique but as evidence toward a thesis that failure's *failure to be known* is its singular most compelling and worthwhile characteristic.

If there is something we *can know* about failure, however, Paul Cook's opening chapter (this volume) represents, in my judgment, the most comprehensive review of failure's systemic meaning that has been written. His genealogy quite effectively glosses all the ways failure has come to have its associations—with capital, with morality, with social position and power, and with the myth of individual striving that pulses beneath it all. Still, it tells us mostly about failure in the abstract. Fitting, then, that the next two chapters that round out part one stage what I read as a dialogic of the most closely held perspectives on failure *as we live it*, revealing in the process one of its more frustrating limitations: its terministic emptiness. Or maybe radioactivity is a better metaphor? An atom is considered radioactive when it has an excess of charged material, rendering it unstable and prone to chaotic behavior. Such atoms seek stability, and they find it either by throwing off charged material or bonding with a more stable element. Elsewhere, I have written that we may have to accept that failure, as a term, is perpetually "unsettled" (Carr, 2024). On its own, it refuses to be stilled. To talk about failure in a critical way, by which I mean to hold it still long enough to make meaning of it, we end up reaching for other ideas and concepts, more stable elements.

In one such example of this phenomenon, Teagarden, Mando, and Commer (this volume) graft failure onto "intellectual risk," emphasizing or promoting a meaning of failure that I would characterize as fundamentally optimistic, inasmuch as "risk" is commonly understood as leading to rewards that are "worth it," i.e., "no risk/no reward." "Intellectual risk" is the optimistic promise upon which the university, as an institution—and by extension, its disciplines—has built itself, and so it makes perfect sense to me that readers, teachers, and students would find this terminology attractive.[1] And while I agree with the authors' assertion that "writing instructors would be better served foregrounding intellectual risk instead of failure" (Teagarden et al., this volume), my agreement hinges on an understanding of "failure" as antithetical to optimism: Yes, writing instructors *would be* better served foregrounding optimistic frames for learning.

As such, I *disagree* with their assessment that a pedagogy oriented around intellectual risk "is a way of pursuing the same goals and enacting the same values" as a pedagogy that adopts "failure" as its lodestar. Quite the contrary: Failure does not *feel good*. It does not promise.[2] Rather, we might say failure threatens. Therefore, the values and goals of one cannot possibly be evident in the other.

Why does this catch my eye? It's not the job of an afterword to dissect the preceding pages. But Teagarden et al.'s atomic maneuvering (if I may be allowed to invoke the above metaphor one last time) serves as a standout example of the

---

1   In fact, if I had to summarize my own pedagogical orientations in a few key phrases, I am certain this would land in the top few; despite being a champion for failure in my scholarly vita, I almost never bring it to the foreground with students.

2   Though, the work on failure that Teagarden et al. reference in building their case (my own 2013 "In Support of Failure") does advance a problematic "pedagogical mandate of happiness" as Johnson and Sheehan (2020) rightly critiqued.

ways failure begs to be made stable. It's a fascinating illustration to me because my interest in failure has always been about bad and unstable feelings, as this chapter (and another they cite, Johnson and Sheehan's [2020] work in *Failure Pedagogies*) fairly and astutely observes, and trying to write about failure *qua* failure has meant trying to sit with and advance, yes, an "epideictic" idea of failure that calls for "living in" those bad feelings (Teagarden et al., this volume), missed goals. I have wrestled with the implications of that interest elsewhere (Carr, 2024), and truth be told, I have had a change of perspective about the ethics of conscripting students into those bad feelings, no matter how well I think I can control it, and regardless of my "good intentions." My interest in "living in" the bad feelings of failure persists, but let's say, on an individual opt-in basis. This requires, I think, a rigorous commitment to self-understanding, among other emotional and material supports. And so, while the notion of intellectual risk is indeed attractive, I wonder if we are still talking about failure at all. I raise this not to undermine the authors, whose work on this idea is extensive and useful, but rather to foreground a question that, for me, lies at the heart of this book (and at the heart of my own scholarly commitments): What are the boundaries of failure? And what is its use to us?

While Teagarden et al. offer a clever pathway for *redirecting* students' fears of failure toward potentially more optimistic outcomes, Wood's chapter (this volume) describing ways to help teachers and students excavate what "feels like" failure strikes me as a second exceptionally savvy way of sidestepping failure's refusal to be known. In asking what failure "feels like," Wood confronts failure's subjectivity head-on without sacrificing the term's use-value altogether. It is an approach that opens a door to failure-as-gathering-place, which others in this volume similarly exemplify. Failure-as-gathering-place is a kind of eternal unknown: where we hold the things we don't understand, where we gently press on the bruise of rejection, still tender in spite of the passage of time.

～～～

This must be my fourth or fifth draft. I keep stalling out here. There are more paragraphs on the next page, but I'm not sure if I want them or how to get there if I do. On my browser right now, I have another tab open with a doc of the lines and paragraphs I've already cut, ideas that don't seem germane (though what isn't germane to failure?). I keep trying to cut the list of worries from the opening, now several months old, but for some reason, I keep coming back to it. That I have it at all—that I haven't left-swiped it out of the Notes app, that I'm interrupting my line of thought right at this moment to reveal something of the backstory of this draft—may be an illustration of what Duffy describes in his chapter (this volume) as another kind of *dwelling place* of failure: the tattered folders in the office, or else the digital files in the ever-present cloud, each holding false starts and abandoned or otherwise unfinished writing, "material evidence of labor I don't want lost." Surely all of us gather here, in these places, not *together* together, but in community around the proof of our existence, of our creativity, of our struggle?

Last spring, a year ago as of the time of this writing, I was the chair of a committee charged with strengthening and promoting the welfare of the faculty when the president of the college initiated a full review of all academic programs, with the implied goal of rank-ordering them on hastily derived, bullshit metrics in order to identify areas of consolidation or elimination. Like every small college without a billion-dollar endowment, the consequences of neoliberal fetishism and failure of imagination had come to roost in our balance sheet, though, of course, we can't say that out loud because it would become a public relations nightmare.

In my role as committee chair, I called a faculty forum; I wrote an open letter summarizing the forum; with my committee members, I weighed the risks of refusing to go along with the directive (leaving the president and Board to own the fallout) against the possibility of proceeding apace (local control); I made resolute remarks at multiple faculty meetings; I privately sought outside advice on what kind of maneuvers a faculty body without the protection of a union might make against a hostile administration; I stopped sleeping and lost my appetite.

How does one uphold their charge to promote the welfare of the faculty in this instance? What use are strongly worded statements and memos against a president and Board of Trustees trying to find many millions of dollars in the cushions of sagging office couches? I did all of the right things procedurally, and it didn't make a difference.

There's more, summed up perhaps as an inadequacy of presence, a failure of attention. This year, I cannot seem to stay on top of student work despite optimizing my pedagogy to my understanding of what I can and can't do. In a job that feels made increasingly intolerable by the consequences of austerity, being accountable to my students feels like the most important use for my energy, and I'm failing at that all of the time. I have less patience with myself.

I keep thinking about The Daniels' 2022 breakout film *Everything Everywhere All At Once*, which follows Michelle Yeoh's Evelyn Wang chasing the big baddie Jobu Tupaki, alter-ego of her daughter Joy Wang (played by Stephanie Hsu) across multiple timelines in a quest to save the universe (Kwan & Scheinert, 2022). To do so, Evelyn must learn to "verse jump" by performing the least likely action imaginable (for example, chewing used gum, giving oneself intentional papercuts) in order to temporarily access some of the more useful skills possessed by other, more successful Evelyns across the timelines: a chef, a movie star, a martial arts master, a rock, a person who never emigrated from China.

Early in the film, it is revealed that *this version* of Evelyn—the one with a failing laundromat and resentment-ridden marriage—is the least successful of all the Evelyns. In other words, she is the failingest Evelyn who ever failed. And it is for precisely this reason that Fail Evelyn is the only one who can save the universe: "She is the least likely, and therefore the one that is perfect. The least likely actions are . . . what allows her to access the skills from the other Evelyns" (Nguyen, 2022). The film is reminiscent, in some ways, of Halberstam's (2011) landmark work on queer failure, which turns to myriad artifacts of "low culture" (animated children's films, avant-garde art) to "think about ways of being and knowing that stand outside of conventional understandings of success" (p. 2). Evelyn has to consistently commit to the unlikeliest actions in direct conflict with what actions may benefit her personally in order to save the world. It is not a critique of established norms so much as a chaotic refusal to engage them.

We may see a similar dynamic at work in the recent demonstrations in support of Palestinian lives by college students across the US and globe, maybe most prominently (as of the time of this writing) by the students at Columbia University, whose ongoing demonstration was finally answered by President Minouche Shafik authorizing the New York Police Department to storm the campus in riot gear. In this case, we have a group of students refusing to ignore their university's complicity (via its investment portfolio) in genocide—a kind of failure of compliance—which provokes a response that, in prioritizing political and capital interests over human rights, reveals yet another failure: the failure of the university to uphold the myth of its mission. Yet, it was a catalyzing moment. Rather than quell dissent, the Columbia University demonstration and raid inspired dozens, perhaps hundreds, of encampments established in solidarity with the cause of Palestinian civilians. A distributed community of refusal.

Weeks ago, a year after my committee's maneuvering failed to alter the decisions that seemed to be preordained, the new committee found a pathway had been cleared to escalate the faculty's concerns. After the previous motions had been ineffective, the faculty have found solidarity and community in other methods of noncompliance, some more organized (outreach to the Board) than others (subversion of performance review documentation).[3]

~~~

Failure as gathering place, failure as dwelling place: This heuristic might comfortably hold perspectives from Driscoll (this volume), Laura Decker (this volume),

---

3   I am sorry to be cryptic, but I hope readers can forgive me.

and Donelson & Cox (this volume). In reflecting on their experiences revising their graduate exams, the latter co-authors call for a "community-oriented approach to failure" to return to when "sometimes, the only answer is to sit with . . . the discomfort . . . [and] bear witness, rather than needing to work to resolve our embodied feelings of despair around rejection-as-failure" (Donelson & Cox, this volume). Isn't this what Driscoll (this volume) models with her CV of Failure? Maybe sharing this document with students doesn't capture the contemporaneous bad feelings of each ungotten grant, each revise & resubmit, but surely there is no shortage of vulnerability and risk here, and it does make plain for junior scholars the knotted terrain of achievement. Laura Decker (this volume), likewise, offers a way of "doing" failure that builds community, repairing one's own rejections and missed opportunities by "planting seeds" in others' gardens. In reading, I was reminded of the legacy of the late Bill Hart-Davidson, who publicly committed to nominating at least one colleague for recognition or award every month. Imagine this ethic in the context of one's own failures: For every gut-churning fuckup, take a turn in the rejection garden, water someone's tomatoes, fertilize the blueberries. This is not unlike what Mario D'Agostino (this volume) takes away from his own unnecessarily strenuous trek through his dissertation process: correcting those harms by refusing to pass them along to his own students, instead prioritizing in himself an ethic of transparent mentorship and communication.

Might this volume—chock full of stories of failure, however, that feels and means to each individual author—be understood as a kind of dwelling for failure, a rejection garden, an offering of community?

I am not sure whether I have said anything interesting here. This is the thing about failure: Its unknowability forces, for me anyway, a certain kind of hesitation in thought. Am I getting it "right?" What would that even mean? I am trying not to worry about it. I am trying to *take a risk*. I am trying to tell you that for me, failure *feels like* not knowing, but not knowing also feels like the only place I want to be, with other not-knowers, spiraling together and taking notes. It feels bad, and it feels fine. All of it, all at once.

REFERENCES

Carr, A. D. (2024). Following failure. *Composition Forum, 53*. https://compositionforum.com/issue/53/following-failure.php.

Kwan, D. & Scheinert, D. (Directors). (2022). *Everything everywhere all at once* [Film]. A24 Productions.

Halberstam, J. (2011). *The queer art of failure*. Duke University Press.

Johnson, G. P. & Sheehan, R. (2020). The uses of queer failure: Navigating the pedagogical mandate of happiness. In A. D. Carr & L. R. Micciche (Eds.), *Failure pedagogies: learning and unlearning what it means to fail* (pp. 127–139). Peter Lang.

Nguyen, H. (2022, April 17). The Daniels on the ADHD theory of *Everything Everywhere All At Once,* papercuts and butts. *Salon.* https://www.salon.com/2022/04/17/everything-everywhere-all-at-once-daniels-adhd/.

Wood, S. (Host). (2022, 27 September). Allison Carr (No. 125) [Audio podcast episode]. In *Pedagogue.* https://www.pedagoguepodcast.com/episodes.html.

CONTRIBUTORS

Elizabeth Blomstedt is Assistant Professor in the Writing Program at the University of Southern California. Her research focuses on writing assessment (including high-stakes writing exams), multilingual writing pedagogies, STEM writing, and writing for sustainability. She has previously worked as the Assistant Director of the Warren College Writing Program at UC San Diego and as a Graduate Fellow in Writing Center Pedagogy and Program Development at the University of Houston.

Allison D. Carr is Associate Professor of Rhetoric and Associate Dean of Student Academics at Coe College, where she also serves as Director of Writing Across the Curriculum and teaches courses in rhetoric and creative nonfiction. She has published widely on failure, including her edited book with Laura Micciche, *Failure Pedagogies: Learning and Unlearning What it Means to Fail* (Peter Lang, 2020). Her co-edited collection on revision, *Revising Moves: Writing Stories of (Re)Making* was published by Utah State University Press in 2024.

Carolyn D. Commer is Associate Professor of English at Virginia Tech, where she serves as the Director of the Rhetoric and Writing PhD program. Her work on rhetorical theory and pedagogy has been published in *Composition Studies*, *Argumentation and Advocacy*, *Literacy in Composition Studies*, *Rhetoric Review*, *Journal for the History of Rhetoric*, and the volume *Teaching Demagoguery and Democracy: Rhetorical Pedagogy in Polarized Times*. She is the author of *Championing a Public Good: A Call to Advocate for Higher Education* (Penn State University Press, 2024).

Paul Cook is Professor of English at Indiana University Kokomo, where he teaches writing, rhetoric, and digital media. Trained as a rhetorician and writing teacher, he has recently been researching solutions to the epistemological crisis of mis- and disinformation in a postdigital landscape. His team won the top prize at the 2018 Misinformation Solutions Forum for their Mind over Chatter modules, which were fully revised and expanded in 2024. His research has appeared in *JAC*, *Across the Disciplines*, *Communication Law Review*, *Workplace*, *The WAC Journal*, and other publications. His first book, *Misinformation Studies and Higher Education in the Postdigital Era: Beyond Fake News* (2024), is forthcoming from Lexington Books.

Steven J. Corbett is Associate Professor of Composition & Rhetoric; Division Head of Communication, Composition & Rhetoric; and Writing Program Administrator at Methodist University. He is the author of *Beyond Dichotomy: Synergizing Writing Center and Classroom Pedagogies* (2015) and co-editor of *Peer*

Pressure, Peer Power: Theory and Practice in Peer Review and Response for the Writing Classroom (2014); *Student Peer Review and Response: A Critical Sourcebook* (2018); *Writing In and About the Performing and Visual Arts: Creating, Performing, and Teaching* (2019); and *Writing Centers and Learning Commons: Staying Centered While Sharing Common Ground* (2023). His articles on writing pedagogy have appeared in a variety of journals, periodicals, and collections.

Anicca Cox is Assistant Professor of English at the University of New Mexico, Valencia Campus. Her work has appeared in *College English, College Composition and Communication, Peitho, WPA Journal, Across the Disciplines,* and several book chapters. Her research primarily focuses on labor equity in academia, institutional change work, and writing program administration with a secondary research area in community engaged food justice/sovereignty work.

Mario A. D'Agostino is Assistant Professor of Writing at Nova Southeastern University, where he oversees numerous visual art and writing initiatives. His work has appeared in *Writing Spaces*; *Diverse Pedagogical Approaches to Experiential Learning, Volume II*; and he served as Editor-in-Chief of *Experiential Learning & Teaching in Higher Education*. He currently serves on the editorial board for *Metropolitan Universities Journal*.

Laura Decker is Assistant Professor of English at Nevada State University, where she serves as the Chair of the Humanities Department. Her recent essays and articles have appeared in *Interrupting, Infiltrating, Investigating: Radical Youth Pedagogies in Education* (2020), *Grassroots Activisms: Public Rhetorics in Localized Contexts* (2024), *English in Texas* (2023), and the *Journal of Writing Assessment* (2024).

Teagan Decker is Professor of English and Dean of the Maynor Honors College at the University of North Carolina at Pembroke. Her recent publications include the co-edited volume *Writing Centers and Learning Commons: Staying Centered While Sharing Common Ground* (2023) and the co-authored book chapter "Honors Colleges as Levers of Educational Equity" in *A Comprehensive Guide to Honors Colleges* (2023).

Jerrice Renita Donelson is Lecturer in Technical and Professional Writing and Rhetoric at the University of Michigan in Dearborn. Her research centralizes narratives and voices of Black users in systems designed for access, using her method UXRS as visual Racial Storytelling combined with UX journey mapping. Her work includes dual enrollment and composition, user experience and UX design, online TPC pedagogy, writing center, and writing with the community. Her non-profit, *Scribe Tribe Writing Tutors*, supports secondary students' literacy practices in Detroit. Her work is in *Wicked Problems, Design Thinking and Technical Communication: Contemporary Approaches to Pedagogy* (2024), *Communication Design Quarterly* special issue on UX pedagogy (2024), *Pedagogy* (2024),

Positionality Stories (2025), and *User Not Found: User Experience as Racial Storytelling in System Design*.

Dana Lynn Driscoll is Professor of English and serves as the Founding Director of the Center for Scholarly Communication at Indiana University of Pennsylvania. She has published widely on learning theory, writing transfer, writing expertise, writing centers, and supporting advanced writers in disciplinary fields. She teaches writing for publication, research methods, and composition pedagogy in the doctoral program in Composition and Applied Linguistics. She has been the recipient of numerous grants and awards, including the 2022 International Association for Writing Across the Curriculum's best article award and the 2012 International Writing Center Association's Article of the Year award. She has served on multiple editorial boards and recently completed her three-year term as co-editor of *Writing Spaces*, an open-access textbook series for first-year composition.

William Duffy is Professor of English at the University of Memphis. His work has most recently been published in *Rhetoric Society Quarterly*, *Present Tense*, *Inside Higher Ed*, and the volumes *Revising Moves* (2024) and *Composition and Rhetoric in Contentious Times* (2023). His book *Beyond Conversation: Collaboration and the Production of Writing* (2021) theorizes a method for navigating the material labor of coauthorship in academia's authorial economies.

Sean Fenty is an instructor at Binghamton University, where he serves as the Director of the Writing Initiative. His work has been published in *ImageTexT: Interdisciplinary Comics Studies*, *Currents in Electronic Literacy*, *Florida Reading Journal*, and in the edited collection *Playing the Past: History and Nostalgia in Video Games*. He has edited multiple editions of *Coming to Voice: Writing Personal, Civic, and Academic Arguments* and *Binghamton Writes: Research and Writing in WRIT 111*.

Tyler Gillespie is Professor at Ringling College of Art and Design. He's the author of the nonfiction collection *The Thing about Florida: Exploring a Misunderstood State* (University Press of Florida) and two poetry collections, *the nature machine!* (Autofocus) and *Florida Man: Poems, Revisited* (Burrow Press). His academic scholarship appears in *College Composition and Communication*, *Community Literacy Journal*, and *The Routledge Handbook of Queer Rhetoric*.

Michal Horton is Clinical Assistant Professor of Business Communication at Baylor University, where she teaches with an emphasis on emotional intelligence and humanizing communication. She also serves as an advisory head of communications for a tech startup. Her research in writing studies has been published in *Pedagogy: Critical Approaches to Teaching Literature, Language, Composition, and Culture* and *Composition Forum*.

Jeffrey L. Jackson is Instructor of First-Year Composition at the State University of New York Cortland. His research areas are academic writing and writing with the help of AI.

Contributors

Justin Mando is Associate Professor and Chair of English & World Languages at Millersville University of Pennsylvania. He specializes in environmental rhetoric, science writing, rhetorics of place, and intellectual risk in the writing classroom. He has published in *Composition Studies, Rhetoric Review, Environmental Communication, Discourse & Communication*, and elsewhere. His book is titled *Fracking and the Rhetoric of Place: How We Argue From Where We Stand* (2021).

Laura K. Miller is Associate Professor of Writing, Rhetoric, and Technical Communication at James Madison University, where she also serves as Executive Director of the Learning Centers. Her research on writing mindsets, noncognitive factors, and tutoring efficacy has been published in *Writing Center Journal, WLN: A Journal of Writing Center Scholarship*, and *Assessment Update*. She is the co-author of *So What? The Writer's Argument*, a first-year writing textbook in its third edition.

Ruth Mirtz is Assistant Professor and Director of the Kansas State University Salina Library. She was formerly a professor of writing at Kansas State, as well as several other universities. She has published on the topics of writing program administration, TA training, first-year writing student research processes, spatial issues around writing instruction, and transfer. She most recently presented at the Computers and Writing 2024 conference on college student research processes and AI.

Suzie Null has worked with elementary through graduate students as a K-12 teacher, composition instructor at UC Santa Barbara, and Professor of Teacher Education at Fort Lewis College. Her research often focused on teacher implementation of organizational policies. She is now retired, so she can focus on her own fiction writing.

Mary Lourdes Silva (she/her) is Associate Professor of Writing and Director of First-Year Writing at Ithaca College. She is a first-generation cisgendered Queer Latina. She has published scholarly articles and essays about the citation practices of first-year college writing students, pedagogical use of multimodal and multimedia technologies and practices, implementation of institutional ePortfolio assessment, gender/race bias in education, movement-touch literacy as a modality to teach reflective thinking in first-year writing, the psychological and financial implications of faculty compelled to review biased student evaluations of teaching, and AI critical literacy in first-year writing.

Alexis Teagarden is Associate Professor of English and Communication at the University of Massachusetts Dartmouth, where she also directs the First-Year English program. Her research interests include writing pedagogy and its intersections with web literacy and intellectual risk-taking, as well as faculty development and evaluation practices. She is co-editor of the 2025 summer issue of

Composition Forum on the theme of Risk and Failure in the Teaching of Writing, and her work can also be found in *WPA: Writing Program Administration, Composition Studies, Forum,* and *Kairos* as well as the edited collections *Composition and Big Data* (2021) and *Toward More Sustainable Metaphors of Writing Program Administration* (2023).

Karen R. Tellez-Trujillo is Assistant Professor at Cal Poly Pomona in the Department of English and Modern Languages. Her educational background and research interests include border, feminist, and cultural rhetorics. She is the Writing in the Disciplines coordinator and Graduate Assistant advisor for Rhetoric and Composition. Karen enjoys working with undergraduate students as a mentor for The Research through Inclusive Opportunities (RIO) program and as the Writing Studies coordinator. Her work has appeared in the interdisciplinary journal *Writers, Craft, and Context* (2023) and the edited collection *Revising Moves* (2024). She also received the 2022–2023 NCTE Early Career Educator of Color Leadership Award.

Josephine Walwema is a faculty member and founding director of the Program in Technical and Professional Writing at the University of Washington, Seattle. She publishes on issues of access, equity, and social justice in writing studies. She has twice won the best article for CCCC Technical Scientific and Communication Award in the category of Best Article Reporting Historical Research or Textual Studies in Technical and Scientific Communication, as well as the Ann Neil Picket Award for best article in *Technical Communication Quarterly*.

Shane A. Wood is Associate Professor and Director of First-Year Composition at the University of Central Florida, where he teaches first-year writing. His research interests include writing assessment, multimodality, and writing program administration. His book, *Teachers Talking Writing: Perspectives on Places, Pedagogies, and Programs* (2023), is a collection of conversations about the theory and teaching of writing in postsecondary contexts.